"An excellent reference book for scholars and students alike. Aldama and González hit it out of the park! Team Latinx Keywords: Home Run!"

—Lisa Sánchez González
University of Connecticut, USA

"With so many Latinx ancestral genealogies, we are like Magellan adrift in a sea of languages and place names, a diaspora whose history is complex and destiny off the charts. Leave it to the sage prolix wisdom of our prolific Latinx savant Aldama, and his trusty scholarly partner in crime, González, to provide us a compass in book form to guide us all."

—William A. Nericcio
San Diego State University, USA

"Given the historical moment and the widespread denigration of Latinx peoples across the US today, it is so important to understand and locate diverse Latinx perspectives in national, international, and global contexts. This wonderful book does just that. A great contribution to a vital field of scholarship, cultural production, and political action."

—Paul Allatson
University of Technology Sydney, Australia

"Aldama and González achieve a remarkable feat. This ambitious, incisive, compact, and well-informed book vitally captures the ever-expanding field of Latinx Studies."

—Silvio Torres-Saillant
Syracuse University, USA

D0226166

LATINX STUDIES

Latinx Studies: The Key Concepts is an accessible guide to the central concepts and issues that inform Latinx Studies globally. It summarizes, explains, contextualizes, and assesses key critical concepts, perspectives, developments, and debates in Latinx Studies. At once comprehensive in coverage and detailed and specific in examples analyzed, it provides over 25 key concepts to the field of Latinx Studies as shaped within historical, social, cultural, regional, and global contexts, including:

- Body
- Border Theory
- Digital Era
- Familia
- Immigration
- Intersectionality

- Language
- Latinidad/es
- Latinofuturism
- Narco Cultura
- Popular Culture
- Sports

Fully cross-referenced and complete with suggestions for further reading, *Latinx Studies: The Key Concepts* is an essential guide for anyone studying race, ethnicity, gender, class, education, culture, and globalism.

Frederick Luis Aldama is Arts and Humanities Distinguished Professor of English and University Distinguished Scholar at the Ohio State University where he is also founder and director of LASER and the Humanities & Cognitive Sciences High School Summer Institute. He is author, co-author, and editor of over 36 books, including the *Routledge Concise History of Latino/a Literature* and *Latino/a Literature in the Classroom*, and recently won an Eisner award for *Latinx Superheroes in Mainstream Comics*.

Christopher González is Associate Professor of English and Director of the Latinx Cultural Center at Utah State University in Logan, Utah. His research and teaching focus on twentieth- and twenty-first century Latinx literature, film, television, comics, and narrative theory. He is the author of *Reading Junot Díaz* (2015) and *Permissible Narratives: The Promise of Latino/a Literature* (2017).

LATINX STUDIES

The Key Concepts

Frederick Luis Aldama and Christopher González

Routledge
Taylor & Francis Group
NEW YORK AND LONDON

First published 2019
by Routledge
52 Vanderbilt Avenue, New York, NY 10017

and by Routledge
2 Park Square, Milton Park, Abingdon, Oxon, OX14 4RN

Routledge is an imprint of the Taylor & Francis Group, an informa business

Library of Congress Cataloging-in-Publication Data
Names: Aldama, Frederick Luis, 1969- author. | González,
Christopher, author.
Title: Latinx studies : the key concepts / Frederick Luis Aldama &
Christopher Gonzâlez.
Other titles: Latino/a studies
Description: New York, NY : Routledge, 2019. | Series: Routledge
key guides | Includes index.
Identifiers: LCCN 2018033533 (print) | LCCN 2018037782 (ebook) |
ISBN 9781315109862 (Master) | ISBN 9781138088436 (hardback :
alk. paper) | ISBN 9781138088443 (pbk. : alk. paper)
Subjects: LCSH: Hispanic Americans–Encyclopedias | United States–
Civilization–Hispanic influences–Encyclopedias.
Classification: LCC E184.S75 (ebook) | LCC E184.S75 A77 2019
(print) | DDC 973/.0468–dc23
LC record available at https://lccn.loc.gov/2018033533

ISBN: 978-1-138-08843-6 (hbk)
ISBN: 978-1-138-08844-3 (pbk)
ISBN: 978-1-315-10986-2 (ebk)

Typeset in Bembo
by Swales & Willis Ltd, Exeter, Devon, UK

CONTENTS

INTRODUCTION

First, we want to mention that we use the term Latinx throughout this book to be inclusive of all genders and sexual orientation as well as to embrace a term generated and deployed by new generations of Latinxs in the US. By no means does this mean that we erase the history and politics that inform the term, Latino/a. However, we side with those who consider this a powerful bottom-up claiming of language in ways that demonstrate inclusivity. As Sandra L. Soto-Santiago succinctly states: "The 'x', the '@', and whatever may come after this, are an invitation to question language and those who impose those rules upon us" (p. 91). She concludes how the category Latinx "dis-mantle[s] what exists and invites us to re-think how individuals with different ideologies, perspectives, and identities are included or rejected from different spaces or communities through language" (p. 91).

Latinx Studies is made up of scholarship in all disciplines (and multi-directionally *across* all disciplines) that seeks to enrich understanding of the history, culture, politics, socioeconomics, policies, and much more that have informed the shaping of US Latinxs with ties to Dominican, Cuban, Mexican, Puerto Rican, Caribbean, Central, South American, and African ancestry and heritage.

This is to say, the category Latinx—along with its orthographic variants Latino/a, Latin@, "Latin/o American," among others—is capacious. In *The Norton Introduction to Latino Literature*, Ilan Stavans identifies Latino/a as "the tension between double attachments to place, to language, and to identity" (p. liii). For Stavans, it is language and cultural ancestral heritage that provides the common ground. It's a category that seeks to acknowledge a common hemispheric experience (culture, language, and history) of those inhabiting the North, Central, and South Americas—as well as those with African origins and indigenous roots. It is a category that captures a history of shared struggle in the struggle against colonial and capitalist material inequities and oppressive ideologies that have led to violence against those in our communities, especially the most vulnerable: children and those discriminated against in terms of gender and sexuality. It's a category that, as Suzanne Bost and Frances Aparicio rightfully point out, is "contested, sometimes fluid, and always relational" (p. 2). Contested because as a fluid category that's meant to be all-encompassing, it can also lose the particularities of important differences that inform *all* Latinx identities and experiences in the US.

Latinx Studies is the multidisciplinary approach scholars take to understand the different threads that make up a resplendent latinidad. Juan Poblete sums up its critical purview as vitally grown from within "the borders of ethnic and areas studies" (p. xv). And, editors of *Key Words for Latina/o Studies*, Deborah R. Vargas, Nancy Raquel Mirabal, and Lawrence La Fountain-Stokes also remark on how Latinx Studies clears space within a cultural studies space that tended to ignore Latinx subjects and non-Anglophone languages. Latinx Studies scholarship aims to disrupt disciplinary borders as well as to radically refocus the objects and subjects of analysis. Its multidisciplinary methodologies and transcultural approaches seek to disrupt "structural and discursive borders" (p. 2), as Paul Allatson states. Latinx Studies seeks to "forge new transnational and transcultural understandings of US and trans-American sociocultural life, and of the USA's global reach as well" (p. 6).

Each Key Concept in this book will identify the vast variety of identities and experiences that make up this umbrella category: Mexican American, Hispano, Chicano, Nuyorican, **Boricuan**, Cubano, Dominican, PortoMexes, Cubolivians, Mexistanis, Blatinos, LusoLatinos, among others. They will uncover the rich variety of ways that Latinxs exist and transform the US: from histories of colonization and displacement to the forming of new contact zones. Indeed, we discover the vast variety of uses of language that rework Standard English and Spanish in newly formed contact zones shaped by "the linguistic reality of [the Latinx] multilingual population" (p. 92), as Lourdes Torres states.

We also discover how each history of Latinx Studies as a record of Latinxs living in time and place as a historical, sociological entity that today is the *majority* minority population in the United States. According to the US census data from April 1, 2010, one out of every six people in the United States is Latinx. Those of Mexican origin represent the largest group: approximately 31 million. Those of Puerto Rican origin: 4 million. Those of Central American origin: 4 million. Those of Cuban origin: 1.6 million. These numbers do not account for the undocumented Latinxs living in the United States that number 10–12 million.

We live in a country where people migrate from all over the world; this mainstream is decisively mixed and multicultural. It is a country where Latinxs and all other groups that make up the general population have grown a rich and diverse appetite for a wide variety of cultural products. Satisfying this diversified demand creates new needs and new demands. And this satisfaction of new appetites implies the education of the senses (tastes, smells, touch, sounds, sights) as well as the education of the cultural needs with respect to these appetites. It implies the education of aesthetic capabilities and interpretations. Scholars of Latinx Studies function as guides to show how our history and presence matters.

Different historical conditions have led to different moments and ways that Latinx communities have moved within the US and across the hemisphere. For instance, the post-WWII Great Migration of Puerto Ricans to US cities was fueled by policies such as Operation Bootstrap, whereby many Puerto Ricans left to find jobs in urban centers in the United States. This led to, as David Colón writes, an "economic disturbance on the island, and a massive wave of migration, sustained over decades and often operating in two directions, to New York City in particular" (p. 272). For Colón, this was the moment of the birth of the Nuyorican subjects who cross all linguistic, social, and cultural boundaries. As Urayoán Noel further identifies, they explored "the complexities of identity and belonging at multiple levels: family, community, city, nation, and beyond" (pp. xiii–xiv). It is this urban demographic that eventually led to, as Vanessa Pérez Rosario (2010) remarks, "a shift in this literature from a rural to an urban focus" (p. 8).

As the Latinx population has increased, so too has its socioeconomic diversity, yielding a sufficiently large number of urban educated, middle-class individuals who, in turn, yield a sufficiently large number of cultural producers, consumers, and interpreters: authors, filmmakers, intellectuals, readers, critics and academics, scientists, and the like.

Over the course of two centuries, Latinx cultural production has been closely linked to the history of Latinxs. Those working under conditions that made it difficult to have the free time to do anything other than sleep to those today who have more of a chance to become authors. For instance, those Mexican workers and immigrants of the 1930s that constituted the majority of the labor force in Texas's cotton industry did not have the time or energy to write novels—or any document for that matter. Under these conditions, even if the will to write or to read was present, there was little time for either a readership or an authorship to grow. Once socioeconomic and political conditions began to change for some of the population of Latinxs then we see a growth in a series of Latinx cultural phenomena and Latinx audiences.

Latinxs have been actively and deeply transforming materially, culturally, and intellectually the everyday lived reality of peoples in the US. Clearly, Latinxs have been transforming the sounds, sights, tastes, and smells of the US for quite some time, and this is especially the case with our increased **urbanization** and population growth. To this end, each Key Concept considers the significant historical, educational, social, political contexts that created the material conditions that have over time solidified the creative, interpretive, and intellectual presence of Latinxs in the US.

To enrich our reader's understanding of what Latinx Studies is, in each Key Concept we discuss the different creative, interpretive, and intellectual threads that weave together this tapestry across time as well as geographical and institutional spaces. We provide a general context for understanding both how Latinx have *shaped* the reality we live in, and also how Latinxs have studied, interpreted, and evaluated our transformative presence in the US. We show how the many different areas of inquiry make visible how the Latinx cultural and material presence (through struggle and victory) has significantly altered the building blocks of reality. We show how the different tributaries feed into this field known as Latinx Studies today and how this deepens our understanding of the cultural and material activities of Latinxs within a global context.

Each Key Concept provides an overview of the critical debates and discussions that gravitate around those foundational areas in which Latinxs have been transforming all aspects of US reality: education, health, public policy, media, sports, language, popular culture, and so much more. We identify the major scholarly branches that make known the variety and vitality of the presence and significant influence of Latinxs in the shaping of the culture, history, politics and policies, and language of the Américas—and beyond. Taken as a whole, the key concepts make clear how Latinx Studies is a dynamic, multiform field that's constantly being shaped as well as shaping what we know of the world we inhabit.

Finally, with a general assault on the Latinx subjects across the country fanned by fake news and xenophobic propaganda, more than ever there's a powerful urgency to our dissemination of Latinx Studies concepts and tools to enrich knowledge about Latinxs today.

Works Cited

Allatson, Paul. *Key Terms in Latino/a Cultural and Literary Studies*. Oxford: Blackwell Press, 2007.

Bost, Suzanne, and Frances R. Aparicio, ed. "Introduction." In *The Routledge Companion to Latino/a Literature*. London: Routledge, 2013, pp. 1–10.

Colón, David. "Other Latino Poetic Method." *Cultural Critique*, vol. 47, 2001, pp. 265–286.

Noel, Urayoan. *In Visible Movement: Nuyorican Poetry from the Sixties to Slam*. Iowa City, IA: University of Iowa Press, 2014.

Pérez Rosario, Vanessa. ed. *Hispanic Caribbean Literature of Migration: Narratives of Displacement*. New York: Palgrave Macmillan, 2010.

Poblete, Juan, ed. "Introduction." *Critical Latin American and Latino Studies*. Minneapolis, MN: University of Minnesota Press, 2003, pp. ix–xxxii.

Soto-Santiago, Sandra L. "What's in an 'x'?: An Exchange about the Politics of 'Latinx'." *Chiricú Journal*, vol. 1, no. 2, 2017, pp. 78–91.

Stavans, Ilan, ed. "Introduction: The Search for Wholeness." *The Norton Anthology of Latino Literature*. New York: W.W. Norton, 2011, pp. lxiii–lxxi.

Torres, Lourdes. "In the Contact Zone: Code-Switching Strategies by Latino/a Writers." *MELUS*, vol. 32, no. 1, 2007, pp. 75–96.

Vargas, Deborah R., Nancy Raquel Mirabal, and Lawrence La Fountain-Stokes, eds. "Introduction." *Key Words in Latina/o Studies*, New York: New York University Press, 2017, pp. 1–6.

LATINX STUDIES

The Key Concepts

AMÉRICAS

The concept of the Américas within US Latinx Studies encompasses a wide range of debates, theories, and scholarship that locate US Latinx subjects, experiences, histories, linguistic practices, and cultural phenomena generally within a hemispheric, transnational north and south continental American framework. As such, the Américas denotes more than a cartographic space. Rather, as Alexandra T. Vazquez sums up, it is an "anti-cartographic object, curricular and aesthetic and alive, that gets us toward a more expansive sense of place and time and people" (p. 11).

Within US Latinx Studies, many scholars aim to understand the historical, social, cultural forces that have shaped and continue to shape the very varied Latinx communities and experiences within and across the regions and nations that make up the north and south American continents. As such, many Latinx Studies scholars have been attentive to the histories and material outcomes of colonial, imperial, and capitalist socioeconomic and ideological forces that have created systemic patterns of disenfranchisement and inequality across the Américas, especially for **mestizo/as**, Afrolatinos, and indigenous peoples. Scholars have attended to the different transcultural networks that grow out of contact zones of cultural creation across the Américas. While seeking to identify historical and cultural common grounds, the aim is to not reduce, as Paul Allatson writes "the Americas to a homogenous whole or a mere space of diversity" (p. 19).

The early histories of **conquest** and colonization of the Américas become a common ground for US Latinx and Latin American scholars to bring a multipronged (historical-material, ideological, and transcultural) approach to their hemispheric scholarship. Many scholars excavate and analyze the early chronicles, or crónicas, of EuroSpanish conquistadores and clergy and the ways that their narratives "invented" and alchemize the physical, geographic, and human material space of the Américas into imaginary spaces in need of filling; that is, these scholars excavate how these conquistadors and clergy created narratives that imagined an Américas *avant la lettre* in need of taming: namely, exploiting, raping, and mass-scale murdering. Several consider the "invention" of the Américas to take place already with Columbus's 1492 diaries and Amerigo Vespucci's pamphlet, *Mundus Novus* (1503) that combined the magical with realism in their narratives. (See also Frederick Luis Aldama's *Postethnic Narrative Criticism*). And for others it happens with early maps of the Américas, beginning with Martin Waldseemüller and Matthias Ringmann's *Universalis Cosmographia* (1500) and its use of the the name America to identify this new world geographic space. For José Rabassa, it is Hernán Pérez de Oliva's use of the concept "invention" in the title of his *crónicas, Historia de la invención de las Yndias* (1528), that solidifies the construction of a Europe-as-civilized vs. the Américas-as-wild Manichean allegory (*Inventing America* 54). Indeed, for Rabassa, it is through the "dismantling of how America was invented in the sixteenth century, and continues to be invented" that we can understand the deep history of colonization that connects the disenfranchised across the Américas. To this end, Rabassa reads the construction of the Américas "as a regime of signs" that can shed light on the "the geographic, cartographic, and historic constituents underlying our present picture of the world" (p. 214). For Jesús Carillo, it is chivalric romance author and conquistador Gonzalo Fernández de Oviedo's *Historia general y natural de las Indias* (1526, 1535; and posthumously as complete volume 1851–1855) that conceived of an Américas that stretched beyond the continent to include the Pacific Rim countries where Spanish conquests continued, including Moluccas and the Philippines (1519 and 1542).

Many scholars have critically excavated these early EuroSpanish *crónicas* to show how expansive this dark, racialized ideological construction of the Américas became over time. However, there have been others who have excavated other early *crónicas* to shed light on how the **pre-Columbian** indigenous presence linked communities and people across the Américas before the conquest and colonization. For some scholars today and important figures in history such as Simón Bolívar, it is texts such as Bartolomé de Las Casas's *Historia de Las Indias* (written in 1542 and published in 1552) that defend the indigenous peoples of the Américas—albeit as primitive, noble savages—that proved counterpoints to those of the conquistadores. Indeed, some consider de Las Casas' text to be the main inspiration of Simón Bolívar who aimed to at once establish sovereign proto-nation-states *and* unite South American peoples in order to liberate the Américas from Spanish rule. (See Paul S. Vickery's "Bartolomé De Las Casas: Prophet of the New World.") And, other Latinx scholars have recuperated Cabeza de Vaca's *Relación* (1542) as an early trans-hemispheric narrative. Indeed, Nicolás Kanellos includes *La Relación* in *Herencia: The Anthology of Hispanic Literature of the United States* as one of the foundational narratives of Latin/o Américas. And, Genaro Padilla considers Gaspar Perez de Villagra's *Historia de la Nueva México* (1610) to be one of the first Latinx narratives as it combines "European and indigenous Mexican figures, rituals, and origin stories into a single tale" (p. 35) along with Aztec symbols (cactus, eagle, and serpent).

Many US Latinx scholars who seek to re-orientate cultural histories with an Américas purview in mind have found inspiration in the work of Cuban author and activist, José Martí. His 1891 essay, "Nuestra América" (first published in New York City then Mexico City), envisions a hemispheric unity in the struggle against divisive US imperialist forces. As Ramón A. Gutiérrez and Elliott Young sum up, "Martí proposed an international order governed by states, organized around a common identity as Americans in the north and in the south, which obliterated the borders of nation-states along with U.S. economic and cultural dominance" (p. 30). Scholars such as José David Saldívar have used Martí as a springboard to conceptualize an analytic framework for understanding the creation of resistant and revolutionary cultural phenomena as grown from shared histories of struggle against colonization and US imperialism across the Hispanophone Caribbean and *latinoaméricas*. Saldívar uses Martí as a sounding board of sorts to give shape to a politically resistant "pan-American literary history" (*The Dialectics of our America* 5). Saldívar deepens the move to articulate a hemispheric Américas in his *Border Matters* (1997) and *Trans-Americanity* (2012). In each we see scholarly moves that expand the borders for studying Latinx cultural phenomena across the Américas—and inclusive of other colonized regions of the planet's southern hemisphere such as Subcontinental India. He articulates a global **borderlands**, a postcolonial trans-americanity that's "outernational" to study US Latinx cultural phenomena like literature within other global south cultural practices.

Other Hispanophone Caribbean and Latin American scholars have proved important for the articulation of a hemispheric Américas critical framework for analyzing cultural phenomena. For instance, Roberto Fernández Retamar's essay "Caliban" (1970 in Spanish and 1974 in English) has proved to be an important inspiration to both Latinx and Latin American scholars today who seek to excavate hemispheric cultural traditions that resist nation-state exceptionalism and US imperialism and that affirm the struggles of mestizos across the Hispanophone hemisphere. Others such as Nestor García Canclini and his concept of hybridity have been used by Latinx scholars to reveal how artificial notions like highbrow and lowbrow culture are ideological constructs that deepen class and social divisions. And, much like Caclini's formulation of a hybrid, transformative cultural production and knowledge making in and across the Américas, so too has the work of Fernando Ortiz proved useful. In his *Cuban Counterpoint* he formulates the concept of "transculturation" to identify how cultures move across nation-state borders, and in multidirectional patterns of mutual transformation that ultimately create a new cultural object. For Latinx scholars, Ortiz's "transculturation" and its generative concept of social and cultural syncretism across the Américas stand in sharp contrast with an acculturation model that's assimilative in its unidirectional move from non-US (inferior) to US culture (superior). Indeed, Ortiz's dynamic model has been useful for today's Latinx scholars to articulate how shared contact zones across the Américas have created powerful transculturative products, and this in an ever continuous and transformative way whereby these new fusions lead to the emergence of new cultural phenomena. (See Aldama and Stavans *¡Muy Pop!*)

Some US Latinx scholars choose to excavate other early narratives that sought to identify an affirming common ground between different subjugated populations across the Américas, including Amerindians, mestizos, and Afrolatinos. Latinx scholars such as Juan Bruce-Novoa, Jesse Alemán, José Aranda, Kirstin Silva Gruesz, Amelia María de la Luz Montes, John Michael Rivera, and Raúl Coronado recover the textual phenomena of earlier epochs to move cultural histories away from English-only, and an East-to-West (or Europe/Anglo Eastern US) orientation. They do so to formulate a multilingual, comparative, trans-hemispheric framework for analyzing cultural phenomena. In *Ambassadors of Culture* Kirstin Silva Gruesz excavates new hemispheric literary genealogies by attending to Spanish language archives that show how this "larger web" of publishers, circulation, and reading communities expand our notions of white, Anglophone centers of cultural production. With Latinx scholars seeking to explore ways that movement of culture and knowledge from Spanish and Portuguese contexts to North American Anglophone contexts creates a more accurate history of transculturation across the *Américas* we've seen the flourishing of new work. Non-Latinxs such as Caroline F. Levander and Robert S. Levine articulate an Américas framework. In *Hemispheric American Studies* the essays identify how literary, cultural, social, political, and economic relationships between the United States and other nations in the Américas have shaped cultural production in the early North American US republic. And, in Anna Brickhouse's *Transamerican Literary Relations and the Nineteenth-Century Public Sphere* (2004) she demonstrates how an Américas orientation can open canonical US literature to other ways of understanding how they work within a larger network of the texts from Mexico, Cuba, Haiti, the Dominican Republic and how they are all shaped by complex intercultural and postcolonial interrelations. (See also Juan Poblete's edited *Critical Latin American and Latino Studies*.)

Indeed, several Latinx scholars have excavated early colonial and post-colonial narratives to identify a borderland hemispheric Américas that affirms pan-Amerindian, feminist, and queer subjectivities and experiences. We see this in the 1970s and 1980s in the work of Gloría Anzaldúa, Cherríe Moraga, Ana Castillo, Lucha Corpí, and Pat Mora. José Vasconcelos' 1925 publication of **La Raza** *Cósmica: Misión de la raza iberoamericana* proved seminal to the articulation of a hemispheric concept of Latinidad—or Latinoness. Rather than see racial mixture (European, African, indigenous) across the Américas—his "bronze continent"—as a deficit, as the colonizers did, Vasconcelos positively affirms **mestizaje** as the next evolutionary phase of humans. Several scholars and activists used this as the springboard to formulate a reconquest of the US Southwest—formerly Mexico's northern territories and the space of the mythic Aztlán. Others complicated Vasconcelos' affirmation of the bronze race ("la raza de bronce") to formulate a borderland, hemispheric space of inclusion. We see this in Anzaldúa's *Borderlands/La Frontera: The New Mestiza* where she claims the space for women and lesbians of color. We see here and elsewhere the work of Latina queer feminists clearing the space for an Américas that affirms racial mixture or *mestizaje* and that celebrates anti-colonial, hemispheric unities out of the diverse indigenous histories and egalitarian politics. (See also *This Bridge Called My Back: Writings by Radical Women of Color*.) Finally, Latinx scholars such as Anzaldúa and others recuperated the Nahuatl word and concept, "Nepantla" to identify their "in-between" existence: one caught up in between the legacies of ancient Aztec knowledge and cultural practice along with the brutal histories of EuroSpanish conquest and colonization. As Walter Mignolo sums up of this Nepantla in-between state of surviving, it is "not a happy place in the middle" but rather "a general question of knowledge and power" (p. 2) for the dislocated and disenfranchised of the Américas. (See Arturo Aldama et al. *Comparative Indigeneities of the Américas: Toward a Hemispheric Approach*.)

The concept of an expansive, ever breathing and growing of peoples and cultures within in-between spaces of the Américas is made explicit not only within US/Mexico borderlands (the focus of Anzaldúa, for instance), but also expansive concepts of Caribbean, Greater Mexico, and the South as the Global South and Nuevo South. (See Jamie Winders's "Commentary: New Directions in the Nuevo South.")

Antonio Benítez-Rojo's "repeating islands" concept of Caribbean archipelago seeks to express the complexity of hybrid transculturative processes and experiences and subjectivities formed across national boundaries. And, Silvio Torres-Saillant identifies Dominican Latinxs also within a hemispheric space whereby a diverse range of Dominican Latinxs speak "with a complex but single voice" (p. 139). And, those such as José Limón and Ramón Saldívar variously use the concept of "Greater Mexico" to expand their study of Latinx cultural production beyond US nation-state boundaries. For instance, in *American Encounters* José Limón uses the concept of "Greater Mexico" (Américo Paredes) to consider how mestizo bodies at once become objects of racialized "eroticism and desire" (p. 4) and resist such objectification. And, in *The Borderlands of Culture* Ramón Saldívar identifies how seminal Latinx scholar and cultural creator, Américo Paredes, embodies the "transnational imaginary" of a Greater Mexico consciousness formed out of a pan-American culture (430). And, Latinx scholars have used the "Global South" concept to enrich understanding of confluences of Latinx and African American coexistence and co-cultural production. For instance, in *Latining America* Claudia Milian uses the Global South concept to identify "Latinities of blackness" that resist brown vs. white racial paradigms. For Milian, Langston Hughes can be seen as providing "critical energy for new articulations, signs, color lines, and assemblages of bodies that pass through the apodictic character of U.S. Latino and Latina brownness and dark brownness as well as U.S. African American blackness" (p. 151).

The Américas has been used by Latinx scholars to expand the ways in which we understand histories of cultural production, dissemination, and consumption. They do so to clear spaces for greater inclusivity of mestizo, African, and indigenous legacies. Ramón A. Gutiérrez writes how nation-state borders and boundaries fail "to contain, to constrain, to delimit, or to fully define how humans live their lives" (p. 29). Indeed, for US Latinx scholars, the proximate location to language and cultures of the Central and South Américas necessarily make this a non-assimilative population. With constant vital growing of Latinx populations from those from the Global South and beyond, Latinx demographics are constantly changing the racial and cultural configuration of the US—and in a transculturative (and not assimilationist) manner. This said, Latinx scholars are mindful that there continue to exist unequal exchanges and flows of cultural (and intellectual) phenomena across the Américas; US mainstream culture and English-language intellectual and creative products continue to overwhelm the lives of those of Central and South America. The

Hollywood juggernaut is a case in point. Latinx scholars are mindful that the nation-state borders and boundaries have artificially cut up the Américas in ways that prevent the movement of real bodies—and with tragic consequences. **NAFTA** is the clearest example of this. It fortified borders against the movement of real people all while dismantling trade policies for the free flow of global capitalism through the exploitation of Latinx workers on the Mexican side of the border. It at once created super exploitable conditions for workers in Mexico as well as divested them of the means for self-sufficiency with its imposition of trade tariffs. In "The Fungibility of Borders" Mary Pat Brady states: "The deportations and disenfranchisement of tens of thousands of U.S. citizens have largely been kept from canonical U.S. histories, but they reveal the extent to which borders serve to establish stratified networks of laborers" (p. 182). And, in *The Fence and the River* Claire Fox asks that we be mindful of theorizing "hybrid or liminal subjectivities" as abstracting into oblivion the real lives of those forced to leave homelands and to traverse dangerous and deadly borders.

Works Cited

Aldama, Arturo, M. Bianet Castellanos, and Lourdes Gutiérrez Nájera, eds. *Comparative Indigeneities of the Américas: Toward a Hemispheric Approach.* Tucson, AZ: University of Arizona Press, 2012.

Aldama, Frederick Luis, and Ilan Stavans. *Postethnic Narrative Criticism: Magicorealism in Ana Castillo, Hanif Kureishi, Julie Dash, Oscar "Zeta" Acosta, and Salman Rushdie.* Austin, TX: University of Texas Press, 2003.

———. *¡Muy Pop! Conversations on Latino Popular Culture.* Co-authored with Ilan Stavans. Ann Arbor, MI: University of Michigan Press, 2013.

Allatson, Paul. *Key Terms in Latinx Cultural and Literary Studies.* Oxford: Blackwell Publishing, 2007.

Anzaldúa, Gloria and Cherríe Morga, eds. *This Bridge Called My Back: Writings By Radical Women of Color.* New York: Kitchen Table, Women of Color Press, 1983.

Anzaldúa, Gloria. *Borderlands/La Frontera: The New Mestiza.* San Francisco, CA: Aunt Lute Books, 1987.

Benítez-Rojo, Antonio. *The Repeating Island: The Caribbean and the Postmodern Perspective.* Durham, NC: Duke University Press, 1992.

Brady, Mary Pat. "The Fungibility of Borders." *Nepantla: Views from South,* vol. 1, no. 1, 2000, pp. 171–190.

Brickhouse, Anna. *Transamerican Literary Relations and the Nineteenth-Century Public Sphere.* New York: Cambridge University Press, 2004.

Fox, Claire. *The Fence and the River: Culture and Politics at the U.S.–Mexico Border.* Minneapolis, MN: University of Minnesota Press, 1999.

Gruesz, Kirsten Silva. *Ambassadors of Culture: The Transamerican Origins of Latino Writing*. Princeton, NJ: Princeton University Press, 2002.

Gutiérrez, Ramón A., and Elliott Young. "Transnationalizing Borderlands History." *Western Historical Quarterly*, vol. 41, 2010, pp. 27–53.

Kanellos, Nicolás. *Herencia: The Anthology of Hispanic Literature of the United States*. Oxford: Oxford University Press, 2002.

Levander, Caroline F., and Robert S. Levine, eds. *Hemispheric American Studies*. New Brunswick, NJ: Rutgers University Press, 2008.

Limón, José. *American Encounters: Greater Mexico, the United States, and the Erotics of Culture*. Boston, MA: Beacon Press, 1998.

Martí, José. "Nuestra América." *Biblioteca Clacso*. http://bdigital.bnjm.cu/docs/libros/PROCE11914/Nuestra%20America.pdf

Milian, Claudia. *Latining America: Black–Brown Passages and the Coloring of Latinx Studies*. Athens, GA: University of Georgia Press, 2013.

Ortiz, Fernando. *Cuban Counterpoint: Tobacco and Sugar*. Durham, NC: Duke University Press, 1995.

Poblete, Juan. ed. *Critical Latin American and Latino Studies*. Minneapolis, MN: University of Minnesota Press, 2003.

Rabassa, José. *Inventing America: Spanish Historiography and the Formation of Eurocentrism*. Norman, OK: University of Oklahoma Press, 1993.

Retamar, Roberto Fernández. *Caliban and Other Essays*. University of Minnesota Press, 1989.

Saldívar, José David. *The Dialectics of our America: Genealogy, Cultural Critique, and Literary History*. Durham, NC: Duke University Press, 1991.

———. *Border Matters: Remapping American Cultural Studies*. Berkeley, CA: University of California Press, 1997.

———. *Trans-Americanity: Subaltern Modernities, Global Coloniality, and the Cultures of Greater Mexico*. Durham, NC: Duke University Press, 2012.

Saldívar, Ramón. *The Borderlands of Culture: Américo Paredes and the Transnational Imaginary*. Durham, NC: Duke University Press, 2006.

Torres-Saillant, Silvio. "Visions of Dominicanness in the United States." In *Borderless Borders*, edited by Frank Bonilla. Philadelphia, PA: Temple University Press, 1998, pp. 139–152.

Vasconcelos, José. *La Raza Cósmica: Misión de la raza iberoamericana*. Baltimore, MD: Johns Hopkins University Press, 1997.

Vazquez, Alexandra T. "Americas." In *Keywords in Latina/o Studies*, edited by Deborah R. Vargas, Lawrence La Fountain-Stokes and Nancy Raquel Mirabal. New York: New York University Press, 2017, pp. 10–11.

Vespucci, Amerigo. *Mundus Novus: Letter to Lorenzo Pietro di Medici*, translated by George Tyler Northup. Princeton, NJ: Princeton University Press, 1916.

Vickery, Paul S. "Bartolomé De Las Casas: Prophet of the New World." *Mediterranean Studies*, vol. 9, 2000, pp. 89–102.

Winders, Jamie. "Commentary: New Directions in the Nuevo South." *Southeastern Geographer*, vol. 51, no. 2, 2011, pp. 327–340.

ART

An important area of Latinx Studies interpretive work is focused on the arts: visual, installation, conceptual, sculptural, photographic, mural, comic book, and tattoo arts. Indeed, we see from this area of material and interpretive production how the Latinx arts variously distill then reconstruct everyday experiences, histories, cultures, and identities. As Rita Gonzalez sums up of Latinx scholarship on Latinx art, it seeks to "negotiate a dual (or even multiple) reality of transnational identity while still understanding how the local or regional inform the works of many artists" (p. 14). Latinx Studies scholars seek to understand how Latinx creators of art in time (history) and space (region) distill then reconstruct Latinx identities and experiences in ways that make new the perception, thought, and feeling of its audiences.

There are several interpretive tributaries that make up the different ways that Latinx Studies approaches the arts. Some seek to recover and make visible historical influences (indigenous and non-indigenous, pre-conquest, colonial, and post-colonial). Some seek to focus on US sociopolitical and material contexts (as connected also to practices in the Hispanophone Caribbean and the hemispheric Américas) that shape artists and their art. Some seek to identify and analyze the shaping devices used in the making of a given art object. Some combine different degrees of the above approaches. All in all, they seek to make visible this important part of Latinx production, dissemination, and consumption of cultural phenomena known as the Latinx arts.

Latinx artists have found ways to dedicate their time and minds to the making of art—and this in spite of gatekeeping policies and practices that have tried to exclude them. Many of the Latinx artists creating before the Brown Power Movements did so largely in isolation and as self-taught. Many that did have access to formal arts education spaces did so because of institutions such as the GI Bill and newly created scholarships and affirmative action policies. As a result of the post-civil rights gains that opened doors more widely to education spaces for Latinxs, many more could sharpen their skills and deepen their knowledge of art history in university settings.

For instance, Carmen Lomas Garza was able to parlay her passion for art—her mother's painting and grandmother's embroidery—into an arts education degree from Texas A&M, Kingsville, followed by an MA from San Francisco State. Others such as graphic artist, painter, and scholar Rupert Garcia used his GI Bill to attend San Francisco School for the Arts. Painter, theorist, and co-founder of the Chicano Arts Movement, Melesio "Mel" Casas used the GI Bill to attend University of Texas, El Paso and then went on to help establish the politicized *Con Safos* art group in the early 1970s. César Martínez, after serving in Vietnam, attended A&I University where he became another important figure in the *Con Safos* arts movement. And Ester Hernandez made her way from fieldworker family roots to UC Berkeley during the mid-1970s where the Chicano struggle empowered her to create politically charged art and to join the "The Mujeres Muralistas" in San Francisco's Mission. Gaspar Enriquez worked as a machinist while honing his portraiture (cholo/as and Chicano historical figures) at East LA Junior College, then University of Texas, El Paso. Studio and mural artist, Judithe Hernández was the first student to win the LACMA awarded "Future Masters Scholarship" to attend LA's Otis Art Institute. She went on to become the only woman of Los Four acts collective that was shaping the Chicano arts vanguard during the 1970s. And, while Patssi Valdez began socio-politically minded painting, photography, and performance art with *ASCO* right out of high school in the early 1970s, she also went on to get a BFA from Otis Art Institute (1985). Found-object artist Raphael Montañez Ortiz (who went on to found El Museo del Barrio in East Harlem) attended Art and Design High School of New York City then went on to get his BFA and MFA at the Pratt Institute in the early to mid 1960s. And, Richard Duardo studied art at Pasadena Community College then UCLA where he got his MFA. He went on to co-found in the late 1970s the political arts collective, Centro de Arte Público.

And, more recently, cartoon artist, muralist, and poster illustrator Eric J. García, after enlisting in the armed services, went on to earn his Bachelors of Fine Arts from the University of New Mexico and to get his Masters of Fine Arts degree from the School of the Art Institute of Chicago. A versatile artist working in an assortment of media, from hand-printed posters, to nationally published political cartoons, to large-scale public murals, they all have a common goal of educating and challenging. And, there's the huge obstacles that digital artist Federico Cuatlacuatl overcame as an undocumented Latinx living in the US who nevertheless managed to find a path to Ball State (BFA) then Bowling Green State University for an MFA in digital arts.

There are many other Latinx artists who are entirely self-taught, honing their craft at home and on the street; this was literally the case for Blatino (Haitian/Nuyorican American) polyglot (English, Spanish, French), Jean-Michel Basquiat. After dropping out of high school and being kicked out of his home, in the mid- to late 1970s he found himself living on the streets all while finding his way to artistic expression in the graffiti arts (his "SAMO" paintings). Alex Rubio's art education space was that of the walls of the Marisol public housing project on San Antonio's West Side; at one point, he even took a bullet. He expanded his graffiti art repertoire to include acrylic and graphite art that draws on **barrio** and prison life. And, Luis Tapia dropped out of New Mexico State to work retail and grow his craft as an artist of santos, retablos, altares, and **bultos**. In the early 1970s he went on to found La Cofradia de Artes y Artesanos Hispanicos group that grew public awareness of Hispanic art in the Southwest.

Of course, these are just a handful of many of the Latinxs that chose the difficult path of becoming artists in a US that was actively discriminatory against them. Even those that found pathways to art education spaces did not find knowledge about Latinx arts or Latin American arts traditions and practices. For instance, while Tejana artist Santa Contreras Barraza made her way to art school at Texas A&I University in the early 1970s, she had to educate herself about Latinx arts and cultural histories.

One way or another, Latinx artists were considered unworthy of museum and other sanctified spaces; many of the curators of the art world (from professors to gallery owners to museum boards) considered anything by Latinxs too lowbrow, regional, primitive, or even peasant-like. And, the US lacked robust institutions of art patronage seen in places such as Mexico and Cuba. So, Latinx artists began displaying their art in public spaces (walls, lowriders, bodies, and more) as well as organizing into art collectives such as *Con Safos, ASCO*, Los Four, and others. These and other grassroots arts movements grew art out of the communities and for the communities. For the most part, they created an art connected to the social and political. Along with those artists mentioned above there are many others, including: Margaret Alarcón, Wayne Alaniz Healy, Chaz Bojorquez, David Botello, Melesio Casas, Gaspar Enriquez, Nicole Limón, Henry Gamboa Jr., Margaret Garcia, Rupert Garcia, Carmen Lomas Garza, Raul Guerrero, Roberto Gutierrez, Adam Hernandez, John Hernandez, Ester Hernandez, Leo Limon, Yolanda López, Alma López, Jose Lozano, Gilbert "Magu" Lujan, Cesar Martinez, José Luis Rivera, Alex Rubio, Marta Sanchez, Eloy Torrez, Jesse Trevino, John Valadez, Vincent Valdez, Pati Vargas, Theresa Ybañez, and George Yepes. For these Latinx creators art served to raise awareness about the identities and experiences of Latinxs in the US—a social tissue ripped apart by racism, oppression, and exploitation. (See the list of Latinx artists at: *A Ver: Revisioning Art History*.)

This isn't to say that Latinx art grew in isolation from other non-Latinx (mainstream) arts practices and movements. Even those such as Luis Tapia who look to Catholic cultural traditions in the making of art *make* something transculturative and new. Afro-Cuban American Andrés Serrano uses all variety of bodily fluid—semen, menstrual, blood, urine, and so on—to radically reframe, and often to great controversy, religious iconography. Other Latinx artists transform cultural iconography from other rituals such as *Día de los Muertos* and *lotería*. Hugo award winning artist, John Picacio, takes the *Día de los Muertos* lithographic work of Mexican artist José Guadalupe Posada and gives it a Latinx science fiction spin. John Jota Leaño's lowrider art sculptures also look to older iconographic *Día de los Muertos* traditions, and do so in ways that seek to decolonize imaginary and real spaces. For instance, he states of his El Muertorider moving art piece (with Artemio Rodriguez) that it "offers social commentary on the policing and silencing of grassroots cruising culture in California rooted in a colonial past rooted in distinctive travel routes from El Camino Real (US 101), the Transcontinental Railroad to Route 66" (www.leanos.net/El_Muertorider.html). Alex Rubio uses his graphite and acrylic art skills to reconstruct *Día de los Muertos* imagery in ways that open eyes to surveillance of Latinx bodies crossing borders and within the prison industrial complex. And, Blatina María Magdalena Campos Pons makes new **Santería** and African diasporic iconography in her photography, painting, and sculptures. While the late Richard Duardo uses the silkscreen, serigraph format, street paint and graffiti style, and iconic Latinx images (lotería, for instance) to Latinx-fy all variety of poster pop art iconography—from Marilyn Monroe to Frida Kahlo, Che Guevara, and Mexican luchadores.

Latina artists were actively creating, but often excluded from within the different Latinx arts collectives and movements. (As mentioned above, *ASCO* and *Los Four* were exceptions to this rule.) For instance, those like Ester Hernandez, Judy Baca, Barbara Carrasco, Judith Hernández, and Yolanda López pushed against the male-dominated **Chicano Movement** (El Movimiento) and its implicit and explicit sexism. They sought to create art that recalibrated viewers' engagement with otherwise macho-oriented, pre-colonial symbols and icons. They often sought to use their art to recover feminist legacies and voices to affirm Latina identities and experiences. In *Walls of Empowerment* Guisela Latorre writes how Judy Baca's "Mi Abuelita" (1971; at East L.A.'s Hollenbeck Park) portrays a grandmother figure with "dark skin, and colorful dress rendered in warm tones" (p. 184), pushing aside the long tradition of Chicano artists who depicted hypersexualized Latinas to clear a space that affirmed the strength and centrality of women in the Latinx community.

Latinx artists recycle anything and everything to make new the perception, thought, and feeling concerning the Latinx experience. In his 1988 essay **"Rasquachismo**, a Chicano Sensibility" Tomás Ybarra-Frausto used the term *rasquachismo* to describe this process that grows from "visceral response to lived reality" and that identified an "aesthetic sensibility of los de abajo, of the underdog" (155–162). We see this in the art of Judy Baca and others mentioned above, as well as cofounder of *ASCO*, painter, sculptor, digital animator, and performance artist, Gronk. We also see it in the fiberglass and plastic pop art sculptures of Luis Jiménez where he uses white and brown color pigments to raise awareness about race and to affirm brown bodies; his rasquache art sensibility grew out of the many hours he spent working on fiberglass and all other kinds of materials in his dad's custom, lowrider body shop. We see this in the Latinx speculative performance art of Guillermo Gomez-Peña that recycles iconography from the past (colonization) and present (US imperialism) to open eyes to Latinxs in an experimental, sci-fi future. And, we see it in the work of Gustavo Crembil and Paula Gaetano with their "AdiTZ'IJK"—a part mud part robotic spheroid art installation that aims to draw awareness to the past (the Mayan creation narrative, Quich) as well as the present (colonial technologies) and the future (a "technoscience that advocates the integration of high and low technological materials, processes and cultures" (http://paulagaetanoadi.com/works/tzijk/). Finally, we see this in the work of installation artist Amalia Mesa-Bains who opens eyes to a *Latina* rasquachismo sensibility. Indeed, Mesa-Bains formally articulated this in a 1996 essay, "Domesticana: The Sensibility of Chicana Rasquache," where she uses the concept of *domesticana* to articulate hers and fellow Latina rasquache art that construct the domestic sphere as place of both paradise and prison. As Rocío Isabel Prado sums up of Latinx art that distills and reconstructs and recycles from anywhere and everywhere: it

> builds upon previous cultural understandings (i.e. folk culture) from many different sources in order to create a sense of relevance within the mestizaje that is Latina/o culture. Consequently, Latina/o pop art does not limit itself to a single source, time period, or language but takes from anything and everything to create work as diverse as the culture it represents.
>
> ("Inexact Revolutions: Understanding Latina/o
> Pop Art," 205–206)

While many Latinx artists choose not to abstract the Latinx experience identity from everyday life, it is important to note that there are Latinx artists who chose more the abstract and found-art routes. For instance, Cuban American Carmen Herrera participated in the New York avant-garde arts movement, working alongside postwar abstractionists, including Mark Rothko, Barnett Newman, and Leon Polk Smith. She developed a very geometric, bold, and angular style that some say anticipated the minimalism of pop art. And Puerto Rican Olga Albizu created thickly painted and gestural canvases (in the manner of German Hans Hofman) that were often reproduced on jazz and bosa nova album covers. While Puerto Rican artist and co-founder of El Museo del Barrio, Raphael Montañez Ortiz, was a central figure in the Destructivism international art movement that used recycled items such as mattresses and pianos to create works that challenged the detachment of the postwar avant-garde.

As mentioned in the beginning of this *Key Concept*, one of the big issues in the Latinx arts has been getting the art out into the public eye. Again, collectives in the 1970s and 1980s formed to clear such spaces. As Prado sums up of ASCO's in your face tactics that demand to be included or else:

> When the Los Angeles County Museum of Art (LACMA) was asked why there was no Chicana/o art in the region's public art institution, a curator replied, "Chicanos don't make art, they're in gangs." In response, the group spray-painted the front of the museum creating the legendary piece, Spray Paint LACMA (Shaked 1059).
>
> (p. 205)

She continues,

> Their critique of the exclusion of Latina/o culture (vandalizing a museum) has become the base upon which artists create a celebration of Latina/o culture (making that vandalism into a piece of art) and has come to define contemporary Latina/o pop art.
>
> (p. 205)

And, while a few Latinxs like Luis Jiménez had made it into the hallowed halls of places such as the Whitney Biennial (where his work appeared along with Roy Lichtenstein in 1973), they had to pound hard on doors that systematically excluded. Los Four's historic 1974 exhibition at the Los Angeles County Museum of Art was the country's first show of Chicano art at a major art institution. ASCO, Los Four, and others mentioned above were not alone. There were others, too, such as the Black Emergency Cultural Coalition and the Art Workers Coalition that advocated for representation of Latinx as well as African American and women in collections and art museums. (See also Carmen E. Ramos's "The Latino Presence in American Art.")

While some Latinx artists and collectives were breaking down doors to sanctified established art museum spaces, others were creating their own spaces. In 1969, artist Raphael Montañez Ortiz founded El Museo del Barrio (operated out of a number of storefronts then moved to a permanent location on Fifth Avenue) to collect, exhibit, and create Latinx arts education (bilingual) programing. In 1970, a group of Chicano artists and community activists in San Francisco's Mission District founded Galería de la Raza as a non-profit community-based exhibition, education, and workshop space. To this day, it continues to support Latinx artists in the visual, literary, media, and performing art fields whose works explore new aesthetic possibilities for socially committed art. And, in 1974 in Philadelphia the Taller Puertorriqueño was established to exhibit Latinx art and build arts education and cultural programming.

Over time, the individual and collective efforts of Latinx artists also showed the nation the significant presence and importance of Latinx art. Today, Latinx artists are not *as* excluded as they were. Indeed, one might argue that Latinx art has been brought into the high-art fold. A case in point: In May 2017, a Japanese billionaire bought Jean-Michel Basquiat's 1982 painting of a skull titled, "Untitled," for $110.5 million. It set the record for the highest price paid for a work by a US artist and for an artwork created after 1980. In 2017, MOLAA, Museum of Latin American Art, Long Beach, variously gave solo exhibition space to the entire life's works of Frank Romero and Luis Tapia, respectively. And, LACMA gave Carlos Almaraz his first major retrospective that traces the evolution of his work from political to more personal and mystical, before his untimely death at the age of 48 in 1989. In 2018, the Walker Art Center in Minneapolis provides exhibition space for the most comprehensive display of Cuban art in the United States since World War II. Cuban-American artist María Brito has her painting and sculpture artwork installed in the Olympic Sculpture Park in Seoul, South Korea, and in the Smithsonian Institution collection. The Smithsonian Coalition for the National Museum of the American People, and the Greater Columbus Arts Foundation seeks to create a museum that "will tell the story of every American ethnic and cultural group coming to this land and nation from every corner of the world, from the first people through today." The Internet has also provided a space for Latinx art that can potentially reach millions of people. Beyond the websites that exhibit the work of individual artists, there are organizations such as the US Latinx Art Forum (www.facebook.com/uslatinoartforum/) dedicated to disseminating knowledge about Latinx art and art history.

Today, too, we have Latinx patrons and collectors with the money to amass huge collections that go on exhibit around the country. We think of the actor Cheech Marin along with businessmen Gil Cardenas, and Joe A. Diaz who have become known as the "Big Three" collectors of Latinx art. Cheech Marin recently announced his plan to open a Center for Chicano Art, Culture and Industry in downtown Riverside. It will house and exhibit Latinx art as well as provide space for lectures, film, and video screening, classrooms, and other spaces.

As we close this *Key Concept* entry on the Latinx arts, we would like to mention that along with the creation and dissemination of art, there has been the interpretation of this art. Shifra Goldman and Tomás Ybarra-Frausto's edited, *Arte Chicano: A Comprehensive Annotated Bibliography of Chicano Art, 1965–1981* published in 1986 provided the first exhaustive bibliography of Chicano art from the colonial era, the 1960s to the early 1980s. The traveling art exhibit Chicano Art: Resistance and Affirmation (CARA) that travelled across the US from 1990–1993 along with the publication *Chicano Art, Resistance and Affirmation* in 1991 were important in solidifying the connection between the Latinx arts and its theorization. It grew out of the first major traveling exhibition of Chicanx art (San Francisco to Denver to San Antonio to New York and Washington) and included discussions and theorizations that articulated its themes of dispossession and disenfranchisement. In 2007, the book series "A Ver: Revisioning Art History" edited by Chon Noriega and run out of UCLA's Chicano Studies Research Center began publishing monographs on Latinx artists, including on Gronk, Yolanda López, Celia Alvarez Muñoz, María Brito, Carmen Lomas Garza, Malaquias Montoya, Rafael Ferrer, Ricardo Valverde, Pepón Osorio, and Luis Cruz Azaceta.

More and more Latinx scholars have been turning their attention to interpreting and analyzing the Latinx arts. We think readily of the work of Alicia Gaspar de Alba, Luz Calvo, Catriona Rueda Esquibel, Gary D. Keller, Richard Griswold del Castillo, Yvonne Yarbro-Bejarano, Richard T. Rodríguez, Laura Pérez, and Guisela Latorre. Scholarly work on Latinx art considers both the formal and political and social underpinnings that informed much of its production since the late 1960s.

Indeed, in 2007 Laura Pérez published the first book-length study on Chicana art, *Chicana Art: The Politics of Spiritual and Aesthetic Altarities* (2007). In her analysis of over 40 Latinx artists and their art created from the mid-1980s and 2000, she formulates a concept of "altarities" to identify a political spiritualist thematic that is "socially transformative, and psychically healing" (p. 25). Latina artists rework pre-Columbian notions of the spiritual, art, and art-making represented in "spirit glyphs" (p. 22), codices and Aztec figures to construct hybrid spiritualities that disrupt capitalistic and materialistic visions of reality.

In 2008, Guisela Latorre published her book length study of Chicano/a mural arts, *Walls of Empowerment*. Focusing on the aesthetic, historical, and political ingredients that inform Chicana/o mural art in the twentieth and twenty-first centuries, Latorre builds a "visual vocabulary" specifically attuned to Chicana/o mural art as it is created in time (history) and place (geographic region and community). Here Latorre studies the use of Mexican indigenous leitmotifs picked up by Chicana/o artists working in the late 1960s and 1970s, critiquing histories of primitivizing and exoticizing indigenous peoples along with showing how Chicana/o artists contest these racist and sexist representations. Recently, Latorre added to this scholarship her coedited, *¡Murales Rebeldes!: L.A. Chicana/Chicano Murals under Siege* that focuses on eight Chicana/o murals from the 1970s to the 1990s. All have endured a lack of recognition—as works of art, as acts of personal expression, and as voices with social, historical, or political relevance. Some of the murals still exist—in both preserved and decaying states—while others have been whitewashed, censored, neglected, and even destroyed. And, in an important essay, "New Approaches to Chicana/o Art: The Visual and the Political as Cognitive Process," Latorre pushes against the idea that "The assumption within the art history establishment has been that a sociopolitical impetus behind the creation of an artwork necessarily negates the possibility of aesthetic value" (p. 112). She considers cognitive science advances useful as this is interested more in how art *moves* one to think and feel differently, and this of course includes the political. This allows one to consider the "visual strategies and devices that Chicana/o artists employ without being concerned with a method that ultimately seeks to distinguish between 'good' and 'bad' art" (p. 112). For instance, we see how Yolanda Lopéz's *Sun Mad* works to wake us perceptually, emotionally, and thoughtfully because it at once uses recognizable prototype narratives and cognitive schemas then radically innovates these; it pulls us in with familiarity, then turns our world upside down.

And, the primary matter of Latinx art scholarship has multiplied to include tattoo, photographic, and other arts. As Rocio Prado reminds,

> The definition of Latina/o art has moved from tangible art to performance art, pirating TV channels, and even graffiti upon a museum wall. What has not changed is the field's inherent unpopularity—a characteristic that has allowed many Latinx pop artists to thrive.
>
> (p. 212)

For instance, in "Illuminated Bodies" Theresa Rojas identifies Kat Von D as a "risk taker who is 'read' in multiple ways that at once challenge the aesthetics of the exoticized Latina body and defy the conventions of the tattooing industry" (p. 119). Moreover, "as a Latina tattoo artist in a traditionally and predominantly male industry, Von D functions as a visual ambassador for others, particularly women, who refuse to use art for the construction and reproduction of synthetic borders" (p. 128). The body as living breathing canvas on the street altering people's perspective about the world—and not something stuck in a museum. Notably, tattoos of the Virgin of Guadalupe are commonly seen on the backs of Chicanos are often regarded as a symbol of Mexican masculinity. And, in *Picturing the Barrio*, David William Foster seeks to "understand what gets photographed and how it situates itself in terms of overall processes of cultural self-understanding" (p. 5). Indeed, Foster provides insight into how photographic shaping devices (angles, lighting, and such) create meaning as situated "within the sociohistorical circumstances from which cultural products arise" (p. 5). Foster analyzes photographs of barrios that run the gamut of nostalgic (Kathy Vargas) to rebellious, "revulsive," and defiant (Gamboa) as well as of Chicana bodies that defy the heteromasculine gaze (Laura Aguilar), gender conformance (José Galvez) to Chicana boxers (Delilah Montoya) and Mexican lynchings (Ken Gonzalez-Day's "Erased Lynchings" series). So, Foster turns away from the ethnographic, documentary approach to study Chicano/a photographs and instead turns attention to "conceptual principles of photography as a creatively 'worked' medium in the same way that painting or sculpture are" (p. 153).

Importantly, too, just as the primary matter has multiplied so too has it ventured into the realm of queer or *jotería* expression. We see this in the scholarship of Robb Hernandez, Rocío Prado, and Richard T. Rodríguez. For instance, in "Drawing Offensive/Offensive Drawing: Toward a Theory of Maricónagraphy" Hernandez formulates the concept of "maricónography" whereby queer Latinx artists trouble straight, masculinist formulations and practices of Latinidad. Prado and Rodríguez both attend to the work of Joey Terrill. Prado analyzes his "The Maricón Series" and Richard T. Rodríguez analyzes Terrill's t-shirt art, 'zines, paintings, and testimonio that articulate both "gay and Chicano/Latino experiences while aligning aesthetics with politics" ("Being and Belonging: Joey Terrill's Performance of Politics," 468). In Rodríguez's analysis of "Dormido" (portraying two men asleep in each other's arms) and "Roberto and Joey" (a cartoon-like, stylized rendition of Terrill and his boyfriend at the time) along with his zine work, *Chicos Modernos*, he creates art that's queer and Latinx affirming. Rodríguez writes,

> Terrill's art and personal testimony assist in collectively remembering these subjects when they are often individually consigned to a footnote or granted a casual nod in historical accounts of both the Los Angeles-based Chicano movement and Chicano art scene.
>
> (p. 486)

This said, Latinx art is still not taught in universities. There are less than a handful of professors trained as Latinx arts scholars. Most of the time, US Latinx and Latin American art history courses are lumped together, if taught at all. As Tomás Ybarra-Frausto states,

> Texts and materials about Latino visual art for high school and even college teachers still do not exist. The books written in the last ten years about American art barely nod toward these alternative stories, these other visions of American art. There are still only a handful of places in the United States where scholars can earn a PhD in Latin American art history, and none where you can earn a graduate degree focused on Latino art.
>
> ("Imagining a More Expansive Narrative of American Art")

However, we remain optimistic. We're seeing the making of regional Latinx art historical archives as well as the arrival of Latinx art professors teaching and researching and excavating Latinx art in ways that show how it at once exists on its own and has interpenetrated and transformed art generally. As Rocio Prado concludes:

> The field's resilience and reaction to its exclusion from mainstream art provides artists a platform upon which to effect change within both the Latinx community and the field of mainstream

art. This further enables the Latinx artist to challenge norms, confront racism, xenophobia, **homophobia**, and sexism, and obtain artistic autonomy. It is this fluidity that has provided Latinx culture with a milieu of misfits to depict and create Latinx identity. We are gifted with nonconformists, oddballs, maricónes, malforas, cybervatos, rebellious art collectives, chingonas, malhabladas, rebels, cholos, pop culture nerds, self-identified illegals, warriors, and overall malcriados. Latinx pop art might not receive much funding, media coverage, or gallery space but it is also never, ever dull.

(p. 212)

Latinx art is its own unique cultural phenomenon, but as formed by many of the techniques, cultures, and histories that shape art within the Américas and the world.

Works Cited

Foster, David William. *Picturing the Barrio: Ten Chicano Photographers*. Pittsburgh, PA: University of Pittsburgh Press, 2017.

Gonzalez, Rita. "Art." In *Keywords for Latina/o Studies*, edited by Deborah R. Vargas, Lawrence La Fountain-Stokes, Nancy Raquel Mirabal. New York: New York University Press, 2017, pp. 12–14.

Griswold del Castillo, Richard, Teresa McKenna, and Yvonne Yarbro-Bejarano. Eds. *Chicano Art, Resistance and Affirmation*. Los Angeles, CA: Wight Art Gallery, University of California, 1991.

Hernández, Robb. "Drawing Offensive/Offensive Drawing: Toward a Theory of Mariconógraphy." *MELUS*, vol. 39, no. 2, 2014, pp. 121–152.

Latorre, Guisela. *Walls of Empowerment: Chicana/o Indigenist Murals of California*. Austin, TX: University of Texas Presss, 2008.

——. "New Approaches to Chicana/o Art: The Visual and the Political as Cognitive Process." *Image & Narrative*, vol. 11, no. 2, 2010, pp. 111–122.

Latorre, Guisela, Erin M. Curtis, and Jessica Hough, eds. *¡Murales Rebeldes!: L.A. Chicana/Chicano Murals Under Siege*. Los Angeles, CA: La Plaza de Cultura y Artes and the California Historical Society, 2017.

Mesa-Bains, Amalia. "Domesticana: The Sensibility of Chicana Rasquache." In *Distant Relations: A Dialogue among Chicano, Irish, and Mexican Artists*, edited by Trisha Ziff. Culver City, CA: Smart Art Press, 1996, pp. 156–163.

Pérez, Laura. *Chicana Art: The Politics of Spiritual and Aesthetic Altarities*. Durham, NC: Duke University Press, 2007.

Prado, Isabel Rocio. "Inexact Revolutions Understanding Latino Pop Art." *The Routledge Companion to Latina/o Pop Culture*, edited by Frederick Luis Aldama. New York and London: Routledge, 2016, pp. 205–213.

Ramos, E. Carmen. "The Latino Presence in American Art." *American Art*, vol. 26, no. 2, 2012, pp. 7–13.

Rodríguez, Richard T. "Being and Belonging: Joey Terrill's Performance of Politics." *Biography*, vol. 34, no. 3, 2011, pp. 467–491.

Rojas, Theresa. "Illuminated Bodies: Kat Von D and the Borderlands of Tattoo Culture." In *Latinos and Narrative Media: Participation and Portrayal*, edited by Frederick Luis Aldama. New York: Palgrave Macmillan, 2013, pp. 117–128.

Ybarra-Frausto, Tomás. "Rasquachismo, a Chicano Sensibility." In *Chicano Art: Resistance and Affirmation, 1965–1985*, edited by Richard Griswold Del Castillo, Teresa McKenna, and Yvonne Yarbro-Belarano. Berkeley, CA: Wright Art Gallery, University of California, 1991, pp. 155–162.

———. "Arte Chicano: Images of a Community." In *Signs from the Heart: California Chicano Murals*, edited by Eva Sperling Cockcroft and Holly Barnet-Sanchez. Albuquerque, NM: University of New Mexico Press, 1993, pp. 54–67.

BORDER THEORY

Since this book's focus is Latinx Studies, this entry will emphasize Border Theory's contributions to understanding literary and cultural production by and about Latinxs, with the well-defined caveat that Border Theory has now moved well beyond its foundational roots in literal understandings of the US–Mexico border and, from that, Chicano and Chicana identity.

Border Theory is the field of study that acknowledges geographic border spaces, and notably, ideological, sociological, and identity borders, as unique spaces of exchange, expression, and transformation that emerged in the 1980s as a "new, multidisciplinary generation of border scholars" (Anzaldúa p. 2). The theory and the area of research it opened has become a crucial and central aspect of Latinx Studies, thanks in large measure to the efforts of noted Chicana feminist Gloria Anzaldúa. Her meditative, mystical, poetic, artistic, book-length exploration of the border, *Borderlands/La Frontera: The New Mestiza*, was destined to become required reading for literary and cultural scholars interested in the ongoing effort of understanding marginalization and power dynamics as they concern the concept of the border.

While Anzaldúa began her book with the literal Texas–Mexico border in mind—as a *tejana*, her personal experiences provided the impetus for the surrounding exploration of the border as a metaphor— the actual geographical border soon became a powerful metaphor for the interstitial and permeable space between abrading cultures, nations, and peoples (p. 4). Others have since taken Anzaldúa's conception of the border as the foundation upon which to build other related theories. For instance, Mary Louise Pratt advanced the related theory of the contact zone—spaces in which cultures meet, push and pull against one another with consequential social results (p. 8). Though Pratt's theory is distinct from Anzaldúa's theorization of the border, the two concepts are clearly related. Specifically, Anzaldúa conceived of a figure she called "the new mestiza," and spoke of with the terms "mestiza consciousness" and "nepantla," which she defines as an "in-between" space. For her, these concepts crumbled binary distinctions and portrayed otherness as a virtue rather than a deficiency.

Both Anzaldúa and Pratt conceived of the border and its related contact zone as a space policed by governmental powers at local, state, and federal levels, meant to control and separate the peoples that happen to reside on either side the border, which Anzaldúa calls, "una herida abierta"—an open wound (p. 25). Literal borders between nations have historically been sites of militarization, violence, and seeming lawlessness. In the late twentieth- and early twenty-first centuries, the border that separates the United States and Mexico is, in places, a heavily patrolled zone where US Border Patrol officers are as likely to encounter someone attempting to enter the United States with illegal drugs as they are an unattended minor desperate for help. As such, the US–Mexico border, as happens in different ways in other nation borders around the world, becomes a site for ideological, political, and national debate.

Border studies used the consequences and subsequent theorization of the actual, geographic border between nations and applies those findings to other so-called "soft" borders that arise when examining the confluence and clash of cultures. Thus, one way of understanding the evolution of Border Theory is that it has as its foundation the physical US–Mexico border (per Anzaldúa), then it moved not only into examinations of other physical borders—not only between nations but also among other differentiated geographic spaces—but also carried the exploration into border concepts wherever any pertinent border exists. As one can readily see, because we are able to distinguish our world at all because borders exist, Border Theory has a tendency to be far reaching, and one could claim this as its major weakness.

Issues concerning identity are often of central concern when Border Theory is applied, and scholars such as Homi Bhabha, David Palumbo-Liu, Anzaldúa, and others have made strides in reconciling identity with border studies. So, despite its name, Border Theory is not myopically concerned with an imaginary line in the sand; it is concerned with difference, that which makes us different, and that which makes difference value-added or value-subtracted within a society. Border Theory stresses the idea that the proximity of two cultures creates a permeable boundary that allows for movement, contestation, **hybridity**, and the creation of something new altogether, among other things. Due to its non-normative, non-binary assumptions, Border Theory has been adapted by scholars and theorists working in feminist, queer, post-colonial, political, sociological, economic, and historical areas of scholarship and thought.

As it applies specifically to Latinx Studies, Border Theory is, as one would expect by now, highly variable. Again, if we return to the example of actual borders, we intuit that not all borders are the same. In fact, though we speak of the US–Mexico border as if it is consistent over the course of its approximately 2,000 miles, the reality is that the California–Mexico border has different affordances and constraints than, say, the Texas–Mexico border. To complicate matters further, the "border" that separates Cuba from the US is much more than even nearly 100 miles of water can indicate—the consequences of Cold War politics, for example. And Puerto Rico, a US unincorporated territory, was reminded after Hurricane Maria in 2017 that its border separation from the mainland, too, is much more than a vast stretch of ocean water might suggest.

José David Saldívar has further developed Anzaldúa's theorization of the borderlands as a site of resistance and change, of development and stagnation (pp. 29–30). Indeed, the border is a paradoxical space, which is what makes it so ripe for exploration and theorization. Further, the border represents not only a fixed geographic location (which it is), by its very nature it invites crossing and movement, even when such crossings are deemed illegal. The border allows for legal and illegal crossing, and when the politics of such crossings lead politicians and activists to cite statistics and numbers, it is easy to forget that there are human beings, not simply numbers, facing very real consequences that shape the border and the nations that lie along either of its sides. This is a key understanding of the border—that it both nurtures and neuters, it gives and it takes away. And, because of the dynamic nature of the border not only as a physical location but also as a larger metaphor, Border Theory is highly interdisciplinary.

One key development in Border Theory is how an understanding of the border can lead to greater understanding of identity. Anzaldúa herself used much of her exploration of the concept of the border as a means of understanding her own identity as a bilingual, Chicana lesbian from Texas. For her, because the border was a non-normative place, it seemed to reflect her own sense of self as a person who did not easily fit into the places dictated to her by society and even her family. While the border was, for Anzaldúa, a place of trauma and a type of wound, it also renewed her self-conception because of its resiliency and fluidity. Debra Castillo reminds us that the border is not just a metaphor; it is an actual place with real consequences (p. 3).

Since the border is an area of interchange, commerce, and cultural exchange, border theorists have applied some of the same ideas of inter-cultural movement as a means of understanding identity formation and understanding between identity groups. The resulting exchange yields something new, what Bhabha theorized as "hybridity" (p. 7)—having a sense of belonging to two or more ethnic identities. It is the intersections of these disparate and distinct identities that yield productive fruit for border theorists. Furthermore, the exchange between borders is a type of border crossing. The act of crossing is an act of defiance, but it is also an act of self-validation. Sometimes the border is an identity border, and so crossing the border in this sense means to step outside of one identity and into another. And this crossing is not a one-time instance; the movement often occurs again and again.

Thomas Nail posits that borders should not be thought of as homogeneous, but rather, they are "complex composites" that indicate multiple borders within any given border (p. 1). Nail further makes the case that the border is much more dynamic and complex than is popularly conceived, and perhaps more importantly, the border is not reducible to a geographic space or location. Incidentally, the vast majority of border theorists agree on this point: it is not just about a geographical, global coordinate. Conversely, not everything is a border, despite the ubiquity of borders in our world. What helps with this problem, according to Nail, is to think of borders in categories rather than as the same sort of thing. These borders are often *related*, but they do not necessarily function in the same way. As Nail states,

> those trying to understand the division of territory between the United States and Mexico are talking about a completely different border than those trying to understand the juridicial borders of immigration enforcement inside the United States. However, the idea that immigration enforcement (juridicial borders) and border patrol (territorial borders) have absolutely nothing in common seems absurd, especially after their political unification under the Department of Homeland Security.
>
> (p. 11)

In the midst of so much theorization of the border, it is notable that a vital aspect of Border Theory is its commitment to activism and activist causes. And some scholars such as Michaelsen and Johnson have theorized the limits of Border Theory (p. 15). So much of the articulation of Border Theory has to do with its influence and shaping power of social justice, which again illustrates the volatile and political nature of the subject. Many scholars of Border Theory are also "activist scholars" that work to effect change in the social policies that relate directly to their areas of scholarship. In particular, these activist scholars work to put into practice, or praxis, such policies that will directly affect the communities in which they have an investment.

Border Theory will continue to resonate with Latinx Studies for the foreseeable future. Its commitment to issues of the border, now an issue of incredible volatility thanks to the Trump administration's dogged resolve to build a border wall, the vilification of undocumented Latinxs among right-wing politicos and politicians in the United States, the continued barriers to equal access to resources and due process for Latinxs, and the commitment by the Trump administration to pursue an anti-immigration, "America First" agenda will ensure the vitality of this much-needed area of study.

Works Cited

Anzaldúa, Gloria. *Borderlands: La Frontera: The New Mestiza*. San Francisco, CA: Aunt Lute Books, 2012.

Bhabha, Homi K. *The Location of Culture*. New York and London: Routledge, 2010.

Castillo, Debra A., and María Socorro Tabuenca Córdoba. *Border Women: Writing from la frontera*. Vol. 9. Minneapolis, MN: University of Minnesota Press, 2002.

Michaelsen, Scott, and David E. Johnson. *Border Theory: The Limits of Cultural Politics*. Minneapolis, MN: University of Minnesota Press, 1997.

Nail, Thomas. *Theory of the Border*. New York: Oxford University Press, 2016.

Pratt, Mary L. *Imperial Eyes*. London: Routledge, 1992.

Saldívar, José D. *Border Matters: Remapping American Cultural Studies*. Berkeley, CA: University of California Press, 2007.

BODY

The Latinx body has been subject to commodification for the vast majority of the history of the United States. Whether in the fields of agriculture or on Hollywood's silver screen, Latinx bodies have made whole industries billions of dollars in profit. Of course, quite often Latinxs are exploited for their efforts, and only rarely do Latinx celebrities attain enough power to be able to dictate the terms of their own profitability and reap the rewards of their efforts. Thus, the Latinx body in the United States can be thought of as a visual product for consumption and also an "invisible" entity that is a tremendous force in the nation's agribusiness. This entry will focus on the former; the latter is explored in the entry in this volume titled "Food."

The Latinx body has consistently appeared in visual storytelling in the United States, quite often to the detriment of the Latinx community. Mary Beltrán notes how the star power of Latinx bodies has a tremendous influence on the perceptions of Latinxs in general (p. 6). Such visualizations that are part and parcel of racial stereotyping and propaganda created with the intent of marginalizing and dehumanizing Latinxs within the popular imagination in the United States. Whether it is the cartoon characters of Speedy Gonzales or "Slow Poke" Rodriguez (1953–present)—literal mice within the Looney Tunes universe, or the "bandido" figure in films such as *Treasure of the Sierra Madre* (1948), Mexican men were historically portrayed as buffoons, clowns, misfits, deviants, or criminals.

Sometimes Mexican men have appeared as caricatures who embody not only criminality and deviancy, but sexual predation. An example of this appears in Clint Eastwood's *The Outlaw Josey Wales* (1976), when hapless travelers from Kansas are set upon by "Comancheros," comprised mostly of Mexican men led by a white man who does the talking. They appear dirty and mute, and very nearly rape the blonde, doe-eyed Laura Lee (played by Sondra Locke). Five years earlier, Eastwood's film *Dirty Harry* (1971) featured a Latinx character named "Chico" who was Harry Callahan's (Eastwood) partner, played by Reni Santoni, an actor of French and Spanish heritage. There are many instances of this sort of lazy stereotyping, as William Nericcio and others have extensively researched. "When one thinks of the relative status of the term 'Mexican,'" claims Nericcio,

> how it is manifest in the textual record available to us as a register of the collective American unconscious, one realizes that some latter-day inheritors of Hitler's visual ideological mandate are still hard at work. One need not be a devotee of the failed European artist/Nazi potentate to suspect that the rules of the semiotic m/adman game still hold true when it comes to the representation of Mexicans and Latinos in mass culture.
>
> (p. 17)

By and large, until the late twentieth century, Mexican men in particular appeared in visual storytelling as clownish or threatening figures, yet always as shallow, cartoonish stereotypes. Some Mexican men, however, avoided becoming a stock character, yet still ended up embodying what came to be known as the "Latin Lover" figure in Hollywood—Latinx men whose sexuality was seemingly near irresistible, was patterned and marketed after the famed Rudolph Valentino persona. Actors Anthony Quinn and Ricardo Montalban easily fit this persona.

On the other hand, Latinx actors not of Mexican descent and not named Quinn or Montalban often appeared to rise above the expected risible stock characters in Hollywood. Such prominent actors include José Ferrer and his son, Miguel Ferrer, both of Puerto Rican heritage, Cesar Romero, of Cuban descent, Hector Elizondo (Basque and Puerto Rican), and Desi Arnaz (Cuban). These actors continually worked against a Hollywood that tended to box in actors based on race and ethnicity, and these men were successful in avoiding limiting careers. On the other hand, there is no question that a majority of these men were also hyper sexualized as "Latin lover" figures, something that continues into the twenty-first century with actors such as Antonio Banderas, Spanish-born Javier Bardem, Andy García, Esai Morales, Benjamin Bratt, and Mexican-born actors Gael García Bernal, Diego Luna, and William Levy. Often these actors are written about in entertainment media with an emphasis on their looks and attractiveness. This concept of the Latin Lover was satirized in 2017 in the film *How to Be a Latin Lover* starring Eugenio Derbez and Salma Hayek.

Embedded within the exploration of Latinx men in Hollywood is the racialization that often dictates the sorts of roles such actors are allowed to play. It is notable that most of the actors who fit the ideal Latin Lover figure have lighter skin tones and do not look mestizo—the browner shades and more "indio" look many Americans associate with the term "Mexican." Such brown bodies have been historically made to take on the role of the stereotype or the buffoon. Thus, we see the sort of slow progress made with the breakthrough of actors such as Cheech Marin, Michael Peña, George Lopez, and John Leguizamo, who are known more for their work in comedy than for their sexual appeal. In fact, comedic roles of substance, not the clownish caricatures that dominated portrayals of Latinxs in the past, have steadily become a force at the box office—thanks in large measure to the work of Peña, Lopez, Leguizamo, Derbez, and others. Leguizamo and Puerto Rican Lin-Manuel Miranda, the genius behind the Broadway smash *Hamilton*, have found success and new audiences in theatre and in film by both **satire** and a rethinking of American history. For Lázaro Lima, the Latinx subject is also to be thought of as a "body politic," that is rigidly situated within history (p. 7). And Arturo Aldama has exposed how "the materiality of violence on … otherized bodies" is a grim reality faced by Latinxs in the US (p. 5).

Latina actresses have endured the sexualization of their bodies in visual storytelling in ways that differ from Latinx actors. As with many "Hollywood bombshells," there is a long history of Latinas' bodies being objectified on the screen. Carmen Miranda and Rita Hayworth are two early examples of this, though they are far from the only ones, as this trend continues unabated into the twenty-first century. Miranda, known as the Brazilian Bombshell, was often cast in roles that high-lighted her exoticness i.e., her dynamic heritage—she was Portuguese-born Brazilian—from the 1930s to the 1950s. Not only was her body a prominent feature of her performances because of her ability to sing and dance, she quickly became a kind of stereotype for Latinx otherness, serving as the basis for Chiquita Banana, a food mascot for the Chiquita Brands International corporation. Thus, when she was not being cast as a sexual object, she was turned into a singing cartoon mascot.

Rita Hayworth was born Margarita Carmen Cansino, the daughter of two dancers, and was steeped in Mexican nightclub, song, and dance culture. Her Spanish and Irish-English descent, as well as her Spanish name, compelled Hayworth to downplay her ethnicity, lighten her hair, and change her name (Hayworth is her mother's maiden name). Hayworth became the iconic American bombshell, and she was a favorite "pin-up girl" for American GIs during World War II. Hayworth's iconic bombshell status is a pivotal plot point in Stephen King's novella "Rita Hayworth and Shawshank Redemption" and its film adaptation directed by Frank Darabont, *The Shawshank Redemption.*

Despite these and other early instances of Latina bodies in visual media in the United States, it is important to note, as Isabel Molina-Guzmán claims, "that Latina performers, producers, and audiences are thus an essential part of global media culture" (p. 1). There is, of course, a problematic issue in viewing women under the sexualized male gaze in Hollywood, but the issue is particularly fraught with racism and prejudice when we consider how Latina performers in visual media must negotiate and navigate such a minefield while attempting to carve out a career for themselves. As Molina-Guzmán asserts, "Ethnicity, and specifically min-ority female ethnic sexuality, can be savored, commodified, packaged, and safely distributed for the consumption of audiences throughout the world" (p. 2). The Latina body is, quite simply, treated and viewed as a product to be consumed. What is more, the Latina body is often made to conform to particular beauty standards in the United States, and these beauty standards have been incorporated into Latinx culture. Dark skin and *pelo malo*, or "bad hair," which refers to black, curly hair often associated with peoples from African descent (Candelario) are typically seen as obstacles to beauty. Hair products, makeup, and other beauty products and enhancers thrive in the Latina community.

In the early twenty-first century, Latinas continue to exert their influence against a power structure that actively works against them. Jennifer Lopez, Penelope Cruz, Salma Hayek, America Ferrera, Sofia Vergara, Rosario Dawson, Zoe Saldana, Eva Longoria, Jessica Alba, Michelle Rodriguez, Eva Mendes, and many other Latinas have made important inroads for Latina representation in visual media, all the while fighting against entrenched sexism and objectification.

In late 2017, in the wake of many #MeToo revelations of sexual harassment and assault, Harvey Weinstein was revealed to be a high-profile studio executive who stood accused of abuse and coercion against women at his company, Mirimax Studios. The *New York Times* report that revealed Weinstein's pattern of behavior led to his ouster. In the wake of the Weinstein revelations, Salma Hayek published an op-ed in the *New York Times*, detailing some of what she had suffered when she worked within Weinstein's purview. Titled, "Harvey Weinstein Is My Monster, Too," Hayek's essay painted a damning portrait of Weinstein and explicitly revealed the sorts of abuses to which women who work in film and television have and continue to face. Hayek says Weinstein often told her that she "was nobody," and that several of her friends, including Robert Rodriguez, Elizabeth Avellan, Quentin Tarantino, and George Clooney, "saved (her) from being raped."

Hayek's heartrending account exposes the difficulties women face in Hollywood, but in particular, it shows how Latinas specifically have this unfair burden placed upon them. As she relates, "Harvey Weinstein had become the wizard of a new wave of cinema that took original content into the mainstream. At the same time, it was unimaginable for a Mexican actress to aspire to a place in Hollywood." Time after time, according to Hayek, she refused his sexual advances, innuendo, and directives, and being threatened with her life was her reward for her bravery. "I will kill you, don't think I can't," Hayek claims Weinstein responded once, in a fit of rage. Most disturbing of all, Hayek's ordeal is not singular.

Scholars of ethnic studies and media studies have long discussed and explored the rampant sexism and objectification women, and especially women of color, must endure throughout a career. But only recently have we seen such women take on the risk and display the courage to give their account, in their own words. The worst of it is not only that these women's bodies are portrayed and represented on screen in ways that are damaging to how society conceives of women in terms of sexuality and beauty standards, but with recent revelations that women in the movie and television industry are literally being coerced, raped, and harassed is both horrifying and contemptible. Latinxs continue to work against a system that treats them as objects, and then is insulted when they refuse to take it anymore.

Works Cited

Aldama, Arturo J. *Violence and the Body: Race, Gender, and the State.* Bloomington, IN: Indiana University Press, 2003.

Beltrán, Mary. *Latina/o Stars in U.S. Eyes: The Making and Meanings of Film and TV Stardom.* Urbana, IL: University of Illinois Press, 2009.

Candelario, Ginetta E. B. *Black behind the Ears: Dominican Racial Identity from Museums to Beauty Shops.* Durham, NC: Duke University Press, 2007.

Hayek, Salma. "Harvey Weinstein Is My Monster Too." *The New York Times.* December 12, 2017.

Lima, Lázaro. *The Latino Body: Crisis Identities in American Literary and Cultural Memory.* New York: New York University Press, 2007.

Molina-Guzmán, Isabel. *Dangerous Curves: Latina Bodies in the Media.* New York: New York University Press, 2010.

Nericcio, William A. *Tex[T]-Mex: Seductive Hallucinations of the "Mexican" in America.* Austin, TX: University of Texas Press, 2007.

DIGITAL ERA

The twenty-first century has witnessed the increased presence of Latinxs within digital spaces, as creators, consumers, and interpreters. While many Latinx artists already began to use and incorporate digital technologies into their work in the 1990s—Alma López's mixed-media digital art and Gómez-Peña's el Mexterminator and Chicano cyberpunk performances, for instance—once the Internet got its legs *and* became accessible to the Latinx community in the 2000s it permeated more deeply Latinx cultural production and consumption practices.

Today, Latinxs are fully working within and actively transforming the world from within different digital spaces. There's a proliferation of Latinx blogs, webnews, art-net, webTV narratives, dedicated YouTube channels and social, cultural, and activist media feeds and platforms, and so much more. In many ways, the digital twenty-first century has thrown open wide the doors for all variety of Latinx creation, interpretation, and knowledge dissemination. Facebook now provides the platform for news broadcasts specific to the Latinx population in Columbus, Ohio. (See www.facebook.com/CanalHispanoTV.) The digital era has allowed for the possibility of satisfying the fast-growing US Latinx population with its complex and layered cultural tastes as well as interpretive and intellectual needs. It has allowed many a Latinx to step into creative, interpretive, and knowledge-making spaces traditionally reserved for a non-Latinx elite.

In response to the increasingly central important role digital tools, cyber platforms, and e-culture generally play in the lives of Latinxs, many Latinx scholars have begun to focus their research on deepening insight into this area. We think readily of the work of Mary Beltrán, Randy Ontiveros, William Nericcio, Ana M. Lopéz, Cristina Venegas, Vittoria Rodriguez, Hector Amaya, Arlene Dávila and Yeidy M. Rivero, Frances Negrón-Muntaner, Chon Noriega, Mari Castañeda, Mark Hugo Lopez, Sergio I. Garcia-Rios, and Matt A. Barreto, among others. These scholars have followed several different scholarly paths, variously seeking to enrich understanding from sociological, psychological, linguistic, educational, political, policy, institutional, industry, and representational analytic methods and approaches. Many such scholars oversee new and exciting scholarship that's emerging from next generations of Latinx scholars. Not only has there been an uptick in dissertations written on Latinxs and media, but they have all been written in the twenty-first century, and especially in the past 5 years. (See *The MLA International Bibliography*.) Latinxs and digital media are fast emerging as a significant part of the digital humanities writ large—an area of scholarly study that has traditionally turned a blind eye to Latinxs and the ethnoracial margins generally.

Before we step into a discussion of the kind of digital media being created and consumed by Latinxs, there's the question of access. On the one hand, today many more Latinxs have access to cyberspace cultural products, information, and knowledge. This is largely the result of the near total ubiquity of smartphones—devices that not only allow one to make phone calls, but also circulate pictures, texts, memes as well as access a variety of visual and auditory cultural phenomena. (See Frances Negrón-Muntaner's research data and conclusions "Latino Media Gap" conducted for Columbia University's Center for the Study of Ethnicity and Race.) And, Latinx access and consumption is multilingual: English and Spanish. As the third largest Spanish speaking population in the world, a significant number of US Latinxs are either bilingual or

Spanish-language dominant; Spanish-dominant émigrés are one of the fastest growing populations to use the Internet within the Latinx demographic, making up about 52% of adult users. According to Anna Brown and Mark Hugo Lopez, "Spanish-dominant Latinos made up 32% of all Latino Internet users in 2015, up from 20% in 2009" (p. 2). The Internet reflects this. Today, there's an abundance of Spanish-language e-news, YouTube channels, and Latinx focused cultural phenomena.

And, as one might expect given the trend in other populations, the highest use of the Internet (and with the majority doing so via smartphones) is among the next generations of Latinxs, especially those aged 18 and under. With these Latinxs trending more toward an English-dominance, we see a tremendous amount of digital culture and knowledge production oriented toward Latinxs in English. And, these Latinxs visit video sharing sites more than any other of the US's main demographic populations. (See the information at the www.pewinter net.org and at the www.pewhispanic.org.)

Access to digital spaces has allowed for different types of social in-group formations. At the most basic, it has facilitated the communication between family members. Skype, FaceTime, Google Chat, and other digital communication platforms connect children with grandparents and other relatives scattered across the US and the Américas generally. E-news platforms connect US Latinxs with events in Central and South America. The Internet facilitates the constant contact and exposure of US Latinxs with language and culture as well as sociopolitical issues. Claire Taylor and Thea Pitman use the term "postregional" to identify the outcomes of this hemispheric digital use and participation. For Taylor and Pitman, postregional is the sense of information and cultural phenomena being at once anchored in local issues *and* simultaneously engaged by Latinxs at distant removes. (See *Latin American Identity and Online Culture*.) And in *Place and Politics in Latin American Digital Culture* Claire Taylor focuses on the creation of locally inflected art that is then circulated and experienced by wider, more geographically distant Latinx communities. In this way, Latinxs artists such as Coco Fusco, Ricardo Domínguez, and Ricardo Miranda Zúñiga create borderland net-art that reconstructs and affirms the local (culture, history, politics) for hemispheric Latinx subjects. Finally, for Sergio I. Garcia-Rios and Matt A. Barreto, the Internet serves as an important space for waking US Latinxs (documented and undocumented, English-dominant and Spanish-dominant) to forces of exploitation and oppression taking place throughout the Américas and thus to greater civic engagement such as seen with the Latinx vote winning Obama's reelection in 2012.

Today, too, we see an emerging area of research in areas where nation-state institutions have historically restricted and censored Latinx digital access and creation. One such scholar, Cristina Venegas, turns her sights to Cuba's cyberculture. In *Digital Dilemmas*, Venegas identifies the Castro Regime's double-edged policies: a regime that actively promotes Internet literacy and digital technology expertise *and* that restricts use for personal gain and censors access for potential political subterfuge. She also identifies how the Internet is used by intellectuals inside and outside "to debate contemporary topics of relevance to Cubans everywhere" (p. 110). And, Venegas notes how the on-the-grounds use of the Internet by regular people overlaps "spheres of legal and illegal activity" (p. 128). Behind closed doors, for these everyday Cuban denizens the Internet becomes "innovative, sometimes unauthorized zones of cross-cultural appropriation that take Cubans outside their country, stimulating a counter-discourse rooted not only in personal lack and frustration but also in community" (p. 129). And, there are Cuban artists such as Ernesto Oroza who use Internet platforms and digital tools (his hacker-inspired "technologies of disobedience" modus operandi) to disrupt the status quo (interview with Alex Gil). And, of course, even within the US there remain a great number of Latinxs who have limited access to the Internet. There are still many Latinx households who can't afford Internet service or smartphones. And, there remain many Latinxs who live in underfunded rural and urban areas without libraries—or other public spaces where one might have Internet access. The access, use, and experience of cyberspace continues to vary widely from one Latinx community to another within and outside the US.

Today, more Latinxs are using digital tools and platforms to create and distribute all variety of cultural phenomena with Latinx content: from blogs, art, wikis, and podcasts to hypermedia fictions, performance art, webisode narratives, and much more.

One such platform that has proved important for Latinx creators has been YouTube. Here you can find all sorts of Latinx content: from lifestyle videos on cooking, hair, and fashion styles (Ximena TV, for instance) to webisodes with Latinx protagonists who overcome issues specific to Latinxs. With primetime network and cable TV historically sidestepping the presence of Latinxs in front of and behind cameras (see Mary Beltrán "Latina/os On TV!"), YouTube and other digital media platforms such as Hulu have become important venues for Latinx creators. Some of the Latinx created WebTV series include: *Los Americans* (2011–), *Becoming Ricardo* (2012–), *Caribe Road* (2011–), *Chutes* (2012–), *East Los High* (2013–), *Encounters* (2011–), *Failing Upwards* (2012–), *Fixing*

Paco (2012–), *Illegal* (2011–), *Justice Woman* (2012–), *Off and Running* (2012–), *Osito* (2014–), *Police Chicks: Life on the Beat* (2011–), *Pushing Dreams* (2013–), *Rag Dolls* (2013–), *Undocumented and Awkward* (2011–), *Ylse* (2008–2010), and *East WillyB* (2011–2013). In each case, the Latinx creators, cast, and crew work with shoestring budgets to produce culturally complex and nuanced, Latinx driven narratives not found in the primetime network and cable media arena. For Mary Beltrán and Vittoria Rodriguez, Latinx created webTV is made with a *rasquache* sensibility: inexpensive, with recycled parts (the sets, for instance), and with an "underdog sensibility" ("From the Bronze Screen to Computer Screens," p. 162). The creators can generate funds from Kickstarter campaigns. They can distribute content via video-sharing websites such as YouTube and Google Channel that can be accessed by Latinx viewers for free. And, free social media platforms (Facebook, Twitter, and Instagram, for example) for publicity and marketing in the building of followers and fans. Take the case of Julia Ahumada Grob and Yamin Segal's *East WillyB*. They ran a Kickstarter that generated enough money to create then launch (March 2013) its first season of 12 episodes. For marketing and publicity, they created the East WillyB website that included a blog, photo galleries, ways to interact with crew and cast, and a "Support Us" tab to help fund more productions (www.eastwillyb.com). And, while the show takes place in a specific location (Bushwick, Brooklyn) that reflects a more Puerto Rican and Dominican Latinx community, its storylines appeal to a wider pan-Latinx audience. There's plenty of content that appeals to Latinxs of Mexican, Cuban, Central and South American ancestry. The smart writing showcases the complex commonalities as well as divergence within US Latinx communities. Its jokes are by Latinxs for Latinxs—unlike, say, those in a typical primetime show such as *Modern Family* where Latinxs are the target of ridicule.

Latinxs are using Internet platforms and digital tools for creation, reclamation, and dissemination of all variety of Latinx cultural phenomena that we don't see in the mainstream. We mentioned already Alma López, Guillermo Gómez-Peña, and Ernesto Oroza. Of course, there are many others, including the Latinx filmmaker, Alex Rivera. He uses Internet platforms and digital technologies in all his films (feature and shorts) and music videos; his www.cybracero.com website ties into his sci-fi feature film about the cybernetic exploitation of Mexicans to build US infrastructure. It exists in the Internet as a "real" corporate entity, Cybracero Systems, that "was created with one objective in mind: to get all the work our society needs done, while eliminating the actual workers and all the difficulties that workers imply: health benefits, housing, IRS, INS, union conflicts, cultural and language differences etc." And, Rivera uses the Internet and digital technology to create installation art—that all lives at www.Rivera.com. For instance, in "Memorial Over General Atomics" and "Lowdrone" Rivera takes the technology of surveillance and destruction (drones used to monitor the US/Mexico border *and, in* their scaled-up versions, drop bombs), strips it down and reconstructs it with new parts—and with a new use: as a cultural object for audiences to apprehend and to make sense of today's reality *and* with a new use function. With his "Memorial" repurposed drone he creates an aerial sculpture that combines drone technology with human radial bones. He asks us not only to fly with this repurposed and re-missioned drone to see what is happening at the factory where they create drones of mass destruction, but also to think about the radial bones that function to hold its propellers: the laboring arm (or *bracero*) worked to death. Rivera's repurposing of the drone in "Lowdrone" similarly asks us to establish a new relationship with the use-function of a tech-object otherwise used for destruction. Here Rivera combines a model of a vintage lowrider (kicking its wheels out to the edges as blades to a repurposed drone) that one can use to watch the surveyor (*la migra*) as one flies or "hops" back and forth across the wall that divides Mexico (Tijuana) from the US (San Ysidro). Before entering the www.Lowdrone.com website, one agrees to "not hold LowDrone.com responsible for the consequences of my transnational hopping." For Rivera, the digital toolbox and cyberspace open up the possibility for audiences around the world "to be able to visualize these liminal spaces and experiences that immigrants have," as he mentions in an interview (Aldama "Toward a Transfrontera-LatinX Aesthetic").

The Internet and digital technologies have also provided important spaces for Latinx interpreters of culture, including, say, older storytelling formats such as the novel and poetry. For instance, at http://labloga. blogspot.com/and www.latinoliteratures.org one can learn about Latinx authors along with their fictional and poetic creations. Remezcla.com and www.latinxspaces.com offer a platform for learning about Latinx music, art, politics, sports, food, film, and culture generally. In discussing the origin and evolution of his www.textmex.blogspot.com, William Anthony Nericcio sees this as the natural evolution of Latinx knowledge dissemination from the limits of the printed page (his book, *Tex[t]-Mex*) to its unbounded presence and circulation in cyberspace. He characterizes his textmex blog as a "post-analog platform" (blog, twitter, Facebook, and the like) that turns upside down all variety of misconceptions of Latinxs. Here and in his Mextasy digital exhibit and *Mextasy* TV show

Nericcio uses the Internet and digital technologies to undertake the necessary "forensic work on American visual culture" to critique the mainstream's denigrative stereotypes of Latinxs as well as to immerse audiences "in the unknowable exquisiteness that is the world of Latina and Latino women and men in the United States and beyond" (Afterword to *The Routledge Companion to Latina/o Pop Culture* 432). Finally, what we see with these creators and interpreters of culture is the use of the Internet and digital technologies to create Latinx content that, in the words of Randy Ontiveros, "preserve their cultural histories and to resist racism" (p. 88).

As William Nericcio succinctly states: "It is the best of times because never before have there been so many avatars of Latinx deliciousness splashing across the televisions, movie screens, and smartphones of the American population" (Afterword 425). And,

> it is the worst of times because never before has racist hate against (primarily, but racists are not picky) Mexican bodies (legal and "illegal," documented and undocumented) and Latinx *gente* been so in vogue in our peculiar nation of once-immigrants/now xeno-phobes (the irony of this too rich to ignore, the Statue of Liberty now reduced from a symbol of freedom to mocking idol).
>
> (p. 425)

Certainly, the number of Latinxs creating, distributing, consuming, and connecting via cyberspace is on the rise—and this across especially with younger generations *and* in English and Spanish language spaces ("Exploring the Digital Nation"). Undoubtedly, it has become an alternative means for Latinx creation, interpretation, and knowledge dissemination. It serves an important tool for growing awareness to social inequities that can and have led to activist movements such as unitedwedream.org,/equalityarchive.com, #latino activism, and many others. It has also cleared a space for creating solidarity across the different Latinx ancestral, ethnolinguistic lines—what others mentioned above identify as the making of a pan-Latinx consciousness. The Internet and digital interpretive and cultural connect populations and redefine the boundaries of Latinx communities. As Ontiveros sums up,

> By giving individuals an opportunity for self-expression and then linking them together in a network of shared passions, digital media is creating new political alliances and new opportunities for cultural exchange. Latinos are only just beginning to mine the possibilities

of these new media technologies and to put them in the service of progressive politics.

("Latino Media in a Digital Age")

Yet, there are still gatekeeping practices that prevent full participation and creative realization. According to the Pew Hispanic Center and the Pew Internet and American Life Project, 56% of Latinxs in the US use the Internet compared to 71% Anglos. Latinxs are less likely to have Internet service at home: 79% compared to 92% of Anglos. Yes, access to digital platforms via smartphones has increased Latinx access. However, the statistics indicate a clear link between income, literacy, and education and Internet access and use. And, even within spaces of learning there's still prejudice against digital modes of knowledge delivery. For instance, after co-developing then running the highly successful Latinx Pop Culture MOOC (Massive Online Open access Course) for the Ohio State University, Aldama's co-instructor was told by the upper administration reviewing her work for tenure that this would not count as part of her teaching portfolio. So, while institutions of higher learning talk about the need for new modes of teaching and collaboration to teach ever bigger audiences there remains a strong prejudice against these new modes of delivery, especially in and around Latinx culture, interpretation, and knowledge. At the individual and institutional levels we need not only to "reboot" (Ana M. Lopéz's notion) the way we analyze Latinx cultural phenomenon within digital and transmedial contexts, but we also have to continue to find, as Tara McPherson declares, "nimbler ways of linking the network and the node and digital form and content, and we need to understand that categories such as race profoundly shape both form and content" (p. 154). We need to actively work within our communities to be sure that new generations have access to the Internet and digital tools to create new cultural phenomena and for themselves to have richer experiences. And, as Beltrán and Rodriguez remind us crowd-source funding has its limits. As successful as *East WillyB* was, it only lasted two seasons. Other Latinx created shows have faced a similar fate. We need to figure out long-term funding sources, perhaps as Beltrán and Rodriguez suggest, "to be coordinated by Latina/o media producers' groups, social advocacy groups, or education organizations with a long-term, vested interest in Latina/o media production and portrayals" (p. 167). And, more systemically, there continues to be a need to collapse the digital divide that already begins in elementary school where Latinxs aren't learning how to understand and utilize productively digital technologies, disallowing them the choice to participate in the use of the Internet and digital tools to transform the world. (See *Digital Tools in Urban Schools*.) This is to say, while the Latinx presence in the Internet is an important cultural and social tool—and can in some instances even help bring Latinxs together to enact social change—it cannot and should not be considered as a replacement for actual work and solidarity by Latinxs in the everyday, material world.

Works Cited

Aldama, Frederick Luis. "Toward a Transfrontera-LatinX Aesthetic: An Interview with Filmmaker Alex Rivera." *Latino Studies*, vol. 15, no. 3, 2017, pp. 373–380.

Anonymous. www.pewinternet.org/2011/07/26/71-of-online-adults-now-use-video-sharing-sites/

Beltrán, Mary. "Latina/os on TV! A Proud (and Ongoing) Struggle over Representation and Authorship." In *The Routledge Companion to Latinx Pop Culture*, edited by Frederick Luis Aldama. New York and London: Routledge, 2016, pp. 23–33.

Brown, Anna, and Mark Hugo Lopez. "Digital Divide Narrows for Latinos as More Spanish Speakers and Immigrants Go Online." www.pewhispanic.org/2016/07/20/digital-divide-narrows-for-latinos-as-more-spanish-speakers-and-immigrants-go-online/

Castañeda, Mari. "Media Policy and the Latino Radio Industry." In *Contemporary Latina/o Media: Production, Circulation, Politics*, edited by Arlene Dávila and Yeidy M. Rivero. New York: New York University Press, 2014, pp. 186–205.

Dávila, Arlene, and Yeidy M. Rivero, eds. *Contemporary Latina/o Media: Production, Circulation, Politics*. New York: New York University Press, 2014.

Fraga, Luis, John A. Garcia, Gary M. Segura, Michael Jones-Correa, Rodney Hero

Garcia-Rios, Sergio I., et al. "Politicized Immigrant Identity, Spanish-Language Media, and Political Mobilization 2012." *RSF: The Russell Sage Foundation Journal of the Social Sciences*, vol. 2, no. 3, 2016, pp. 78–96.

Gómez-Peña, Guillermo. "The New Global Culture: Somewhere between Corporate Multiculturalism and the Mainstream Bizarre (A Border Perspective)." *TDR: The Drama Review*, vol. 45, no. 1, 2001, pp. 7–30.

Lopéz, Ana M. "Calling for Intermediality: Latin American Mediascapes." *Cinema Journal*, vol. 54, no. 1, 2014, pp. 135–141.

McPherson, Tara. "Why Are the Digital Humanities So White? Or Thinking the Histories of Race and Computation." In *Debates in the Digital Humanities*, edited by Matthew K. Gold. Minneapolis, MN: University of Minnesota Press, 2016, pp. 139–160.

Negrón-Muntaner, Frances. "The Latino Media Gap: The State of Latinos in U.S. Media." July 2, 2015. www.youtube.com/watch?v=U6PC0gix1Yk

Negrón-Muntaner, Frances, et al. "The Latino Media Gap: A Conversation with Frances Negrón Muntaner." June 14, 2014. http://nacla.org/news/2014/6/19/latino-media-gap-conversation-frances-negr%C3%B3n-muntaner

Nericcio, William. "Tex[t]-Mex, Seductive Hallucinations of the 'Mexican' in America, 2.0: A Diary Chronicling the Transmogrifying Metamorphosis of a Neurosis from Book to Museum and on to the Internet." In *Latinos and Narrative Media: Participation and Portrayal*, edited by Frederick Luis Aldama. New York: Palgrave Macmillan, 2013, pp. 91–109.

——. "Afterword: A Latino Pop Quartet for the Ontologically Complex Smartphone Age." In *The Routledge Companion to Latinx Pop Culture*, edited by Frederick Luis Aldama. New York and London: Routledge, 2016, pp. 424–433.

Ontiveros, Randy. "Latino Media in a Digital Age." In *Latinos and Narrative Media: Participation and Portrayal*, edited by Frederick Luis Aldama. New York: Palgrave Macmillan, 2013, pp. 85–90.

Oroza, Ernesto. "Interview with Ernesto Oroza." In *Debates in the Digital Humanities*, edited by Matthew K. Gold. Minneapolis, MN: University of Minnesota Press, 2016, pp. 184–193.

Rodriguez, Vittoria and Beltrán Mary. "From the Bronze Screen to Computer Screens: Latina/o Web Series and Independent Production." In *The Routledge Companion to Latina/o Media*, edited by María Elena Cepeda and Dolores Inés Casillas. New York and London: Routledge, 2016, pp. 156–170.

Taylor, Claire. *Place and Politics in Latin American Digital Culture: Location and Latin American Net Art*. New York and London: Routledge, 2014.

Taylor, Claire, et al. *Latin American Identity and Online Culture*. New York and London: Routledge, 2013.

Tryon, Chuck. *On-Demand Culture: Digital Delivery and the Future of Movies*. New Brunswick, NJ: Rutgers University Press, 2013.

Venegas, Cristina. *Digital Dilemmas: The State, the Individual, and Digital Media in Cuba*. New Brunswick, NJ: Rutgers University Press, 2010.

EDUCATION

The education system in the United States presents significant challenges when it comes to students from Latinx communities (Urbina; Gándara). Such challenges arise in the form of language, cultural expectations, geographic region, increasing demographics, and the economics of education. In many ways, the history of Latinxs in education mirrors the education struggles African Americans faced until the late-twentieth century, in terms of access. In other words, the segregation of educational resources. Yet Latinxs often face additional and distinct difficulties when navigating the education system than African American students, language and bilingualism often being two of these. At times, students and activists were led to protest inequalities and injustices they saw in their schools, at times shutting down entire school districts in the process. This entry will present a historical overview of these challenges, along with emerging obstacles and opportunities that have manifested in the first part of the twenty-first century.

Often, Latinxs attended segregated schools until schools were integrated in the late 1960s; Richard Rodriguez depicts this in his breakout memoir *Hunger of Memory*. In other parts of the US, especially in rural and smaller communities that did not have segregated schools, Latinxs attended the same schools as white children. But these schools followed an assimilationist model where Latinx students had to conform to the strictures of the education system with disdain and disregard for their Latinx heritage. For students who could only speak Spanish, this put them at an immediate disadvantage. The barrier of language prevented the acquisition of grade-level knowledge, the result of which yielded failing grades and increased dropout rates. Further, speaking Spanish in many schools yielded punitive measures, where students received corporal punishment for speaking their native tongue at school.

Such a draconian approach to language often created a divide at home, where students were forced to learn English while continuing to speak Spanish at home. The division of language, while creating students who were at ease in the language of two worlds, at times led to an isolation of parents from their children's lives outside the home. Thus, early English acquisition has proven to be a crucial yet difficult issue to resolve in Latinx education. When schools are unprepared or indifferent to the needs of their Spanish-speaking students, the students are all-too often marginalized in a curriculum that already expects students to understand English fluently and makes relatively few accommodations for them.

This situation for Latinxs and education was untenable, and change had to come. The impetus for change came in the form of protests and activism. During the 1960s, in concert with other forms of civil rights protests that were occurring all over the country, Latinx students and civil rights leaders took to the streets and also walked out of the schools themselves as an unequivocal rejection of the status quo. These protests came to be known as "blowouts," and they became a force, particularly in the state of California (Garcia; Berta-Ávila et al.).

In East Los Angeles, on March 6, 1968, over a thousand high school students left their classrooms and marched into the streets in an effort to bring about better resources, teaching, and services as a part of their public education (Woo). Their demands were not outrageous. In fact, it was embarrassing that they even had to protest for such things as schools that weren't literally falling apart, ill-qualified teachers, counselors who cared little for Latinx students who, as the statistics they cited bore out, would most likely drop out anyway. The students demanded a curriculum that not only was relevant to their experiences outside of the school, they wanted their education to look like they did. They wanted teachers and principals who could empathize with their plight and lessons that drew from their own rich albeit ignored culture and history.

The blowouts were not a single afternoon affair. It would be days before the blowouts ceased, spreading out to more than a dozen schools of the East Los Angeles School District. The power of the movement was palpable. High schoolers, who tend to be viewed as apathetic and uninterested in causes larger than themselves or their own education, rose above their stereotype in more ways than one. Here were these so-called underachieving Latinx students demanding better resources for a worthwhile education. Though the blowouts did not lead to a complete turnaround for Latinxs in education, school boards and districts around the country were put on notice that substandard educational services and teaching would not be tolerated.

The struggle for a superb education for Latinxs persists into the twenty-first century. Two examples will serve to highlight the difficulties Latinx students have confronted since the blowouts of 1968 and show that this is not a problem of the past. In 2010, Arizona Republicans pushed for the passage of Arizona HB 2281, which effectively banned Tucson school district's Mexican-American Studies program—a program designed to educate students on the importance and vitality of Mexican American culture, from literature and film, to history and food traditions, and more. It is exactly the sort of program the students involved in the California blowouts had asked for: a curriculum that, for once, reflects Latinx history and the significance of Latinx culture to the United States.

Indeed, the law was designed to limit the presence of ethnic studies programs in Arizona public schools, going so far as to claim that ethnic studies courses "promote the overthrow of the United States government," and that they tended to "promote resentment toward a race or class of people," and so on. The law led to protests both in Arizona and across the United States. Advocates for the Tucson students claimed their constitutional rights had been violated. In the fall of 2017, a federal judge rendered a decision on behalf of the students, claiming the law was politically motivated, premised on "race-based fears." Such is the power in keeping Latinxs ignorant of their history and culture that the chance that Latinxs would have a more accurate perspective of their own identity literally terrifies white politicians and many of their white constituents.

Texas has also had it issues with the inclusion of Mexican American history within the curriculum. In 2016, the Texas School Board, in a response to a demand for more of an emphasis on Mexican American history and culture, ostensibly due to the large demographic of Mexican American students in the state, invited the submission of textbooks in this subject area. Initially, the only textbook submission they received was titled *Mexican American Heritage*, a book lambasted by scholars for being rife with errors, omissions, and misrepresentations. The book propagated stereotypes of Latinxs and was so problematic that experts in the area claimed it was irredeemable and not easily corrected or revised.

The controversy of the textbook was endemic of the larger issues surrounding public education in Texas, namely, the odd emphasis on religious matters and casual disregard of such momentous historical events as the institution of slavery and the fundamental causes of the American Civil War. Activists such as Tony Díaz, who goes by the nom de guerre "El Librotraficante," (or booksmuggler), continually brought attention to both the textbook issue in Texas as well as the Arizona HB 2281 law. Ultimately, the Texas State Board of Education refused to approve *Mexican American Heritage*. Both the repeal of the Arizona law that banned ethnic studies and the problematic textbook in Texas may not have been rejected were it not for the efforts of students, parents, civil rights activists, and politicians who work tirelessly to ensure that Latinxs are receiving the best education this nation can provide.

When the vast majority of Latinx students are US citizens (95% according to the National Council of La Raza), the challenge of making education equitable and accessible for Latinx students is a moral imperative, but one that is making progress, albeit at an uncomfortably slow pace. While it is recognized that Latinxs are the fastest-growing demographic in the United States, Latinx students remain, incredibly, among the most segregated student demographic in the nation. Though Latinx student achievement continues to improve, it still lags behind other student demographics. On the other hand, the high school dropout rate fell from 32% in 2000 to 12% in 2014, according to the Pew Research Center. One of the biggest factors in Latinx student success is the amount of resources, or relative wealth, of a given school. The general trend is that the more resources and investment in Latinx student education, the more those Latinx students tended to achieve at a higher level, and it often paves the way to success in higher education. These resources often contribute directly to college preparedness, and when they are absent, students are not as ready for the challenges of higher education.

To be sure, there is a well-established link between poverty and underachievement in education (Krogstad). Over one third of Latinx children live in poverty. Such impoverished conditions at home tend to concentrate the family's priorities on economic matters. The result of this is that parents are often preoccupied with financial burdens or they devote more time to providing for the family. When parents are unable to encourage and help their children in educational tasks at home (i.e., homework), projects and essays that take many days to complete, children are more apt to become frustrated and stop caring about how they perform in their grades. Research has shown how impoverished conditions at home lead to increased absenteeism, increased chronic illness, decreased opportunities for school-sponsored extracurricular activities, and increased risk for dropping out of school altogether (Krogstad).

In a positive development, many institutions of higher learning have now set their sights on becoming and remaining what is designated as a "Hispanic-serving Institution" (HSI). Such institutions are a part of a federal program that provides assistance and resources to universities that are dedicated to giving aid to first generation, low income Hispanic students. Universities who participate must meet certain criteria, such as the designation of a not-for-profit university, must offer accredited degrees of two years or beyond, and most significantly, they must have at least 25% Hispanic undergraduates that are "full-time-equivalent" enrolled students. Through the efforts of the Hispanic Association of College and Universities (HACU), which persuaded Congress in 1992 to give recognition to universities with high enrollment of Hispanics with the designation of HSI, thousands of Latinx students have benefited from this additional funding and apportionment of resources.

However, since the election of Donald J. Trump as President of the United States in 2016, Latinx immigrants have been put on edge due to Trump's divisive comments on Mexicans, as well as his promise to let the Obama-Era programs of DAPA (Deferred Action for Parent Accountability) and DACA (Deferred Action for Childhood Arrivals) expire in late 2016. These programs, and DACA especially, allowed motivated and talented Latinx students of undocumented parents, who themselves are undocumented, the opportunity to continue their education without the fear of being deported to a nation they can scarcely remember, having been brought to the United States at an early age. DACA is not, as some have claimed, amnesty. Rather, it is a temporary solution that is very much tied to the productivity and efforts of the recipients. DACA status is renewable once every two-years, and it bestows upon the recipients the right to work. With the number of recipients close to 800,000, so-called DREAMers (as a result of the DREAM Act) were enrolled into DACA. But in September 2017, the Trump administration allowed the DACA program to expire. As of early 2018, a resolution to address DACA recipients still had not been achieved, thanks in large measure to President Trump's insistence that DACA is resuscitated only with a commitment to building his signature border wall.

The history of Latinx education has been long and frustrating, with only the occasional breakthrough achieved after massive protests and activism. The need for improved funding and resources for Latinx students has led to the advent of organizations that are dedicated to this notable cause. As the Latinx demographic continues to swell, it is unsustainable to have inadequate resources for Latinx students. They are a significant part of the future of the United States, and to ignore them seems to carelessly disregard the nation's future.

Works Cited

Berta-Ávila, Margarita, Revilla A. Tijerina, and Figueroa J. López. *Marching Students: Chicana and Chicano Activism in Education, 1968 to the Present.* Reno, NV: University of Nevada Press, 2011.

Gándara, Patricia C., and Frances Contreras. *The Latino Education Crisis: The Consequences of Failed Social Policies.* Cambridge, MA: Harvard University Press, 2010.

Garcia, Mario T. *Blowout!: Sal Castro and the Chicano Struggle for Educational Justice.* Chapel Hill, NC: University of North Carolina Press, 2014.

Krogstad, Jens Manuel. "5 Facts about Latinos and Education." *Pew Research Center*, 28 July 2016, www.pewresearch.org/fact-tank/2016/07/28/5-facts-about-latinos-and-education/#

Noguera, Pedro A. "Saving Black and Latino Boys: What Schools Can Do to Make a Difference." *Phi Delta Kappan*, vol. 93, no. 5, 2012, pp. 8–12.

Rodriguez, Richard. *Hunger of Memory: The Education of Richard Rodriguez: An Autobiography.* New York: Dial Press Trade Paperbacks, 2005.

Urbina, Martin G., and Claudia R. Wright. *Latino Access to Higher Education: Ethnic Realities and New Directions for the Twenty-First Century.* Springfield, IL: Charles C. Thomas, 2016.

Woo, Elaine. "'60s 'Blowouts': Leaders of Latino School Protest See Little Change." *Los Angeles Times*, 7 March 1988, articles.latimes.com/1988-03-07/local/me-488_1_lincoln-high-school-graduate

EMPIRE

Latinx Studies scholars have focused their analytical lens on the topic of empire to make visible, as Lázaro Lima writes how "scattered remains throughout the Americas cross national borders as well as affective states of being" (p. 55). For Latinx Studies scholars, the aim is to uncover the material and ideological histories of empire as they effect the past, present, and future of Latinx subjects. They seek to unsettle, in Lima's words, "empires founding conceits premised on freedom" (p. 56).

Sesshu Foster's 2005 published novel *Atomik Aztex* is an interesting creative case in point. It is a novel that reimagines the *mestizo* and Aztec empire as victors in world history. Had the Euro-Spaniards won, the narrator Zenontli speculates, "they'd wipe us out [and] enslave our peoples down at the corner liquor store, crush all resistance thru germ warfare and lawyers, lie, cheat, kidnap, ransom, burn our sakred [sic] libraries [...] install Christian theokratik [sic] dixtatorships [sic]" (p. 2). However, in this storyworld it's the Aztec empire who reign victorious, spreading their reach through wonton destruction throughout a Europe characterized as backward and primitive and in need of salvation from its self-destructive tendencies. Of course, Foster makes it clear that in this tongue-in-cheek speculative revision of history the reader is supposed to recognize the *actual* history of European empire building with its conquest, colonization, and genocides across the Américas.

Foster's *Atomik Aztex* flips tables on history. It also directs attention to the debates and discussions within Latinx Studies in and around the history of domination, exploitation, and oppression of indigenous, mestizo, and African descended peoples within Spanish Iberian and US empire-building histories. To understand just how ripped apart our contemporary social tissue is, many Latinx scholars, creators, and activists have turned their sights to the past: to excavate and make known the racism, coercion, violence, expropriation, and genocide that forms the backbone to empire building histories in the Américas. They have done so and continue to do so to understand the past in order to challenge and resist imperialist policies at home and throughout the Américas that continue to disenfranchise those at the ethnoracial margins. They do so to clear a critical space in and around the legacies of empire that continue to harm those pushed to the class, gendered, ethnic, and sexual margins. They do so in defense and affirmation of a pan-Latinx, mixed-race (African, indigenous, European) hemispheric people that have historically stood against empire's destructive presence.

For Latinx Studies scholars, empire building begins with the Spanish and Portuguese conquests of the Américas; it's the wealth built on the back of exploited Africans and indigenous peoples that fueled the huge conquests of territories and people in the Old and New Worlds. Latinx scholars and creators have dissected and made visible the consequences of European empire building on material, ideological, and cultural levels: 1) the violence, torture, murder, *and* rape of African and indigenous peoples in the New World; 2) the ideological master narratives constructed and circulated by the Catholic church and European monarchic centers of power that systematically sought to dehumanize African and indigenous peoples as barbarian, savage, non-humans to justify their exploitation, rape, and murder; and, conversely, the heroizing of the European as pure, civilized, and savior; this myth making also serving the function of hiding Spain's long histories of ethnoracial mixings of Jews, Muslims, Galicians, Basques, and Moors. 3) the recognition of transcultural (and linguistic) byproducts that resulted from the new contact zones created as a result of (and in spite of) the violence of empire building in the New World. In *Local Histories/Global Designs* (2000) and *The Darker Side of the Renaissance* (2003) Walter Mignolo makes clear how material and ideological forces of empire building went hand in hand to justify Euro-Spanish expansion at any cost. For instance, he identifies how during the European conquest of the Américas, cartographic and written technologies and practices were upheld as the records of truth (geographical and historical) in opposition to the unreliable oral and visual cultures of New World natives. That is, the material conquest of the Américas went hand in hand with the ideological framing of the New World space and its peoples as a blank slate absent of history and culture to be written on by technologies of empire.

*

For scholars of Latinx (and Latin American) Studies seeking to understand the present by looking to the past, the weakening of Europe's empire in the Américas during the nineteenth century has proved particularly important. During the early nineteenth century when many were pushing out the Spaniards and Portuguese across the Américas, some were asking who should be recognized in the formation of new republics. For instance, on February 15, 1819 when Simón Bolívar gave his inaugural speech at the Second National Congress of Venezuela at Angostura he articulated the complex relationship *criollos* (second generation descendants of Spaniards) had to the Américas and Europe:

Americans by birth and Europeans by law, we find ourselves engaged in a dual conflict: we are disputing with the natives for titles of ownership, and at the same time we are struggling to maintain ourselves in the country that gave us birth against the opposition of the invaders.

Moreover, for many Latinx Studies scholars, it's his gesture of ethnoracial inclusion that mattered. He declares: "We are not Europeans; we are not Indians; we are but a mixed species of aborigines and Spaniards." This and other articulations of protean nation-states that recognize mestizos, Africans, and indios as the *new* citizenry that would stand against further attempts at incursion and control by Europe become important for Latinx Studies scholars today.

As one moves deeper into the nineteenth century we see Latinx Studies scholars making visible the impact of the rise of the US empire just as Europe's crumbled. For scholars such as John Morán González, Jesse Alemán, Rodrigo Lazo, Laura Lomas, Amelia María de la Luz Montes, José Aranda, Genaro Padilla, Marissa K. López, Nicolás Kanellos, José Limón, Kirstin Silva Gruesz, among others, the US's empire building strategies include physical, political, and ideological maneuvers. For instance, with the proclamation of its manifest destiny, the US massively expanded its territories into the northern areas of Mexico (now Texas, New Mexico, Arizona, Nevada, and California) and the Caribbean. Indeed, the 1823 Monroe Doctrine is seen by many Latinx scholars today less as the US protecting the Latin/o Américas from repeats of European empire building incursions and expropriations, and more the clearing of a path for its own imperial rise. And, the signing of the Treaty of Guadalupe Hidalgo in 1848 is considered a land-grab (half of Mexico's territories) and disenfranchisement of Tejanos, Californios, and other Latinxs who lived in the northern Mexican territories; with borders being drawn and racist policies instituted, Latinxs in the US became the backs upon which the US would continue building its wealth.

The US's continued empire building maneuvers (the "Big Brother" free-market trade policy, for instance) in Cuba, Puerto Rico, and the Dominican led to US companies such as United Fruit Company and many others turning the Hispanophone Caribbean into repositories of exploitable labor. And, the 1898 American-Spanish-Cuban War is seen as the US's economic, political, and ideological empire building in the Caribbean. The US empire was flexing its imperial muscle and selling individualism and free market capitalism as the path to democracy all while expropriating lands, exploiting people, and creating new forms of material and economic dependency for non-US territories. Indeed, the very fact that the US government and media began to identify as "America"—a single nation assuming the name of a whole hemisphere—is indicative of this period's rise of empire along with its concomitant exceptionalism and narcissism.

In the face of this rise of a US empire, scholars of Latinx Studies have identified pockets of resistance in historical figures and the production of cultural phenomena. To the list of scholars already mentioned above, we think readily of others also collected in Rodrigo Lazo and Jesse Alemán's *The Latino Nineteenth Century* (2016) along with Louis A. Pérez, Jr.'s *Cuba in the American Imagination* (2008) and Laura Lomas's *Translating Empire* (2008). One such figure who has become part of the Latinx Studies canon: Cuba's anti-imperialist writer and activist, José Martí. With pen and gun, Martí fought against the physical and ideological appendages of US empire building that framed the Afrolatino Caribbean as backward, provincial, and in need of domination. Many scholars have championed his essay "Nuestra América" as a call to a protean, hemispheric, and resistant pan-Latinidad. (See José David Saldívar's *Dialectics of Our America*.) Indeed, Martí is held up as formulating this pan-Latinidad inclusive of mestizo, indio, and Afrolatino in the face of the US empire's policies of militaristic, economic, and physical violence that targeted Latinxs of the Caribbean and the US mainland. Martí's call for a unified front of all Latinxs—African, indio, and mestizo—has led to important scholarship on regions of the Américas impacted by US imperial **hegemony**. (See also Claudia Milian's *Latining America: Black-Brown Passages and the Coloring of Latinx Studies*.)

US empire building throughout the Américas has resulted in increased economic dependency as well as displacement of people. For instance, in 1954, the US supported military coup in Guatemala put in power a dictatorship that led to the murder and displacing of hundreds of thousands of people. Juan González refers to this as "the unintended harvest of the US empire" (p. xvii). In *Harvest of Empire* González provides a detailed social, political, historical account of the consequences of empire building, especially in the displacing of Mexicans, Puerto Ricans, Cubans, Dominicans, Colombians, and Central Americans. With the twentieth century US empire building in **Central America** funding civil wars and later the implementation of the North American Free Trade Agreement that destroyed local, village economies, families from Mexico and Central America have been forced from land and home; just to survive another day, they've become the exploited, undocumented labor pool that has made rich capitalists and continued to fuel the US's empire building with its, in González's words, "vicious and relentless drive for territorial expansion, conquest, and subjugation of others—Native Americans, African slaves, and Latin Americans" (p. 270).

Indeed, Latinx scholars like myself and others have identified the period after WWII as a time when the US had come into its own as an empire. When its "Latin American Backyard," as Juan González calls it, had amassed massive wealth for US capitalists; indeed, between 1950 and 1967, US investments in this proverbial Latin American Backyard had created extravagant profits. However, as the US empire's reach expanded, it needed to implement a system of pro-capitalist, enlightened despots. As Frederick Luis Aldama discusses in *Why the Humanities Matter*, during this period US imperialism needed bought intellectuals and culture specialists to function as "mandarins to sell such destructive methods as necessary for the establishment of 'democracy'" (p. 117). Indeed, like the mandarins of imperialist China, to sustain itself as an empire, the US had to manufacture a professional and intellectual class —from writers, to teachers, to factory managers, and even presidents— to keep safe capitalist interests throughout the Américas. During the 1960s, the CIA and Ford Foundation funded institutions such as the Alliance for Progress, Peace Corps, and the Congress of Cultural Freedom (CCF); notably, too, the UN funded the Economic Commission for Latin America and the Caribbean (CEPAL) that promoted the creating of mixed economies controlled by local and global capitalists. Indeed, we see these appendages of empire working to fund pro-US capitalist journals in Latin America such as *Cuardernos* (1953–1965) and *Mundo Nuevo* (1966–1971) and fellowships and travel grants that one way or another bought important Latin American scholars, artists, and writers; *Mundo Nuevo* featured interviews with Carlos Fuentes and excerpts from García Márquez's *Cien años de soledad*. (See Patrick Iber's *Neither Peace nor Freedom: The Cultural Cold War in Latin America*, Frances Stonor Saunders's *Who Paid the Piper?: The CIA and the Cultural Cold War*, and Noam Chomsky's *American Power and the New Mandarins*.)

Given the deep destructive presence of European followed by US empire building histories in the Américas, it's not surprising that a strong impulse informing the shaping of Latinx (and Latin American) Studies has been its identification of a modus operandi of resistance. During the 1960s and 1970s **el movimiento**, for instance, artists, activists, and scholars identified and celebrated pre-Columbian histories, myths, and figures that represented a resistant epistemology and ontology. Within Latinx Studies, then, as David Luis-Brown sums up, this has linked "the racial struggle to the anti-imperial struggle" (*Waves of Decolonization* 66). Indeed, Ana Patricia Rodríguez identifies just such a struggle and anti-imperial resistance in Central American authors such as Ruben Darío, Máximo Soto Hall, Ramón Amaya Amador, and Carlos Gagini; for Rodríguez, this conjoining of struggle with anti-imperialism can be seen in the work of Joaquín Beleño that makes visible and challenges the US militaristic intervention, construction, and control over the Panama Canal. This is to say that Latinx Studies with its formation of a hemispheric, trans-Latinx worldview (José David Saldívar's "outernational" postcolonial "trans-americanity") has grown in response to the material, social, economic, and political conditions and consequences of US empire building.

*

In 2000, Michael Hardt and Antonio Negri published *Empire*. They argue that global capitalism had dissolved traditional nation-states, created networks of power, and reconfigured empire as an "outopia or really a nonplace" (p. 166). Resistance and revolution happen as "counterpower" and by a "multitude, without mediation" (p. 237). As there are no "emperors" ruling bounded nation-states (no sites of power), political struggle and activism are now "completely open" (p. 237). For Hardt and Negri, empire is a new world order not based on class struggle, but characterized by a fluid, infinitely expanding and highly organized "supranational organism" that says power is everywhere and therefore resistance can be everywhere: it is where the fight for a true democracy can happen as a simple negation in "the will to be against." Some Latinx and Latin American scholars have used Hardt/Negri's formulation to identify a posthegemonic empire at work today. For instance, in "Beyond Hispanic Studies? Interdisciplinary Approaches to Spain and Latin America" Jon Beasley-Murray identifies the rise of new "transnational networks" of intellectual work on Latin American and US Latinx cultural production throughout the Américas and globally that "offer examples of new ways of connecting and interacting, forming perhaps something like a globalization from below" (p. 179). Accordingly, the posthegemonic empire as outopia leads to the rise of networks of global counterpower from the indigenous of Chiapas and Subcomandante Marcos to the protestors of Seattle and Genoa. (See also Jon Beasley-Murray's *On Posthegemony: Political Theory and Latin America* as well as Román de la Campa's "Deconstruction, Cultural Studies, Capitalism.") For Arnaldo Manuel Cruz-Malavé, this formulation of empire as outopia and resistance as the counterpower of the multitudes is given expression in Puerto Rican author, Giannina Braschi's poetry and novels. For Cruz-Malavé, Braschi's *Empire of Dreams, Yo-Yo Boing!*, and *United States of Banana* embody a transformative teleology from "a totalizing performative poetics of inversion to a rhyzomatic poetics of deterritorialization, singularity, and appositional, horizontal camaraderie 'from below'" (p. 804). Indeed, Braschi realizes through fictional form Hardt and Negri's conception of power and resistance to empire today that's not based on the class struggle within the nation-state class, but as located within the rhyzomatic, deterritorialized multitude. Indeed, he identifies Braschi's *United States of Banana* as a

> political–poetic, anti-imperial book [that] does not seek to attain a new space of sovereignty from which to exert an alternative, progressive hegemony; instead, it attempts to imagine and foster, as Neil Harvey has suggested with respect to the political practice of the Zapatistas, new forms of interaction, communication, and cooperation "from below," literally from below.
>
> (p. 815)

Moreover, *United States of Banana* clears a space for "new urban-inspired, anticolonial spatial forms that would foster networks of interaction and cooperation, camaraderie, compañerismo, and yes, love" (p. 816). Yet others (ourselves included) are critical of Hardt and Negri's formulation of networks of power as outopic empire with its concomitant multitudinal resistance. (See Aldama's *Why the Humanities Matter.*) In "Revolutionary Love: Bridging Differential Terrains of Empire" Cathryn Josefina Merla-Watson is critical of their formulation of a spontaneous uprising of the multitude within and against global capitalist networks of power as material and ideological empire building strategies continue to work today based on a clear understanding of the nation-state's function in its repression of the working class. More pointedly, Merla-Watson is critical of Hardt and Negri because they erase very real struggles of real people, especially women of color. The Latina queer feminist formulation of inclusive borderlands rooted in indigenous women's history is a more powerful site of resistance to very real violence, oppression, and exploitation of empire. And, in *Latinamericanism after 9/11* (2011) John Beverly argues that within today's global capitalism and neoliberalism we need to recognize the real, trans-American radical social movements that seek to expand notions of citizenry within and across recognizable nation-states. In *Why the Humanities Matter* Aldama argues how for Latinxs in the US we don't see in any way the boundaries of the nation-state becoming permeable and networks of power creating necessarily counterpower multitudes. It's exactly the opposite. The militarization of the US/Mexico border has never been so intense as it is today. Hardt's and Negri's idea of borderless empire and resistant multitude doesn't deal with the problem of accountability. As more and more Latinxs become the target of immigration enforcement and are increasingly forced to cross dangerous borders, with many real Latinxs dying everyday as a result, we object to Hardt/Negri's transformation of the people and the people's struggles as an immeasurable and class-less multitude of counterpower along with the erasure of the nation-state as outopic empire. We remind that Marx and many others have insisted that the idea of a people as a unit is a false idea: you have the working people and on the other hand the bourgeoisie—not as a unit of people with shared interests and shared representation. This is why, for example, working class Latinxs in the US have more in common with workers in Canada than they do with bourgeois Latinxs in the US.

*

As has been shown, there's the dark side of empire building that has been choking the Américas since 1492. Today, we continue to struggle with its dark legacies with the uprooting, exploitation, oppression, and disenfranchisement of Latinx Americans. And, as we've also shown, there are the byproducts of empire building in the Américas that have led to the ethnoracial mixtures, movements of peoples and forming of new contact zones, and transcultural productions that Latinxs live and experience today. (See Earl Shorris's *Latinos: A Biography of the People*.) To fight empire, Juan González proposes that we stand in solidarity and support of working class unions that transcend nation-states; that we abolish the concept of "illegal" and fight for equal legal, civil, and economic rights for all workers; that we end the colonial status of Puerto Rico; that we recognize language minorities and promote the widespread study of Spanish; invest in public schools and public infrastructure; and, end US militarism along the border and in Latin America and sanctions against Cuba. In his Afterword to *The Darker Side of Western Modernity* Mignolo asks his readers to think critically of the epistemologies built to justify the empire building conquests of the New World. In so doing, he asks that his readers consider alternative, **pre-Colombian epistemologies** as a way to envision alternative futures that affirm community, life, and the planet itself. (See also Paloma Martínez-Cruz's *Women and Knowledge in Mesoamerica*.)

Works Cited

Aldama, Frederick Luis. *Why the Humanities Matter: A Common Sense Approach.* Austin, TX: University of Texas Press, 2008.

Alemán, Jesse, and Rodrigo Lazo, eds. *The Latino Nineteenth Century.* New York: New York University Press, 2016.

Beasley-Murray, Jon. *On Posthegemony: Political Theory and Latin America.* Minneapolis, MN: University of Minnesota Press, 2010.

Beverly, John. *Latinamericanism after 9/11.* Durham, NC: Duke University Press, 2011.

Braschi, Giannina. *Empire of Dreams.* New Haven, CT: Yale University Press, 1994.

———. *Yo-Yo Boing!* Pittsburgh, PA: Latin American Literary Review Press, 1998.

Chomsky, Noam. *American Power and the New Mandarins.* New York: Pantheon Books, 1969.

Cruz-Malavé, Arnaldo Manuel. "'Under the Skirt of Liberty': Giannina Braschi Rewrites Empire." *American Quarterly*, vol. 66, no. 3, 2014, pp. 801–818.

De La Campa, Román. "Deconstruction, Cultural Studies, Capitalism." In *Critical Latin American and Latino Studies*, edited by Juan Poblete. Minneapolis, MN: University of Minnesota Press, 2003, pp. 154–170.

Foster, Sesshu. *Atomik Aztex.* San Francisco, CA: City Lights, 2005.

González, Juan. *Harvest of Empire: A History of Latinos in America.* New York: Viking, 2000.

Hardt, Michael, and Antonio Negri. *Empire.* Cambridge, MA: Harvard University Press, 2000.

Iber, Patrick. *Neither Peace nor Freedom: The Cultural Cold War in Latin America.* Cambridge, MA: Harvard University Press, 2015.

Lima, Lázaro. "Empire." In *Keywords in Latina/o Studies*, edited by Deborah R. Vargas et al. New York: New York University Press, 2017, pp. 55–58.

Lomas, Laura. *Translating Empire: José Martí, Migrant Latino Subjects, and American Modernities.* Durham, NC; Duke University Press, 2008.

Luis-Brown, David. *Waves of Decolonization: Discourses of Race and Hemispheric Citizenship in Cuba, Mexico, and the United States.* Durham, NC: Duke University Press, 2008.

Martínez-Cruz, Paloma. *Women and Knowledge in Mesoamerica: From East L.A. to Anahuac.* Tucson, AZ: University of Arizona Press, 2011.

Merla-Watson, Cathryn Josefina. "Revolutionary Love: Bridging Differential Terrains of Empire." In *The Un/Making of Latina/o Citizenship: Culture, Politics, and Aesthetics*, edited by Ellie Hernández and Eliza Rodriguez Y Gibson. New York: Palgrave Macmillan, 2014, pp. 167–189.

Mignolo, Walter. *Local Histories/Global Designs: Coloniality, Subaltern Knowledges, and Border Thinking.* Princeton, NJ: Princeton University Press, 2000.

———. *The Darker Side of Western Modernity. Global Futures. Decolonial Options.* Ann Arbor, MI: University of Michigan Press, 2003.

Milian, Claudia. *Latining America: Black-Brown Passages and the Coloring of Latinx Studies*. Athens, GA: University of Georgia Press, 2013.

Pérez Jr., Louis. *Cuba in the American Imagination: Metaphor and the Imperial Ethos*. Chapel Hill, NC: University of North Carolina Press, 2008.

Saldívar, José David. *Dialectics of Our America: Genealogy, Cultural Critique, and Literary History*. Durham, NC: Duke University Press, 1991.

——. "Looking Awry at 1898: Roosevelt, Montejo, Paredes, and Mariscal." *American Literary History*, vol. 12, no. 3, 2000, pp. 386–406.

Saunders. Frances Stonor. *Who Paid the Piper? The CIA and the Cultural Cold War*. London: Granta Books, 2000.

Shorris, Earl. *Latinos: A Biography of a People*. New York: W.W. Norton, 1992.

FAMILIA

Latinx *familia* is a very richly varied kinship network. Influenced by ancestral origin cultures from the Dominican Republic, Cuba, Puerto Rico, Mexico, Central America, and South America. Influenced by regional location such as rural or urban. Influenced by different US immigration policies as tied to differences in the histories of wars, natural disasters, and expropriation of lands. And, within the family unit, there's much diversity in terms of race and sexuality as well as class and citizen status.

Yet, while the Latinx *familia* is complexly configured and stratified, there is much that Latinx families share in common, including religion (Catholicism), connection to homelands, and trans-language (English and Spanish). Indeed, it is the geographic proximity of US Latinx families to ancestral homelands that creates a constant infusion of ancestral cultural ties across Latinx families of different national origins. Unlike other ethnoracial groups from Europe and elsewhere that make up the US demographic as a whole and whose ancestors crossed big bodies of water, Latinx families continue to be in close contact with kinship networks in the Hispanophone Caribbean as well as the central and south Americas. And, with the history of the Southwest as expropriated northern Mexico's lands (the 1848 signing of the Treaty of Guadalupe Hidalgo), this region of the US continues to be majority Latinx and steeped in Latinx culture. Additionally, histories of forced migration (wars and natural disasters) that continue today often mean that Latinx families in the US are constantly shaped by the arrival of kin (blood and non-blood) from national origin countries. For instance, already in 2001 *Crossing Over: A Mexican Family on the Migrant Trail* Rubén Martínez wrote about how such a Latinx **diaspora** from Mexico was already radically changing the demographic of Los Angeles. The result of this and birth rates within Latinx families has led to this demographic becoming the majority minority in the US.

Our geographic and cultural proximity to ancestral homelands has also meant the constant presence of the Spanish language in family life. While certainly the push–pull effects of an English-only education system has led to the general trend among new generations of Latinxs to be less fluent in Spanish, it remains a living, breathing part of Latinx family life. As Luis Fraga et al. summarize, "Even those Latinos who are further removed from the immigration experience either acknowledge these cultural elements or attempt to maintain or even recover them" (*Latino Lives* 175). That is, it is not dying as it did with Italian, German, or any other language that US immigrants of earlier generations brought with them.

Historically, Latinx families have tended to live in similar neighborhoods. This is the result both of city planning impositions (Red-lining) *and* by self-design. For instance, San Francisco's Mission District proved attractive to many Latinxs of Mexican and Central American origin because of its history of being a rent-controlled area in an urban core where jobs could be found; with Latinx families setting up *tiendas* and *cantinas* and cultural events and where Spanish could be heard everywhere, the area became a gravitational pull for more and more Latinx families to live. Until the Silicon Valley tech industry began to take over the neighborhood in the late 1990s and especially today, the Mission District was a *barrio* made up of a majority of Latinx families.

With costs of living on the coasts becoming prohibitively high for Latinx families, there has been a migration to the Midwest and the South—regions where the Latinx demographic is growing the fastest. Again, availability of jobs, low cost of living, and existing Latinx family members have led to an internal diaspora where Latinx families and communities are setting roots in traditionally underpopulated Latinx urban and suburban places. In Chicago, there's been a steady reverse migration out of the urban core. And, it's the **suburbs** of Columbus, Ohio, where we see the relocating of Latinx families from the expensive coasts and the Southwest. The suburbs offer less expensive housing (subdivisions and low-rise apartment complexes) and access to better funded and resourced schools.

Internal diasporic patterns and new regions of settling are changing the way Latinx families are growing in the US. For instance, in the research findings of scholars such as Luis Fraga, John A. Garcia, Rodney

E. Hero, Michael Jones-Correa, Valerie Martinez-Ebers, and Gary Segura, we see these Latinx families developing "extensive interactions with non-Latinos, even as they maintain the majority of their social and economic interactions with other Latinos" (*Latino Lives in America: Making it Home* 175). And, as Founder & Director of OSU's LASER: Latinx Space for Enrichment & Research, Frederick Luis Aldama sees how Latinx families in Columbus's suburbs are constantly working to overcome obstacles such as high schools run by non-Latinx staff and teachers as well as stressors of life living among non-Latinx neighbors, police officers, and shop keepers who see Latinx families as a threat; Latinx family and community organized events such as quinceañeras and other Catholic church rituals, Cinco de Mayo, Puerto Rican Day Parade, Latinx Festivals, low-rider parades, and many others. (For more on quinceañeras, see Rachel V. González-Martin's "Barrio Ritual and Pop Rite: Quinceañeras in the Folklore-Popular Culture Borderlands.")

Raúl Homero Villa identifies these cultural and social affirmations of family as *barriological* practices that gel together the *familias* that make up these Latinx communities. (See Homero Villa, *Barrio-Logos*.) Indeed, Latinx urban planners today put these family and community centered practices in the daily activities of Latinxs front and center in their work on *barrios* but also in the designing of new urban spaces generally. For instance, Aldama's colleague, Jesús Lara, considers such family-oriented and directed barriological practices as vital to seeing how one can revitalize cities without the stratification and ejection of working families that result from gentrification processes. (See Lara's *Placemaking and Planning*, as well as the work of Michael Mendez, James Rojas, Henry Muñoz, and Johana Londoño.)

Whether in the suburbs, urban core, or rural regions of the US, the family unit has proved to be a space of resilience, refuge, and action within a nation that has systematically discriminated against Latinxs with its wage gaps and push-out/lock-out school system policies. As with African Americans and other discriminated against ethnoracial demographics in the US, maintaining cohesion among family members has held at bay capitalist forces that seek to exploit by dividing and isolating people from one another. Often, we see how all family members work not only to pay bills, put food on tables, and keep roofs overhead, but also to open clear space for educational pursuits. The Latinx family unit and community building initiatives and traditions are a means of survival within a socioeconomic system aimed to exploit and oppress.

Immigrant policy and citizen status continue to be tools used to divide Latinx families. We see this clearly and tragically when undocumented Latinx parents are forcefully separated from their documented children. Fighting for members of our Latinx families who are Deferred Action for Childhood Arrivals (DACA) recipients have proved a lightning rod for pulling the Latinx community together. However, the rhetoric within the mainstream media and generated by US politicians and civic leaders that frames the path to citizenship as one of good vs. bad family members has been rightfully questioned by activists in the Latinx community because of the way it slips into the "model minority" ideology: DACA recipients are good and productive vs. the parents and other family members who are bad and criminal. For Amalia Pallares this rhetoric falls squarely within a "neoliberal framework that posits undocumented youth as highly talented potential individual producers" (*Family Activism* 98). Activists such as Immigrant Youth Justice League (IYJL) and Latino Action Youth League (LOYAL) have mobilized to protest this rhetoric (and potential policy making) to protect all members of the Latinx family. And, the UndocuQueer movement has importantly enlarged the scope of this activist work to include queer and trans undocumented family members.

Preservation of the Latinx family has proved historically to be important in defending against exploitative and oppressive policies. However, there is within this history a dark cloud. Because of deep-seated sexism and homophobia within Latinx families, political activism of the 1960s and 1970s sidelined and willfully erased women and LGBTQ kin. The two central concepts used to unite members of the Chicano Movement were *la raza* and carnalismo; both concepts were tied to the championing of the straight male when in actuality the family and community is much more complexly configured. The different Latinx movements and their cultural products—from Luis Valdez's *teatro* to the poetry of Miguel Algarín and Miguel Piñero and the Nuyorican Café—celebrated a heteromasculine idea of the Latinx family unit that violently erased and subordinated women and LGBTQ family members.

Many Latina feminists, creators, and activists countered this message by calling attention to the hard work and deep contributions to Latinx family and community. In the case of Puerto Rican author, Judith Ortiz Cofer, she put front and center in her fiction and poetry grandmothers, mothers, and sisters (see her *Silent Dancing* and *The Line of the Sun*). Such Latina creations, as Moreno writes in *Family Matters*, "undermine the privileged site of la casa patriarchal—the 'primal scene of the nation'—by revealing the anachronistic and exclusionary power structure embedded in la gran familia" (p. 13).

Activists, scholars, and creators have recognized the importance of family to organize against forces of oppression. However, they have also been setting the record straight concerning the *actual* make-up of the Latinx family. In *Next of Kin* Richard T. Rodríguez calls out the damage done by creating and naturalizing a hetero-patriarchal conception of the Latinx family that willfully ignored and violently excised from existence huge numbers of our kin who identify as **LGBTQ**. Today, nearly 1.4 million Latinxs identify as LGBTQ. And, Latinx same-sex couples are making families and raising children at a rate not seen in other same-sex demographics (Rodríguez's "Family" 63).

This concept of *familia* became hotly contested by queer activists, scholars, and creators. The 1981 publication of *This Bridge Called My Back* edited by Cherríe Moraga and Gloria Anzaldúa proved seminal in clearing an affirming space for LGBTQ subjects. Anzaldúa's celebration of queer women of color as *atravesados* demanded that the heteromasculine activist movements reconfigure its concept of family to be gender, queer inclusive. Contemporary LGBTQ scholars continue to add to and expand these seminal recognitions of *actual* Latinx families and communities made up of complex intersectional identities. For instance, in *Reading Chican@ Like a Queer* Sandra K. Soto uses the indexical "*Chican@*" to identify a performative Latinoness made up of "the unpredictable, polymorphous, and often contradictory representations of the mutual constitution of racialization and sexuality" (p. 121). Richard T. Rodríguez insists that our "reconfigured kinship arrangements need not be established in mutual exclusivity from biological relations" (*Next of Kin* 167). And, Ellie D. Hernández has excavated the rich array of jotería pop cultural phenomena to show how it embraces another aspect of Latinx ancestral heritage: indigeneity. (In addition to Ellie D. Hernández's "Cultura Jotería: The Ins and Outs of Latina/o Popular Culture" see the work of José Esteban Muñoz, Yvonne Yarbro-Bejarano, Ricardo Ortiz, Licia Fiol-Matta, and Ray González, among others.)

So as much as there is that unites members of the Latinx family—and differently origin-culture Latinx families across the nation—there are internalized ideologies that create divisions within the Latinx family. In addition to the gender and sexuality structural striations just mentioned, there are also issues that grow from internalized racism. EuroSpanish conquest of the Américas introduced the ideology of the *casta* system: light-skin and European features were seen as superior and brown-skinned, indigenous features were seen as inferior. This *casta* ideology continues to play out in Latinx families today.

Many Latinx authors have brought to the fore how this casta system and internalized racism plays out in everyday ways within the Latinx family. In the memoir, *Down These Mean Streets*, Piri Thomas recounts his violent experiences within the Nuyorican family that disowned him for being a too-dark-skinned Afrolatino along with those of a racist US society. Indeed, novelist, poet, and scholar Arturo Islas gives creative expression to this when he creates the character of Mama Chona in *The Rain God*. No matter how hot the Texas desert is, she wears long sleeves and carries an umbrella. She doesn't want the sun to darken her skin like *los indios*. She refuses to do dishes as it's beneath her idea of being light skinned and therefore superior to manual labor.

As Islas recreates with the character of Mama Chona, **classism** and racism often go hand in hand with some members of some Latinx families. In *The Dirty Girls Social Club* Alisa Valdes-Rodriguez creates a series of upwardly mobile Latina characters (all born during the 1970s *movimientos*) from different cultures of origin—Mexican, Puerto Rican, Dominican, and Cuban—who betray this linkage between class and race. For instance, the light-skinned affords the privilege of slumming it with Chicano activists and her embracing of a Mexica identity; but when she's actually faced with real contact with working class, dark Latinxs she's repelled. Whereas the dark-skinned Puerto Rican born Usnavys rejects her African, indigenous roots as a way to *think* herself superior. The Hispano character, Rebecca, from New Mexico finds her perch of superiority by claiming a pure Spanish bloodline; and, even after she betrays her parent's wishes for her not to date a black man, when she does it is with an exotic African born and raised black man and not an African American. One way or another, they all fall into the *casta* ideology to distance themselves from lower class association. They buy into the racist ideology as they distance themselves from accepting the complexity of class and race in their proximate and distant kinship relations. They distance themselves from real political and social activism and awareness.

Latinx creators have also reconstructed non-sanctioned Latinx kinship networks such as gangs. In *Always Running: Gang Days in East LA* Luis Rodriguez chronicles his days as a teen when he joined a gang. With a fractured and largely absent family, the gang became a surrogate family for him. We see this also chronicled in Edward James Olmos's film, *American Me*. In *Gang Nation* Monica Brown analyzes Edwin Torres and Piri Thomas (Puerto Rican) as well as Xyta Maya Murray and Mona Ruiz (Chicana) to identify how the gang has become an alternative family (and not one she condones) within a social tissue that's ripped apart by legacies of colonialism and today's capitalism that has created systemic structural inequities such as "entrenched poverty, failing educational and health care systems, a debilitated infra-structure, as well as the seeming lack of hope and the existential despair that accompany these material conditions" (p. xiv). Gang life becomes an alternative community and family for those completely ejected from society. And yet, as Luis Rodriguez reflects, his membership in this ad hoc family came at a high cost: violence and murder.

The Latinx family is an important focus in the making of mainstream cultural phenomena such as film and television. The Latinx family has been the center piece of prime-time sitcoms and dramas such as *Desperate Housewives, Cristela* (2014–2015), *The George Lopez Show* (2001–2007), and *Modern Family*. The family in *Cristela* is of Mexican origin, with many of the jokes driven by generational differences or **machismo** (masculine entitlement). *The George Lopez Show* reconstructs a more complexly configured Latinx working-class family living in Los Angeles: George (George Lopez) is the ancestrally Mexican-origined Latinx married to the ancestrally Cuban-origined Latina, Angie (Constance Marie). Most of the punchlines are built around the differences between the two cultures. *Ugly Betty* featured an urban, working-class Latinx family that showed the first gay Latinx teen, the nephew Justin Suarez, on prime-time TV. With *Ugly Betty* there's much importance placed on food (Mexican), dance, and **code-switching** (especially during heightened emotional moments and by the older generation represented by the father who peppers his English with "Dios mio!" and "mija," and so on) as expressions of their Latinidad, however, the show subordinates this to its fairytale vision of the Latinx family: the naïve idea that hard work and the pursuit of one's passion will lead to a Cinderella-like, socioeconomic transformation. In *Desperate Housewives* the Solis family are upper-middle class, with Gabi Solis as a stay at home mama until the husband Carlos (Ricardo Antonio Chavira) goes blind, loses his job, and takes up massage therapy. The show depicts them as a Latinx family with a fragile hold on status: they quickly slide down the class ladder when they are shown the servant's entrance to the country club—an indication generally of their lower status in the community once they are not members of the professional, bourgeois class. In *Modern Family* Sofía Vergara plays the role of a Colombian first-generation Latina where the butt of the jokes gravitate around her thick accent and malapropisms. She's married to a divorcee Anglo, reconstructing another type of Latinx family that's ethnoracially mixed.

We even have the Latinx family reconfigured in another galaxy. In the SyFy show, *Caprica* (2009–2010) the Adama family comes to represent the minority and émigré—(from another planet) identified population living in the majority white, Caprica City. The well-known Chicano actor, Esai Morales (*La Bamba, Zoot Suit, Mi Familia*) plays the head of the family, Yosef Adama. The Adama family code-switch (English/Spanish/Hebrew) and live in an older, crowded part of the city ("Little Tauron") that the show's camera lens washes in a gold-hued sepia light; they are a family close to their cultural roots (performing various rituals) and nostalgic for the loss of their homelands. The three generations that live under one roof reveal a close-knit family, even though each has their own respective patterns of behavior and world-view. For instance, along with the upwardly mobile Yosef, there's the gay uncle, Sam, who is a politicized hit man. The abuelita holds strong to their cultural values, imparting these to the third generation of Tauron such as Yosef's son, William. All members of the family have a varied phenotype; some are darker and others lighter skinned. In many ways, the Adama family is a snapshot of today's Latinx family.

There are many mainstream films that also reconstruct the Latinx family. There are those Disney productions such as *Camp Rock* (2008), *Wizards of Waverly Place* (2012), and *Bratz*, among others, where we see Latinx families but that are seemingly totally assimilated. For instance, in *Camp Rock* and *Wizards* Cuban-American actress María Canals plays the mother figure but her Latinoness is only tangentially referred to in that she's a cook. And, the casting of Latina actresses Selena Gomez (Alex in *Wizards*) and Demi Lovato (Mitchie Torres in *Camp Rock*) are very lightweight cultural indexical referents to Latinoness.

With the animation feature, *Coco* (2017), Disney might have finally gotten the Latinx family right. Not only in terms of creating a complex range of characters that make up the Latinx family that's the core of the story (and this with the help of Latinxs on the set and as the voices of the characters), but also by doing so Disney acknowledged the fact that it is the Latinx familia that are the main demographic paying to watch movies. The film's release made a record number of dollars, and this largely because of Latinx families going to see the film—families on both sides of the US Mexico border.

In other films, we see the Latinx kinship network as a palimpsest overlay to the affirmation of an ad hoc multicultural family. We see this in the *Fast & Furious* franchise where car chases and fighting bad guys increasingly revolve around protecting this Italian, Mexican, Irish, African American, Haitian, rag-tag family unit: Dom Torreto and sister

Mia Torreto along with Letty Ortiz, Michelle Rodriguez, Brian O'Connor, among many others. We see them praying before dinner as well as increasingly speaking Spanish, as in the case of Dom. However, because the Latinx family markers lack any substance along with the prominent place of other Latinx signifiers such as music (reggaeton) inflected with a gangster **ethos**, the reconstructions of Latinx familia here slip into a simplistic rendering of the Latinx family as a type of "utopian multiculturalism" (p. 89), as Mary Beltrán writes.

There's a long tradition of Latinx filmmakers who have countered this mainstream simplification of the Latinx family. We see this in films like *La Bamba* (1987) and *My Family/Mi familia* (1995), *Star Maps* (1997), *Girlfight* (2000), and *Mosquita y Mari* (2012), *Spy Kids* (2001), and *Cesar Chavez* (2014). In each we see different complex configurations of the Latinx family—and this to a radical degree in *Star Maps*. Arturo Aldama identifies how in *Star Maps* the director Miguel Arteta chooses to make visible how "external forces (racism, the state, and colonialist consumption patterns) and internal factors (machismo, Americanization, active complicity)" (p. 136) lead to sexism and gender oppression within the Latinx family. In *Girlfight* Karyn Kusama creates the character Diana Guzman (Michelle Rodriguez) who literally boxes her way out of a troubled family life (an aggressive and violent father). She decides to grow her skill in an otherwise highly gendered (male) sport as a form of empowerment and way out of an otherwise suffocating Latinx domestic space. In *Mosquita y Mari* film director Aurora Guerrero celebrates the role of mothers and comadres (godmothers, or co-mothers) along with the bond between two young women; that is, she celebrates the positives of Latinx kinship networks as not necessarily built from blood relations, but out of a long tradition of *comadrazgo*. And, with the *Spy Kids* franchise (2001–2011) Robert Rodríguez puts front and center the Latinx family as complexly built, including through non-blood relations. Finally, in a biopic like *Cesar Chavez* director Diego Luna focuses on the male figure, Cesar Chavez (Michael Peña), but also gives screen time to the hard work and sacrifices made by his wife, Helen Chavez (America Ferrera); it attempts to intertwine personal history and family life with the history civil rights struggles and organization.

The Latinx family is formed by and within historical, social, political, and cultural forces. It is shaped by ancestral origins as well as geographic location. The Latinx family is complex, to say the least. And while mainstream representations of the Latinx family often get this wrong— and some to a racist degree as with those road signs that appeared along the freeway in southern California depicting a migrant family running against the bright yellow backdrop or other representations of the Latinx family as an invasive threat—there are many that seek to celebrate the presence of Latinx families in the US. We think here of the Monumento a la Familia Puertorriqueña in Hartford, Connecticut with its inscription: "Honoring the contribution of the Puerto Rican families to the development of the United States of America."

Works Cited

Aldama, Arturo J. *Disrupting Savagism: Chicana/o, Mexican Immigrant, and Native American Struggles for Self-Representation.* Durham, NC: Duke University Press, 2001.

Anzaldúa, Gloria and Cherríe Moraga, eds. *This Bridge Called My Back: Writings by Radical Women of Color.* New York: Kitchen Table, Women of Color Press, 1983.

Beltrán, Mary. "Fast and Bilingual: 'Fast & Furious' and the Latinization of Racelessness." *Cinema Journal*, vol. 53, no. 1, 2013, pp. 75–96.

Brown, Monica. *Gang Nation: Delinquent Citizens in Puerto Rican, Chicano, and Chicana Narratives.* Minneapolis, MN: University of Minnesota Press, 2002.

Fiol-Matta, Licia. *A Queer Mother for the Nation: The State and Gabriela Mistral.* Minneapolis, MN: University of Minnesota Press, 2002.

Fraga, Luis, John A. Garcia, Michael Jones-Correa, Gary M. Segura, Rodney Hero, and Valerie Martinez-Ebers. *Latino Lives in America: Making it Home.* Philadelphia, PA: Temple University Press, 2010.

González, Ray, ed. *Muy Macho: Latino Men Confront Their Manhood.* New York: Anchor Books, 1996.

González-Martin, Rachel V. "Barrio Ritual and Pop Rite: Quinceañeras in the Folklore-Popular Culture Borderlands." In *The Routledge Companion to Latino/a Pop Culture*, edited by Frederick Luis Aldama. New York and London: Routledge, 2016, pp. 279–290.

Homero Villa, Raúl. *Barrio-Logos: Space and Place in Urban Chicano Literature and Culture.* Austin, TX: University of Texas Press, 2000.

Lara, Jesús. *Placemaking and Planning: Cultural Resilience and Strategies for Reurbanization.* Tucson, AZ: University of Arizona Press, 2018.

Londoño, Johana. "Barrio Affinities: Transnational Inspiration and the Geopolitics of Latina/o Design." *American Quarterly*, vol. 66, no. 3, 2014, pp. 529–548.

Martínez, Ruben. *Crossing Over: A Mexican Family on the Migrant Trail.* New York: Metropolitan Books, 2001.

Moreno, Marisel C. *Family Matters: Puerto Rican Women Authors on the Island and the Mainland.* Charlottesville, VA; London: University of Virginia Press, 2012.

Muñoz, José Esteban. *Disidentifications: Queers of Color and the Performance of Politics.* Minneapolis, MN: University of Minnesota Press, 1999.

Pallares, Amalia. *Family Activism: Immigrant Struggles and the Politics of Noncitizenship.* New Brunswick, NJ: Rutgers University Press, 2014.

Rodríguez, Richard T. *Next of Kin: The Family in Chicano/a Cultural Politics.* Durham, NC: Duke University Press, 2009.

———. "Family." In *Keywords in Latina/o Studies*, edited by Deborah R. Vargas, Lawrence La Fountain-Stokes, Nancy Raquel Mirabal. New York: New York University Press, 2017, pp. 61–63.

Soto, Sandra K. *Reading Chican@ Like a Queer: The De-Mastery of Desire*. Austin, TX: University of Texas Press, 2010.

Yarbro-Bejarano, Ybarra. *The Wounded Heart: Writing on Cherríe Moraga*. Austin, TX: University of Texas Press, 2001.

FOOD

Few things have moved beyond the bounds of Latinx culture like the flavors and aromas of its tradition of food. But, like with many things that are appropriated from Latinx heritage, the foods and culinary practices of Latinxs have at times fallen the route of the bland stereotype. When taken on its own terms, however, encountered as vital and vibrant pieces of authentic culture, *la comida latina* serves as a key aspect of the culture's identity and history. Because food traditions can be passed down from generation to generation, there is the sense of a family tradition imbued within recipes and ingredients that come together with passion and meaning. And, as with many peoples, the culinary practices of Latinxs reveal a deep sense of community, nationalism, and regionalism. As Gustavo Arellano puts it,

> It's too easy to say Mexican food is an all-American food: to say as much is to ignore the tortured relationship between Mexicans and their adopted country. But Mexican food is as much of an ambassador for the United States as the hot dog, whether either country wants to admit it or not.
>
> (*Taco USA* 5)

But Latinxs have another significant connection to food, and in particular the production of food and the agribusiness industries of the United States. Latinxs comprise a sizable portion of the workers who plant and harvest crops, slaughter and process meat, and they often put their bodies and lives at risk for low wages and jobs that keep them ever on the move as they follow the ebb and flow of seasonal crops. These migrant workers have been foundational to the agricultural sector of the US economy, though often it appears that they are not paid their true value and worth to this multi-billion dollars a year industry. As a result, the issue of food and how Latinxs help shape food-related industries are not simply relegated to the flavors and recipes alone; a great deal of this discussion should reflect the impact food industries have on the Latinx body, which affects wages, insurance, health, liability, exploration, and the transience of life for many Latinxs in the US. This entry will first provide an overview of the foods that are influenced and shaped by Latinx culture, and it will close with the cost of food production and sustainability on the Latinx body. After all, "Eating is a border crossing," according to García et al. (p. 1).

Latinx cuisine has long been a part of the United States, and indeed of the Américas. The Hatch chiles that thrive in New Mexico, the *barbacoa* of Texas—the slow and low methods of cooking the undesirable parts of the cow—the myriad dishes made from the humble corn and bean, the plantains of the Caribbean, and so much more have not only come to characterize Latinx culture but also to impress these specific flavors upon the United States. And, with the globalization of the late twentieth- and early twenty-first centuries, the food pathways of Latinoamerica continue to thrive and flourish, further shaping the taste buds of the United States as well as changing how Latinxs are conceived of within the American imagination.

To begin with, as with the conception of the idea of Latinidad, it is best and correct to think of Latinx food as being diverse within itself, with the common foods manifesting as variations on a theme, based on the specific locations and the regional ingredients available. Take the *tamal* as an example. The basic characteristics of a *tamal* is a cooked filling with a doughy exterior called *masa*, made from maize kernels, wrapped in a husk or leaf, steamed by the dozen or two in a large pot. The resulting food is recognizable as a *tamal*. In the American Southwest, *tamales* most often appear with braised pork shoulder filling, a corn and lime *masa* called *nixtamal*, wrapped in a corn husk and steamed. But Costa Rican *tamales* are made with specific variations. Rather than a dried corn husk wrapper, Costa Rican tamales are wrapped in fresh banana leaves, and further tied with a string. As another brief example, Latinx cuisine of the American Southwest, which draws heavily on the Mexican food tradition, tends to feature pinto beans as one of its staples. In Florida and along the East Coast, black beans tend to appear much more frequently, thanks to the influence of Caribbean Latinx culinary traditions. Thus, one should not think of iconic dishes of pan-latinx cuisine as monolithic or consistent across all specific Latinx cultures. Variations appear often, and such variation gives rise to notions of authenticity within the Latinx food community. Which *tamal* is more authentic, the Mexican or the Costa Rican? Which type of *frijoles* are more authentic, pinto beans or black beans? Such discussions do arise, but they often discount or dismiss the idea of regionalism as another key ingredient of Latinx *comida*.

The rise of Latinx food culture has led to both a productive and problematic consumerism in the United States. The negative consequences are obvious. There tends to be both commodification and cultural appropriation at the heart of the expansion of Latinx foods. One of the most obvious and controversial figures in this sort of dynamic is Rick Bayless, a chef and host of the public television show *Mexico: One Plate at a Time*. Bayless, an Anglo American, owns several fine dining restaurants in Chicago, most notably Topolobampo and Frontera Grill. His show often incorporates his restaurants, with the conceit of each episode being that Bayless first travels to Mexico and learns the history and method for making a specific dish that is native and authentic in its preparation. He is often shown speaking Spanish with the locals, which gives the impression that he is not merely a trespasser but rather a member of the community. In the second half of a typical episode, Bayless then takes the knowledge he has garnered from his visit to Mexico and then appropriates the knowledge, either in his home kitchen or literally in the kitchen of one of his restaurants, where he presumably sells what he has learned for profit. He calls himself a "translator of Mexican cooking" (Mason). Bayless's defenders say he brings these Mexican communities to the larger masses and thus gives them the benefit of such exposure. But it is hard not to see that Bayless literally takes the culinary knowledge of Mexican peoples and makes money from it. Latinx cultural critics such as Gustavo Arellano have spoken about this at great length. In an *OC Weekly* column, Arellano says that Bayless's reaction to his critics that call out his cultural appropriation of Mexican food as a kind of racism is, in fact, a claim of "reverse racism" (Arellano). As one can see, Bayless serves as a kind of lightning rod for the appropriation of Latinx cuisine in the US.

Bayless is not the only one who appropriates Mexican food culture, to be sure. To his credit, he is always clear and open about where he takes his influences, and his open acknowledgment does give positive attention and advertisements for the various places he visits in Mexico. By all appearances, Bayless does respect and appreciate his Mexican food influences.

Moving from the fine-dining chef to the fast food industry, restaurants have attempted to capitalize on bastardized versions of authentic Mexican food. The most prominent is Taco Bell, now owned by Yum!

Brands, which has perfected the Americanized fast food version of Mexican food. Taco Bell is a worldwide brand, and it continues to produce its brand of Mexican food to people all over the world. And all across the United States, there are fast food restaurants that attempt to cash in on the Mexican food niche. Del Taco, Taco John, Taco Villa, Casa Taco, TacoTime, and many more that remain unnamed here, are all fast food restaurants that put their particular spin on Mexican take out. Some have curious menu items. Taco John and TacoTime serve tater tots. And in 2018, Taco Bell announced that they would begin serving French fries.

The antithesis of these fast-food Mexican restaurants is the mobile taco trucks and taco wagons. What began as savvy, on-the-spot, authentic Mexican food at construction job sites (work often done primarily by Latinxs in the Southwest) has now become an upscale, foodie trend that shows little signs of abating. (See also Paloma Martínez-Cruz's *Food Fight!*) The key difference with these trucks, as opposed to something like Taco Bell, is that the food aspires to be more than fast food. They are also very tech smart, using social media apps to generate buzz and customers.

Incidentally, it should be noted that there are variations of Mexican food in America. In Texas, the Mexican and Texan influences have created a Frankenstein's monster called "Tex-Mex," a particular confluence of flavors and cooking techniques that are specific to the Texas region. In point of fact, the type of food Taco Bell sells is a kind of Tex-Mex, rather than authentic Mexican or New Mexican or California Mexican food. Such restaurants reveal how popular Mexican food (and foods based on Mexican food) are, and how adaptable it is to different regions and palates across the United States. As Zilkia Janer maintains, "Whether as inheritors and creators of sophisticated cuisines, or as the workforce that sustains the food system from the fields to the table, Latinos are a vital force in the food culture of the United States" (p. xiii).

If we think of the other side of the food industry, the side that is involved in the production of food—that is agribusiness—we see that Latinxs literally do the heavy lifting in the industry. From planting and harvesting crops by hand in rough conditions for relative low wages, to the prominent role Latinxs play in the meat industry—an undeniably dangerous job—Latinxs are often at the knife's edge in the agribusiness industry. They are skilled labor, but they are seen as replaceable, or worse, disposable.

Television celebrities such as Stephen Colbert and Morgan Spurlock have gone to great lengths to expose the powerful and persistent falsehood that Latinxs, and specifically, undocumented Latinxs, are taking jobs away from hardworking (read, White) Americans. Farmers have actively recruited workers to harvest their crops, and the workers who were not Latinx quit before the end of the day. The United Farm Workers (UFW) of America, to make the point, showcased a "Take Our Jobs!" initiative meant to highlight the difficult work farmworkers do. While over eight thousand people were interested in the farm jobs, "only seven American applicants in the 'Take our jobs' campaign were actually picking crops" ("Field of Tears").

Harvesting oranges, cucumbers, watermelons, onions, apples, peaches and so on is still mostly done by humans, and most humans refuse to work so intensely for such little pay. Spurlock, in an episode of his series *Inside Man*, working for a few days harvesting oranges, proclaimed, "This is the hardest I've ever worked for 93 cents" (CNN). Colbert, while still in his Republican character, testified before Congress concerning the backbreaking work of Latinxs in agribusiness. Near the end of his approximately two-hour hearing, Colbert seemed to break character and became serious. "I like talking about people who don't have any power," he said, the bravado gone from his voice as he worked his way to a downer of a punch line.

> It seems like the least powerful people in the United States are migrant workers who come here.... . And at the same time, we invite them here and ask them to leave.... I don't want to take anyone's hardship away from them (but) migrant workers suffer and have no rights.
>
> (Stephen Colbert)

Journalist and novelist Héctor Tobar has chronicled some of this in his book, *Translation Nation: Defining A New American Identity in the Spanish-Speaking United States*, and especially Latinxs who work in meat processing plants in the American South. The work is harrowing and grueling, but Tobar shows the dignity and determination with which Latinxs earn a living filling America's larder of vegetables and animal protein.

Whether it is in the authentic flavors of Mexico, the fast food iterations of Mexican food, the appropriation of Mexican food culture, or the Latinxs themselves working hard often under exploitative conditions to supply the brute labor of agribusiness, Latinxs are very much an essential ingredient in America's culinary tastes, desires, and ambitions.

Works Cited

Arellano, G. *Taco USA: How Mexican Food Conquered America*. New York: Scribner, 2013.

———. "The Problem Isn't Rick Bayless Cooking Mexican Food—It's That He's a Thin-Skinned Diva." *OC Weekly*, February 21, 2017, www.ocweekly.com/restaurants/the-problem-isnt-rick-bayless-cooking-mexican-food-its-that-hes-a-thin-skinned-diva-7075113

CNN, Cable News Network. transcripts.cnn.com/TRANSCRIPTS/1307/14/se.01.html

"Fields of Tears." *The Economist*, The Economist Newspaper, December 18, 2010, www.economist.com/node/17722932

García, M., DuPuis, E. M., and Mitchell, D. *Food Across Borders*. New Brunswick, NJ: Rutgers University Press, 2017.

Janer, Z. *Latino Food Culture*. Westport, CT: Greenwood Press.

Martínez-Cruz, Paloma *Food Fight! Millennial Mestizaje and the Dilemmas of Ethical Eating*. Tucson, AZ: University of Arizona Press, 2019.

Mason, A. "Rick Bayless Describes Himself as a Translator of Mexican Cooking and He's Been Doing Just That in the Windy City since 1987." *CBS This Morning*, n.d. EBSCOhost, dist.lib.usu.edu/login?url=http://search.ebscohost.com/login.aspx?direct=true&db=n5h&AN=32U1678276215CTM&site=eds-live

"Stephen Colbert, in GOP Pundit Character, Testifies on Immigration in D.C." *The Washington Post*, WP Company, September 25, 2010, www.washingtonpost.com/wp-dyn/content/article/2010/09/24/AR2010092402734.html

Tobar, H. *Translation Nation: Defining a New American Identity in the Spanish-Speaking United States*. New York: Riverhead, 2006.

GLOBAL

Latinx Studies' approach to the global is multifold. It includes an awareness and deep criticism of colonial and capitalist global expansions that have led to the systematic oppression, exploitation, and genocide of indigenous, mestizo, and Latinx subjects. It includes a critique of how such subjects are controlled by the imposition of policies, surveillance, and physical borders that operate to control the flow of real bodies across the Américas and beyond. It includes an affirming sense of how Latinx subjects have survived colonial and imperialist global expansions. It includes a strong scholarly impulse to shed light on the creating of Latinx cultural phenomena within this colonial, postcolonial, global capitalist history. Global and globalization in Latinx scholarship at once identifies multinational capitalism and worldwide markets that are built through their oppression and exploitation of vulnerable populations.

However, it is within this space that Latinx scholars also seek to identify forms of resistance, or local acts of what Paul Allatson calls "productive hybridization" (p. 114). To this end, the scholarship seeks to identify how Latinx cultural phenomena interface with cultural phenomena created by global-Other communities in its *transculturative* fashioning of music, art, literature, films and so much more. (See Mark Overmyer-Velázquez and Enrique Sepúlveda III's *Global Latin(o) Americanos*).

For Latinx Studies scholars, the concept of the global goes hand in hand with conquest, **colonization**, empire building, imperialism, and capitalist neoliberalism. The tragic history of the European conquest of the Américas includes centrally the exploitation, subjugation (rape), oppression (torture), and genocide (murder) of indigenous peoples. The enslaved labor of indigenous and African peoples in the Américas fuel European colonial expansion and global empire building practices. To justify this physical, material exploitation of peoples in the Américas and in other non-European regions of the world, a whole network of ideologically driven documents that codified global-Others as primitive and uncivilized—without subjectivity, history, and culture—grew. These ideologically driven texts included anything from maps of the New World to Euro-Spanish cronicas and **testimonios**. Scholars such as José David Saldívar identify a "Global South" so as to create historical, cultural, political linkages between global-Others historically colonized, displaced, exploited, and oppressed across the Américas (Caribbean inclusive), Africa, and Asia. (See also Walter D. Mignolo's *Local Histories/Global Designs*.) We see the effects today in the US of this long history of settler **colonialism**, imperialism, and capitalist neoliberalism in the continued use of propaganda (the Latinx Threat Narrative, for instance), policy, and surveillance practices that continue to create conditions across the Américas that, in the words of Gina E. B. Candelario, "make it impossible for some segment of our population to live out their lives in the countries of their birth" ("Transnationalism" 236).

The global for Latinx Studies scholars is deeply implicated within histories of colonization, empire building, and imperialism that have led to current neoliberal policies and practices that spin propaganda about post-race societies, affirmative diversity practices to cover over global free trade practices that lead to corporate profits through the exploitation of increasingly controlled, surveilled, and marked Latinx (and global-Other generally) subjects as laboring bodies. Internal policies within the US have led to legalized racial profiling along with the increased integration of civil police forces with Immigration and Customs Enforcement. Latinx Studies scholars are critical, too, of how manufactured goods that travel freely across global marketplaces are built by increasingly exploitable pools of policed and surveilled Latinx laborers, from the low-paying, dangerous jobs in foreign-owned factories (*maquiladoras*) on the Mexico side of the US/Mexico border to factories and agri-business fields in the US, the threat and implementation of workplace raids and anti-union policies and practices generally have continued to destroy Latinx populations. (See also Josue David Cisneros's *The Border Crossed Us*.)

Latinx Studies scholars consider localized, material effects of corporate globalization practices on different regions of the US: from the US/Mexico borderlands to the New England states and beyond. For instance, several scholars included in Daniel Arreola's edited *Hispanic Spaces, Latino Places* identify the effects of global, national, and local policies that have shaped places like the borderland communities of Tijuana and San Diego. As a result of industrial practice, corporate tourism, and controlled movement of laboring bodies, Lawrence A. Herzog considers just such a US/Mexico borderland space to be "inherently globalized" ("Globalization of the Barrio" 107). The global corporate policies and practices that create a "cross-border supply-demand relationship" (p. 107) has radically altered the social and economic health of US Latinx barrios as well as those along the northern Mexican border. This has introduced all sorts of new problems, including Latinx communities having to deal "with political actors and decision makers who are based far from the region, such as investors in global enterprises whose head-quarters are in New York, Chicago, London, or Tokyo" (p. 124). However, these communities have also pushed back, creating US/Mexico worker's alliances in the struggle to guarantee affordable housing, public transportation, and wages.

Policies that favor global corporate interests impact the everyday lives of Latinx communities within the US and its commonwealth countries such as Puerto Rico. In *Sponsored Migration*, Edgardo Meléndez identifies the very global economic, material, social, and political practices that connect Puerto Rican Latinxs to the US mainland. Today, there are more Puerto Ricans who live in the US mainland than in Puerto Rico. Much like Central Americans and Mexicans who are pushed from homelands (wars, violence, poverty) for the US, there's a long history of policies (social, political, economic, linguistic) that have disenfranchised Puerto Ricans who move to the US, turning them also into exploitable transmigrants; in theory, they can move back and forth between Puerto Rico and the US mainland, but these policies curtail such freedom.

Capitalist globalization policies and practices have radically transformed the demographic makeup of communities and regions across the US. For instance, historically regions with few Latinxs in the South, Midwest, and New England states are experiencing massive demographic transformations. Latinxs are the fastest growing ethnoracial demographic in Columbus, Ohio. And, with transmigrations of Dominicans and Puerto Ricans directly or via New York to work in factories (beginning in the 1940s), cities such as Waterbury and Hartford in Connecticut are becoming dominant Latinx spaces. With bodegas, cultural festivals, and population density generally of Puerto Ricans and Dominicans in Waterbury actively shaping the social, cultural, and economic life of the city. (See the scholarship in Andres Torres edited *Latinos in New England*, especially that of Ruth Glaser's "Mofongo Meets Mangú").

Importantly, too, there's new scholarly work that seeks to identify other Latinx/global-Other interrelations that have arisen out of globalization processes. For instance, Rudy P. Guevarra Jr. puts the spotlight on transpacific empire building histories and global capitalist practices that have brought Latinx and Asian peoples together; for instance, whether the result of slave galleons of empire building epochs or workers on today's modern cruise liners, different repositories of Mexipino, mixed-race communities and in places such as Mexico and California. For Rudy P. Guevara colonial and capitalist global practices have created "a long historical web of interconnectedness that underpins the *mestizaje* that began in the sixteenth century") (p. 327).

Empire-building and global capitalist policies and practices have forced Latinx peoples from homelands, creating transnational solidarity networks as well as transforming the demographic makeup of US regions. Latinx scholars have also been interested in analyzing the concomitant creation of cultural phenomena by global-Others that grows from this history of displacement, exploitation, and oppression. Foundational Latinx scholars such as Jovita González, Américo Paredes, Tey Diana Rebolledo, María Herrera-Sobek, and others sought to excavate Latinx cultural phenomena that was informed by local and global cultural phenomena. Ramón Saldívar identifies, for instance, Paredes's scholarly and creative impulse as grown from a "transnational imaginary" formed out of global cultural encounters (*The Borderlands of Culture* 430).

For Latinx scholars such as Paredes, the local and global influences on music creation have proved a particularly rich area of investigation. There are many scholars working to enrich understanding of the globality of Latinx music, including Frances Aparicio, Peter J. García, Ignacio Corona, Deborah Pacini Hernandez, Ruth Glaser, Josh Kun, Kristie A. Dorr, Deborah Paredez, José Limón, Raquel R. Rivera, among many others. In *La Verdad: An International Dialogue on Hip Hop Latinidades*, editors Melissa Castillo-Garsow and Jason Nichols bring together scholarship (US and Latin American based) that considers the creation and dissemination of Latinx hip hop and hip-hop culture across more than a dozen countries. The scholarship also importantly considers the way that global-Others from Costa Rica, Bolivia, Nicaragua to Mexico, the US, and Taiwan actively transform hip hop by creating multilingual (Creole, Portuguese, Aymara, among other languages) socio-politically aware soundscapes. At once grown from particular soils and locations, the scholarship considers global influences as well as transculturative interactions with soundscapes from across the world. The common understanding is that these global-Other creators are not passive absorptive sponges of globally distributed, manufactured cultural objects (music or otherwise). Rather, they are locally situated, active transformers of all global cultural phenomena, creating hip-hop cultural landscapes that speak to and resist global practices of capitalist production driven by profits that homogenize the cultural marketplace.

Latinx scholars attend to how the creation and consumption of cultural phenomena takes place within local and global contexts. Indeed, such scholars seek to enrich our understanding of how locally produced cultural phenomena can push against global capitalist processes—those processes that seek to profit at the expense of flattening and homogenizing the cultural landscape. When it comes to art (from graffiti to tattoo, mural, photographic, and plastic arts), literature creation, and dissemination, scholars consider at once the power of cultural gatekeepers (US East Coast curators and editors, for instance) that create unidirectional flows (from the US to the rest of the Américas, for instance) as well as how Latinx artists and authors create works that *transcend* borders and complicate capitalist-driven marketplace ebbs and flows.

Scholars have also examined other kinds of global-Other Latinx intersections and its cultural products, including Latinx and Asian. In *The Transpacific Geographies of Chicana/o Literature* Jayson Gonzáles Sae-Saue demonstrates how Latinx literary authors such as José Antonio Villarreal, Valdez, Paredes, Oscar Acosta, Miguel Méndez, Virginia Grise, Daniel Cano, Alfredo Véa, Rudlofo A. Anaya, and Rolando Hinojosa evidence a history of "cross-racial links" between traumatized and exploited Latinxs and Asian Americans: from Japanese internment camps of WWII to Asian dislocations during WWII, the Korean War, and the American War in Vietnam. He demonstrates how material reality (WWII, Korean War, American War in Vietnam, internment camps, migratory field work, and Chinese migration to northern Mexico, for instance) leads to locally and globally (transpacific) grown Latinx identities. As such, Gonzáles Sae-Saue widens the borderland consciousness concept to include Asia and Asian Americans impacted by forces of globalization. By charting the shared histories of exploitation between Asians and Latinxs as well as histories of US imperialism generally, he provides an expansive critical frame for understanding the formation of borderland identities as at once *local* and pan-Pacific *global*. (See also Camilla Fojas's *Islands of Empire* and *Cosmopolitanism in the Americas*.)

This dual focus on the local and global creation and dissemination of Latinx cultural production has opened up the field of Latinx Studies to many ways of approaching and analyzing US Latinx cultural phenomena from a global-*outside* scholarly perspective. Indeed, in universities such as Mexico City's UNAM, the study of Latinx culture is seen as an important way of growing and complicating Mexican studies. In Europe, we see a similar impulse, especially among scholars focused on the creation and dissemination of non-dominant cultural traditions such as Turkish-German, French-Maghrebian, Spanish-Moroccan, Spanish-Basque literatures.

Such global-Other/Latinx transactional scholarship has found many ways of growing, including in digital spaces (Hispa USA) and yearly academic conferences. (See Frauke Gewecke's "Latino/a Literature in Western Europe.") After the inaugural conference on Chicano/a literature and culture took place in Germersheim, Germany in 1984 followed by Paris in 1986), other conferences have sprouted up across Europe that bring together scholars that seek to study Latinx culture from global, outside-the-US perspectives. With the institutionalizing of the annual "Chicano Literature and Latino Studies Conference" has also grown a journal, *Camino Real: Estudios de las Hispanidades Norteamericanas*, as well as a visiting scholars program whereby US Latinx scholars can spend a month at the university sharing their work on Latinx literature as well as learning from scholars on Spanish scholarship on its *mestizaje* borderland identities: how Islamic, Basque, **Iberian**, and other ethnoracial cultural cross pollinations shed light on US Latinx identities and experiences as recreated in its cultural phenomena. For instance, Cañero Serrano examines how Islamic cultural phenomena inform "the hybridity of identities, practices, and expressions in the Spanish-speaking 'Nuevo Mundo.' Even the exclamation 'Olé!' is a hispanicized form of 'Allah!'" (p. 271). For Timothy Marr a non-Americas-based scholarly approach makes for a "longitudinal interculturalism" that enlarges the field of American studies.

In "Latin@ Studies Abroad" Jennifer Reimer (who teaches at the Bilkent University in Ankara, Turkey) argues for a global, transnational approach to the study of Latinx culture that balances between "honoring what remains site specific to Latin@ studies—the material realities of the US–Mexico border, for instance—while identifying sources of shared conflict between US Latin@ communities and Turkish students" (p. 260). For Reimer, this is not just a matter of scholarly inquiry. It provides a productive pedagogical approach that alerts students in Turkey to shared commonalities with good and bad cultural practices such as machismo, patriarchy, and community rituals. By teaching Latinx literature to Turkish students Reimer creates a space for solidarity "between Turks and Latin@s in the struggle against male-dominated systems globally" (p. 261). In the end, Reimer seeks to clear a pedagogical space with her Turkish students whereby they might "experience how theorists like Anzaldúa can change the way we apprehend our world and ourselves" (p. 261). It opens up possibilities within a rigid Turkish education system for the students to "discover the value of their own personal lives, identities and stories as a legitimate form of knowledge, one of the core values of US Latin@ and ethnic studies" (p. 261). Finally, it enriches the students' understanding of how "subjects, cultures, ideas and forms of learning and knowing transact between varying local and global forces [. . .] can silence or destroy [as well as identify] sites of active resistance" (p. 264). (See also Jennifer Reimer and Christopher Rivera's 2015 special issue on Latinx Studies for the *Journal of American Studies of Turkey*.) For Francisco A. Lomelí, Latinx literary scholarship from abroad, or "*de allá*" (from there), opens eyes to new "ways to approach Chicano criticism in relation to other national and international minority literatures and cultures" (Foreword *Spanish Perspectives on Chicano Literature* 15).

In addition to special issue journals, other scholarly venues have proved important to establishing a study of Latinx experiences, identities, and culture from a global-Other perspective. For instance, there's the "Global Latin/o Studies" scholarly series with the Ohio State University Press that publishes edited volumes and monographs that focus on the Latinx experience in its totality as set within a global dimension. Its scholarly titles include several mentioned above such as *La Verdad* and *Sponsored Migration* as well as others that are committed to building knowledge around the variety and vitality of the presence and significant influence of Latinxs in the shaping of the culture, history, politics, and policies around the world. And, there are special issue journals around the world that are dedicated to publishing scholarship on Latinx Studies from a non-US perspective.

A global approach to the study of Latinx identities and experiences has enriched understanding of the pernicious effects of colonization, empire-building, and capitalist neoliberalism that continue to result in the displacing, oppressing, and exploiting of Latinx peoples. It has also opened eyes to how Latinx cultural phenomena at once works within and against global capitalist networks of creation, distribution, and consumption.

Works Cited

Allatson, Paul. *Key Terms in Latinx Cultural and Literary Studies*. Malden, MA: Blackwell, 2007.

Arreola, Daniel, ed. *Hispanic Spaces, Latino Places*. Austin, TX: University of Texas Press, 2004.

Candelario, Gina E. B. "Transnationalism." In *Keywords in Latina/o Studies*, edited by Deborah R. Vargas, Lawrence La Fountain-Stokes, Nancy Raquel Mirabal. New York: New York University Press, 2017, pp. 236–238.

Cañero Serrano, Julio. "'Tendiendo puentes, compartiendo conocimientos': The International Conference on Chicano Literature in Spain (1998–2014)." In *Spanish Perspectives on Chicano Literature: Literary and Cultural Essays*, edited by Jesús Rosales and Vanessa Fonseca. Columbus, OH: Ohio State University Press, 2017, pp. 109–120.

Castillo-Garsow, Melissa, and Jason Nichols. eds. *La Verdad: An International Dialogue on Hip Hop Latinidades*. Columbus, OH: Ohio State University Press, 2016.

Cisneros, Josue David. *The Border Crossed Us: Rhetorics of Borders, Citizenship, and Latina/o Identity*. Tuscaloosa, AL: University of Alabama Press, 2014.

Fojas, Camilla. *Cosmopolitanism in the Americas*. Purdue University Press, 2005.

———. *Islands of Empire: Pop Culture and U.S. Power*. Austin, TX: University of Texas Press, 2014.

Gewecke, Frauke. "Latino/a Literature in Western Europe." In *The Routledge Companion to Latino/a Literature*, edited by Suzanne Bost and Frances R. Aparicio. New York and London: Routledge, 2013, pp. 107–115.

Gonzáles Sae-Saue, Jayson. *The Transpacific Geographies of Chicana/o Literature*. New Brunswick, NJ: Rutgers University Press, 2016.

Guevarra, Rudy P., ed. "Introduction to the Special Issue." *Journal of Asian American Studies*, vol. 14, no. 3, 2011, pp. 323–329.

Herzog, Lawrence A. "Globalization of the Barrio: Transformation of the Latino Cultural Landscapes of San Diego, California." In *Hispanic Spaces, Latino Places*, edited by Daniel Arreola. Austin, TX: University of Texas Press, 2004, pp. 103–124.

Lomelí, Francisco A. "Foreword." In *Spanish Perspectives on Chicano Literature: Literary and Cultural Essays*, edited by Jesús Rosales and Vanessa Fonseca. Columbus, OH: Ohio State University Press, 2017, pp. ix–xiii.

Marr, Timothy. "'Out of This World': Islamic Irruptions in the Literary Americas." *American Literary History*, vol. 18, no. 3, 2006, pp. 521–549.

Meléndez, Edgardo. *Sponsored Migration: The State and Puerto Rican Postwar Migration to the United States*. Columbus, OH: Ohio State University Press, 2017.

Mignolo, Walter. *Local Histories/Global Designs: Coloniality, Subaltern Knowledges, and Border Thinking*. Princeton, NJ: Princeton University Press, 2000.

Overmyer-Velázquez, Mark, and Enrique Sepúlveda III, eds. *Global Latin(o) Americanos: Transoceanic Diasporas and Regional Migrations*. New York: Oxford University Press, 2018.

Reimer, Jennifer A. "Latin@ Studies Abroad: Making the Transnational International." *Latino Studies*, vol. 14, 2016, pp. 258–264.

Reimer, Jennifer A., and Christopher Rivera, eds. "Latin@ Studies in Transnational Contexts: Reading, Writing, and Living Lives on/in the Margins." *Journal of American Studies of Turkey*, vol. 42, 2015, pp. 1–10.

Saldívar, Ramón. *The Borderlands of Culture: Américo Paredes and the Transnational Imaginary*. Durham, NC: Duke University Press, 2006.

Torres, Andres, ed. *Latinos in New England*. Philadelphia, PA: Temple University Press, 2006.

IMMIGRATION

The subject of immigration in the United States, as it pertains to those entering from Latin American nations, is a subject fraught with nationalism, xenophobia, political strife, and ongoing dysfunction. Due to the massive border between the United States and Mexico, incidentally one of the longest contiguous national borders in the world, coupled with the many nations that lie to the south of this border, a majority of immigrants that sidestep the legal protocol of entering the nation by adhering to the US government's laws, creates a difficult and charged situation. To add to this already complex situation, not all immigrants from Latin American nations are treated the same upon entry into the United States. "The Latino Threat Narrative," according to Leo Chavez, "posits that Latinos are not like previous immigrant groups, who ultimately became part of the nation" (p. 3). Not only are they treated differently, at times they are all homogenized as if they all have the same backgrounds, nation of origin, and histories. So, it is important to remember, as it is with all of the entries within this volume, that not all immigrants from Latinx nations are the same, which means they are not recognized in equal ways. The consequences of this fact will be discussed in greater detail shortly.

The first inconvenient fact stems from the Treaty of Guadalupe Hidalgo in 1848 that ended the **Mexican–American War**. In this treaty, the United States compelled the sovereign nation of Mexico to relinquish what was approximately half of its land mass into the custody of the United States (Griswold). While Mexico ceded this immense piece of land, the US acquired large portions of present-day New Mexico, Arizona, Nevada, California, Colorado, Utah, Wyoming, and the Rio Grande as a border. Not only was the acquisition of so much land a key change to both nations and that part of the world, it also directly affected everyone who was already living in the land that exchanged hands. Within the affected area, Mexican citizens ostensibly (as enforced by the treaty) became US citizens immediately. However, though there were many conditions embedded within the treaty, the United States government, as history has shown time and again with other treaties made with indigenous peoples of America, often ignored the conditions of the Treaty of Guadalupe Hidalgo. As a result, Mexicans became a part of the US overnight, though they were not welcomed as newest members of the land in which they now found themselves.

To further complicate things, the immigration laws of the United States have changed over time and have been applied inconsistently, and in the view of some, unfairly. In the early twentieth century, the United States made several impactful decisions that would affect future immigrants, and particularly immigrants from Latin American countries. In 1917, Puerto Ricans were granted US citizenship, and the US government passed the Immigration Act of 1917, requiring immigrants to meet a literacy requirement. Continuing in this fateful year of 1917, as a result of the entrance of the United States into World War I, the government moved to grant Mexican workers "temporary" status to fill the void of men who left to fight against Germany. This law would not be the first time the US temporarily gave legal status to Mexicans when it conveniently served American interests.

Shortly thereafter, the US would enact laws and policies that would continue to affect Latinx immigrants. The US put a limit on the number of immigrants in 1921, marking the first time this step had been taken. Over the next decade, the US government created the Border Patrol and began to deport Mexicans, as many as half a million. But, as with the lack of work force that occurred in WWI, the US again invited Mexicans to become temporary workers during World War II; these workers, known as braceros or laborers, were brought in to work specifically in agriculture. This policy, known as the Bracero Program, was officially ended in 1964, but not before the US launched an effort to oust the braceros and gain control of the large numbers of undocumented workers. Through this effort, known as "Operation Wetback," the US, via the Immigration and Naturalization Service (INS), began deporting hundreds of thousands of undocumented workers.

In subsequent years, the cycle of undocumented workers from Mexico and Central America has waxed and waned, and US regulation departments such as INS, ICE, and the Border Patrol have had mixed results in deporting undocumented workers. In the twenty-first century, when politicians running for office speak of the immigration problem, they are mostly speaking of the Mexican and Central American influx of undocumented workers, though with the election of Donald J. Trump as the 45th President of the United States, immigration policy has targeted, according to the judicial system, Muslim-majority countries as well.

Other Latinx immigrants from different nations of origin have had significantly different experiences with immigration status. Of course, Puerto Ricans are US citizens. For many years, Cubans enjoyed the policy of protected status if they were able to make it to the shores of the United States. This policy, known colloquially as the "wet foot, dry foot" policy, initially known as the Cuban Adjustment Act, implemented in 1966, allowed Cubans who fled their country the ability to pursue citizenship a year later. However, President Barack Obama, as one of his final acts as president in January 2017, put an end to the policy. Obama is also noted for the high number of deportations that occurred during his two terms in office.

By examining just how differently these two Latinx subgroups have access to immigration in the United States (Mexicans and Cubans), one can understand why these subgroups have such difference of political views and opinions on this subject. Cuban Americans often tend to align themselves politically with the right-wing of the US political spectrum, while Mexican Americans generally align with left-wing politics. Cuban Americans tend to be in support of stringent immigration policies, yet for many decades they were beneficiaries of an exception to the rule. Mexicans have never been given such a policy, and instead they have periodically been welcomed to do strenuous and sometimes dangerous labor jobs, only to be told to leave when they were no longer wanted. Those who attempt to cross into the United States via the Mexico/US border are often portrayed in the media as criminals, while statistics reveal that a great number of undocumented immigrants actually arrive in the United States via an airplane ticket—immigrants on HB1 visas who overstay their permitted time in the US.

The dichotomy between Mexican and Cuban immigrants to the United States also reveals the impetus for what makes them leave their nation of origin in the first place. For much of the second half of the twentieth century, Cubans were under a strict Communist government. Cold War politics influenced how the US viewed Cubans who wanted to leave the island. However, Cuban President Fidel Castro ensured that many of the nation's criminals and "undesirables" were sent to the US as a part of what came to be known as the Mariel Boat Lift. Despite this disingenuous move by Castro, Cubans have been given extraordinary flexibility in their citizenship process in their path to becoming US citizens. Thus, Latin American peoples who are caught in the midst of political unrest or refugee status are given wide latitude concerning citizenship status in the US. These peoples include, at various times, Salvadorians and Hondurans.

Mexicans, on the other hand, and many of those who come to the United States by crossing the southern border, are not fleeing Communism or fascist regimes. Yet their reasons for leaving their homeland is concentrated very much on the idea of the American Dream, which leads them to believe that opportunity is to be had in the United States if only one is willing to work hard enough. Often the situation south of the border can be so dire for some people that mothers and fathers will send their children, some younger than ten years old, to make the voyage north alone. While this speaks to the hearts of any humanitarian, there is also the incontrovertible fact that illegal drugs and firearms often make it into the United States through the southern border. Thus, while on the one hand you have humanitarian reasons for wanting to provide an opportunity to those who seek it, on the other hand the US cannot abide a porous border that also allows dangerous substances and materials to enter. At times, the two have been conflated. Drug empires will use a person as the means of conveyance for their product. These people, called "mules," are often forced to engage in these dangerous endeavors.

Part of what makes the continuous influx of undocumented workers such a vexing issue for the United States is that there are billion dollar a year industries that rely on exactly this type of worker to generate their profits. Despite continued innovation and mechanization of agribusiness and other labor-intensive industries, much of this backbreaking work must still be done by humans. When no one else will do the work for so little money, these businesses hire undocumented workers to do the heavy labor, turning a blind eye to the law or willing to pay the nominal fine for hiring undocumented workers. Though these workers see an opportunity to make money, they also ignore or disregard the risks such work puts them in.

One of the last immigration policies of substance came in 1986, when President Ronald Reagan was forced to deal with this very issue of undocumented labor in the agribusiness sector. The Immigration

Reform and Control Act (IRCA) was passed with the intention of strengthening the border and ensuring employers were aware of the legal status of their workforce. On the other hand, Reagan also provided something that has, in the early twenty-first century, come to be anathema for many conservative politicians: amnesty. IRCA granted amnesty to approximately three million affected peoples living in an undocumented status since the 1970s. Since then, however, no president, despite their efforts, has made any substantive change to the way the immigration process is handled in the United States. President Barack Obama, through executive order, enacted the policies of Deferred Action for Parents of Americans (DAPA) and Deferred Action for Childhood Arrivals (DACA). The policies sought to ameliorate the issue of undocumented citizens by not penalizing qualifying individuals who met very specific parameters. DAPA was ultimately found to be unconstitutional, and President Trump allowed DACA to expire at the end of 2017. As of January 2018, with the threat of a government shutdown looming, the fate of hundreds of thousands of DACA recipients was still unknown. Further, as Leal and Limón demonstrate, "The immigration debate often appears to exist in a parallel universe where policymakers ignore research, pundits present opinions as facts, politicians endorse obvious falsehoods, and the media boil complexities down to sound bites" (p. 3). Research by Maria Chavez et al. shines much-needed light on the struggles, aspirations and plights of those DREAMers affected by DACA:

> Undocumented Latino youth who have been raised in the United States from childhood and have carved out a precarious place for themselves as Americans are constantly reminded that they are not "real Americans," challenging our ideals as a "nation of immigrants" and requiring a shift in the identity, dreams, and goals of undocumented youth.
>
> (p. 5)

At the state level, California passed what came to be known as Proposition 187 in 1994, which banned undocumented immigrants in California access to public services such as schools, welfare, or health care. Even more severely, Prop 187 made the creation of forged citizenship documents a felony. Two years later, Prop 187 was ruled unconstitutional because it overstepped its authority into what is the purview of the federal government. While on the national level, in 2006, H.R. 4437 inflamed protest even before the 2016 election (Mohamed).

Since the year 2000, the issue of immigration has only intensified. In 2005, civilian patrols calling themselves "Minutemen" began taking matters such as finding and reporting border crossing into their own hands. Later, in 2010 in the state of Arizona, Republican governor Jan Brewer signed SB-1070, a far-reaching law to curb undocumented immigrants. State and local governments have attempted to implement their own immigration policies, but they are often challenged on the same grounds that unraveled California's Prop 187: immigration policy is set by the federal government.

The United States takes pride in its history of immigration. The symbol often associated with immigration is the Statue of Liberty and the poem "The New Colossus," which positions the Lady Liberty as a beacon and invitation to those who are not wanted in their native lands. Yet many Latinxs who have traversed to the US from the south, far from the Statue of Liberty, have not always been afforded the same ease of entry into the US as immigrants of the past. Further, all Latinx **migration** into the US has not taken the same route, and the variance of such immigrants, based on their nation of origin, raises in relief the differences in the Latinx immigrant experience. And as Lisa García Bedolla notes, Latinx immigrants "influence and are influenced by the larger social, economic, and political environment" (p. 2). It seems that, despite grand pronouncements of bigger, better walls and mass deportations, Latinx immigrants—both documented, naturalized, or the undocumented—as well as US-born citizens of Latinx ancestry, remain and continue to flourish in a nation in whose presence they have been found since its earliest stirrings.

Works Cited

Chavez, Leo R. *The Latino Threat: Constructing Immigrants, Citizens, and the Nation.* Stanford, CA: Stanford University Press, 2013.

Chávez, Maria, Jessica Lavariega Monforti, and Melissa R. Michelson. *Living the Dream: New Immigration Policies and the Lives of Undocumented Latino Youth.* New York: Routledge, 2016.

García Bedolla, Lisa. *Fluid Borders: Latino Power, Identity, and Politics in Los Angeles.* Berkeley, CA: University of California Press. 2005.

Griswold, del C. R. *The Treaty of Guadalupe Hidalgo: A Legacy of Conflict.* Norman, OK: University of Oklahoma Press, 1992.

Leal, David L., and José Eduardo Limón. *Immigration and the Border: Politics and Policy in the New Latino Century.* Notre Dame, IN: University of Notre Dame Press, 2013.

Mohamed, Heather Silber. *The New Americans? Immigration, Protest, and the Politics of Latino Identity.* Lawrence, KS: University Press of Kansas, 2017.

INTERSECTIONALITY

The concept of intersectionality is widely acknowledged as coined in 1989 by black feminist legal scholar, Kimberlé Williams Crenshaw. (See Crenshaw's "Mapping the Margins: Intersectionality, Identity Politics, and Violence against Women of Color.") She used the concept to articulate a coalitional politics formed by straight and queer men and women of color to push against targets of oppression. She used it to identify how multiple oppressed groups could create coalitional movements based on race, ethnicity, gender, sexuality, class, and region. However, while not necessarily identified as "intersectional" per se, the recognition that Latinxs are a complex *intersection* of identity categories that include gender, race, ethnicity, class, sexuality, region, and differently abled was beating at the heart of Latinx feminist and queer theorists and cultural practitioners long before 1989. As Bonnie Thornton Dill and Ruth Enid Zambrana sum up, intersectionality can provide a lens for understanding the multiple factors forming "systemic inter-relationships" (p. 1) across identity/categories (race, gender, class, sexuality, nationality, and physical ability) that determine/shape oppression and inequality in the US. It can provide a "lens for reframing and creating new knowledge because it asserts new ways of studying power and inequality and challenges conventional understandings of oppressed and excluded groups and individuals" (p. 5).

While Latinxs exist as intersectional subjects, it's not always been the case that Latinx Studies recognized intersectional identities. Indeed, during the time of the Chicanx and Latinx movements of the late 1960s and early 1970s, race and ethnicity took the forefront, building the struggle based on a straight male subjectivity that actively marginalized women and excluded LGBTQ. While the various Brown Power Movements made strides in identifying systemic racism, they made voiceless and invisible all non-straight male identities that make up the Latinx communities across the nation.

First wave Latina feminists and queer creators such as Gloria Anzaldúa, Cherríe Moraga, Chela Sandoval, María Herrera-Sobek, Norma Cantú, Emma Pérez, among legions of others, embraced and affirmed Latinx intersectional identities. In theories, cultural objects, and boots on the street, they identified how situated intersectional identities (race, gender, sexuality, class, region, for instance) were mutually inclusive; that one could not talk about or raise awareness about Latinx oppression and struggles if one excised, say, gender or sexuality from race and ethnicity.

Chela Sandoval articulated the concept of "differential consciousness," Anzaldúa that of the borderlands and interstitial identity, Moraga's Third World feminist resistance, and Pérez as a site of decolonial resistance.

In Anzaldúa and Moraga's edited *This Bridge Called my Back* and Anzaldua's single-authored *Borderlands/La Frontera* we see the formal articulation of an intersectional praxis. The concept of the borderlands along with the inclusion in *This Bridge* of all variety of Latina authors, scholars, creators, and activists importantly embraced marginalized women and LGBTQ populations from the US/Mexico border to the Afrolatina Caribbean and beyond. It also sought to provide road maps for a *mestizaje*-grounded decolonial resistance and revolution empowered by coalitional, intersectional praxis. The concept of "nepantla" proved important for articulating this decolonial resistance as coming from intersectional identities that have been displaced but who can use the power of this existence in-between spaces—in the borderlands—to enact communal empowerment, transformation, and resistance. So while she identifies how Latinxs forced to exist in this displaced state suffer from psychological and physical paralysis, the embrace of borderlands as a space of intersectional affirmation turns *los intersticios* into a space of empowerment: "Su cuerpo es una bocacalle [Her body is an intersection]" (p. 80).

The work of Anzaldúa and others built on and expanded the work of other women of color resistance movements, including the Third World Women's Alliance—a more expansive and inclusive woman of color front to its earlier iteration as the Black Women's Alliance. The coalitional activism of women of color was intersectional politics in action. It brought together Latina, African American, Asian American, Arab American, and other oppressed demographic groups to fight against state repression and oppression (economic, body/reproduction, political) as well as to challenge the prevailing Anglo, male centric Latinx, African American, and other movements of color attempts to control and exploit women's fertility and to subordinate them in revolutionary struggle. Indeed, in *The Latina Advantage* by Cristina Bejarano we learn of how Latinas have used a strategic intersectionality to gain important footholds in political office.

These and other early Latina feminists and queer activists, scholars, and cultural practitioners variously conceived of the exploitation and oppression of Latinxs as happening simultaneously and in multilayered ways on subjects Othered because of gender, sexuality, class, race, and ethnicity. As María Eugenia Cotera sums up, the Latina feminist and queer scholars, creators, and activists worked within an intersectional framework that included an acute awareness and embrace of "other struggles for liberation and decolonization" (*Keywords* 65). They broke from and pushed against the dominant, hetero-patriarchal narratives of the Latinx movements. They also broke from and pushed against white feminist practices that ignored issues of race and ethnicity in their push to liberate Anglo women. They gave voice to the infinitely more complex, intersectional ways that Latinxs exist.

The legacy of these early borderland, interstitial, and intersectional scholars, creators, and activists continues to be seen in much Latinx Studies scholarship today. We think readily of the work of Juana María Rodríguez, Michael Hames-García, Ernesto Javier Martínez, Catrióna Rueda Esquibel, José Esteban Muñoz, Sandy K. Soto, Richard T. Rodríguez, Priscilla Ybarra, Lorena García and Lourdes Torres, for instance. In *With Her Machete in Her Hand* (2006) Rueda Esquibel uses the borderland concept to articulate how a focus on intersectional identities (sexuality, gender, class, and *language*) in Chicano/a literature and visual culture "acknowledge queer desire as always-already present in the Chicano/a communities" (p. 182). For Rueda Esquibel, this distinguishes a cultural genealogy that's different to a middle-class, Anglo-European queer one, and thus makes for a more complete understanding of the Chicano/a cultural imaginary and consumption within a hemispheric Americas, feminist, and queer political activism. In *Next of Kin* Richard T. Rodríguez excavates an intersectional cultural imaginary grown from Latinx queer contingent kinship and discourse practices (para. 3). In *Reading Chican@ Like a Queer*, Sandra K. Soto foregrounds her own performing of intersectionality. She opens her book declaring, "My queer per-formative 'Chican@', signals a conscientious departure from certainty, mastery and wholeness, while still announcing a politicized subjectivity" (p. 2). She goes on to radically expand the concept of intersectionality itself, writing how Chican@ subjectivity resists fixed categories such as race, sexuality, and gender. For Soto, the categories themselves are "unpredictable, incommensurable, and dynamic, certainly too spatially and temporally contingent" (p. 6). So, she decides to embrace states of unfixity: the "manifold ways that our bodies, our work, our desires are relentlessly interpellated by unequivalent social processes" (p. 6). Likewise, in *Identity Complex* Hames-García understands that Latinx subjectivity is shaped by class, by gender, by sexuality and how "any social identity *always* depends fundamentally on relations to other social identities" (p. 6). However, for Hames-García, the concept of intersectionality, by assuming the fixing of pure identities, thus structurally isolates what is actually a blending of multiple identities, and chooses not to use it. He talks instead of interstices and fragmentation to describe the interaction of social identities—but always as incomplete, blended, and fractured. For Hames-García, Latinx identities grow within a historical process of "gender and sexual domination of racially subordinated peoples" (p. 106). And, sociolinguists Lourdes Torres and Lorena García use an intersectional lens to publish ethnographic linguistic analysis on how race, ethnicity, class, and *sexuality* inform Latina everyday lives. She writes how research on Latinas as intersectional subjects—and with an especial light focused on sexuality—deepen understanding of how "desire, danger and pleasure, cultural and political representation and activism" inform "human rights and social justice, among other topics" (p. x). In these and the work of other scholars we see how everyday life for Latinxs differently materializes these inseparable intersectional nodes of existence. As María Lugones sums up: "It is only when we perceive gender and race as intermeshed or fused that we actually see women of color" (p. 93).

As we've begun to show, intersectional, borderland identity, intersticio, and so on identifies the different main categories that inform Latinx identity. As we've also begun to show, some scholars, artists, and activists choose to focus more on one of the categories than the others, and this without erasing the presence and concern for how the other categories identify nodes of crisscrossing identities that inform Latinx subjectivity. In the instance of those who focus on LGBTQ identities, we see how sexuality is reclaimed as a site of affirmation and defiance to other normalizing and normative categories; that is, it becomes a site for scholars to identify how one might push against normalizing systems of categorization. In her coedited *Tortilleras* Lourdes Torres focuses on queer sexuality to identify how the "intersectionality of oppressions" (p. 228) acts on Latina subjects—and this even with a violence of coming out of the closet that Anglos don't experience.

In addition to sexuality, Latinx scholars focus on highlighting other categories such as land, nation, citizenry. In *Writing the Goodlife* Priscilla Ybarra puts the environment under the microscope as an important shaper of intersectional identity. For Ybarra, the Latinx relation with the environment has been a significant site of oppression and resistance; Latinx identity is very much informed by long histories of working the land as well as being exploited in and through this work. In this way, one can't really understand Latinx subjectivity without considering this history—environmental injustices and activism. In *Erotic Journeys* (2005) Gloria González-López focuses on the intersectionality of *migrancy* and sexuality as centrally shaping Latinx identities, troubling notions that Latinx subjects in Mexico are more sexually repressed than in the US. Eithne Luibhéid and Lionel Cantú Jr. and the scholars included in their edited *Queer Migrations* point to the ways that the categories of race, gender, sexuality, class, and citizenship do not simply intersect but are mutually constitutive when we consider immigration practices. Here we see clearly how non-citizenship and the immigration control apparatus violently act on queer and trans migrant subjects; that is, as the editors write, fixed and normative identity categories of sexual, gender, racial, class function to violently discipline non-citizen, trans, and queer migrant bodies. To this end, when considering Latinxs as intersectional subjects, one must raise awareness around how sexuality interacts with national status (citizenship, undocumented/documented); that migrant and **exiled** Latinx queer subjects experience the violence of the border differently. Here, the work of artist and activist Julio Salgado is important. As one of many behind The UndocuQueer movement, Salgado in his art and in his political protesting organizes for the rights of undocumented queers in the Latin/a community—subjects not only exploited as non-citizens and undocumenteds, but also violently acted on because of sexual orientation and transgender visibility.

An intersectional lens has come to inform the way Latinx literary and cultural studies takes place today. It informs pedagogical practice in universities and beyond. In this way it can and has complicated our understanding of *mestizaje* as not just indigenous and European, but also African in ancestral heritage. In *Latining America* Claudia Milian provides a systematic study of Latinx with African ancestry and African Americans to enlarge the concept of Latinidad; Milian uses the new concept of *latinities* to capture this. Also, to identity the deep history of intersectional African racial identities within Latinx communities in the US and across the Americas.

With the formation of Ethnic and Latinx Studies departments across the country (first seen with the post-liberation movements that led to San Francisco State University and Berkeley's establishing of Ethnic Studies departments), there's been a move to bring this intersectional, borderland concept into pedagogical practices whereby students can learn to attend to the multiple social, cultural, and material practices that act on and that are resisted by Latinx subjects. This continues to be seen in women's studies, lesbian, gay, bisexual, and transgender studies, cultural studies, critical legal studies, labor studies, multicultural studies, American studies, and social justice education. The intersectional concept centrally informs the pedagogical practices within these spaces, opening student's eyes to how ethnicity, race, region, and sexuality inform the psychological, social, and conceptual ways that Latinxs live.

As mentioned already with Soto and Hames-García, there's been a certain holding-at-arm's-length of the concept of intersectionality. These scholars along with others are careful to use it as it assumes that there are fixable identity categories. They are weary that the concept further reifies identity categories and that these fixed, essentialist categories will act to divide peoples. There's also a weariness to how intersectional has become a mainstream buzzword evacuated of any sense of it being a political tool of analysis to uncover the coalitional, interactivity of race, class, gender, sexuality, and so on.

That said, we've seen how productive concepts such as borderlands, intersticio, and nepantla have been in Latinx Studies. They have alerted us to the multiple ways that Latinxs exist intersectionally across categories of gender, class, race, sexuality, and citizenship; how this can work as an analytical model for understanding Latinxs' existence at the individual, communal, and national levels. While there was much discussion of the US being a post-race society after Obama was elected we know this is far from the case. Identity categories continue to be used to exploit and oppress. They continue to be used by Latinxs to identify a resistance to this exploitation and oppression and for social and political change.

Works Cited

Anzaldúa, Gloria. *Borderlands/la frontera: The New Mestiza*. San Francisco, CA: Aunt Lute Books, 1987.

Anzaldúa, Gloria, and Cherríe Moraga, eds. *This Bridge Called My Back: Writings By Radical Women of Color*. New York: Kitchen Table, Women of Color Press, 1983.

Bejarano, C. L. *The Latina Advantage: Gender, Race, and Political Success*. Austin, TX: The University of Texas Press, 2013.

Cotera, María Eugenia. "Intersectional." In *Keywords in Latina/o Studies*, edited by Deborah R. Vargas, Lawrence La Fountain-Stokes, and Nancy Raquel Mirabal. New York: New York University Press, 2017, pp. 64–68.

Crenshaw, Kimberlé Williams. "Mapping the Margins: Intersectionality, Identity Politics, and Violence against Women of Color." *Stanford Law Review*, vol. 43, no. 6, 1991, pp. 1241–1299.

Dill, Bonnie Thornton, and Ruth Enid Zambrana, eds. *Emerging Intersections: Race, Class, and Gender in Theory, Policy, and Practice*. New Brunswick, NJ: Rutgers University Press, 2009.

Esquibel, Catrióna Rueda. *With Her Machete in Her Hand: Reading Chicana Lesbians*. Austin, TX: The University of Texas Press, 2006.

González-López, Gloria. *Erotic Journeys: Mexican Americans and Their Sex Lives*. Berkeley CA: University of California Press, 2005.

Hames-García, Michael. *Identity Complex: Making the Case for Multiplicity*. Minneapolis, MN: University of Minnesota Press, 2011.

Lugones, María. "Heterosexualism and the Colonial/Modern Gender System." *Hypatia*, vol. 22, no. 1, 2007, pp. 186–209.

Luibhéid, Eithne, and Lionel Cantú, Jr., eds. *Queer Migrations: Sexuality, U.S. Citizenship, and Border Crossings*. Minneapolis, MN: University of Minnesota Press, 2005.

Milian, Claudia. *Latining America: Black-Brown Passages and the Coloring of Latinx Studies*. Athens, GA: University of Georgia Press, 2013.

Rodríguez, Juana María. *Queer Latinidad: Identity Practices, Discursive Spaces*. New York: New York University Press, 2003.

Rodríguez, Richard T. *Next of Kin: The Family in Chicano/a Cultural Politics*. Durham, NC: Duke University Press, 2009.

Sandra, K. Soto. *Reading Chican@ Like a Queer: The De-Mastry of Desire*. Austin, TX: The University of Texas Press, 2010.

Torres, Lourdes, and Lorena García. "New Directions in Latina Sexualities Studies." *NWSA Journal*, vol. 21, no. 3, 2009, pp. vii–xvi.

Torres, Lourdes, and Immaculada Pertusa, eds. *Tortilleras: Hispanic and U.S. Latina Lesbian Expression*. Philadelphia, PA: Temple University Press, 2003.

Ybarra, Priscilla. *Writing the Goodlife: Mexican American Literature and the Environment*. Tucson, AZ: University of Arizona Press, 2016.

LANGUAGE

Language, specifically that of Spanish and English, has played a particularly important role in Latinx Studies scholarship. This is for good reason. From education practices, policy, and legislation making to mainstream representations of language use as tied to Latinx identities, this has been the focus of scholars working in education, law, sociology, cognitive and neuro sciences, and the humanities, among other fields. And while we see and hear Spanish everywhere today in the US, it continues to be a hotbed of contention in terms of who belongs and who does not. It continues to divide the country among the pro-assimilationists (English-only advocates) and xenophobes (Spanish as subpar and aligned with Latinxs who threaten to take jobs) versus those who see Spanish/English fluency as dynamic, multicultural, inclusive, and ancestrally affirming. As John Nieto-Phillips sums up: "Among Latinas and Latinos, language is a complex and sometimes vexing matter. Inextricably bound up in notions of identity and civic belonging, language lies at the center of contemporary discourse about immigration, education, and citizenship" (p. 109).

The dominant language in the US is English. This is, of course, an accident of history. It could have just as easily been Spanish—or even bilingual English/Spanish, given that the Spanish and British empires played significant roles in its early, nascent nation-state shaping. John Nieto-Phillips identifies how because English became a tool of US imperialism, the "adoption of the English language by Spanish speakers in the United States was commonly cited as a prerequisite for the enjoyment of 'full' citizenship, including the right to vote or to participate in self-government" (p. 111). However, while English was the lingua franca of US empire building, Spanish was never entirely displaced. The history of expropriating northern Mexican territories (the US Southwest today), Spanish–American war (1898), US imperial incursions in the Hispanophone Caribbean, as well as the constant migration of Spanish-speakers into the US from the Caribbean, Mexico, and Central America, has led to a long history of the presence of Spanish in the US. Today, Spanish can be heard nearly everywhere in public places in the Southwest, parts of Chicago and Florida, as well as in New York, New Jersey, and urban centers in New England states. Spanish-only and bilingual speakers in the US provide a huge demographic demand for Spanish language TV and radio across the country.

This said, the US has had a fraught history with Spanish. Scholars have identified how, for instance, nineteenth century Spanish-language newspapers in places such as New Mexico and Texas were maligned as degenerate, fake, sloppy, subpar news sources. There's the long history, too, of discrimination within education, with Spanish being attacked by teachers and policy makers alike. Others have studied how the fluent movement between English and Spanish in the formation of a new, third, and urban language among zoot suiters of the 1940s was also a target of discrimination. Today's news is filled with people who express their distaste for Spanish, aligning the language with Latinxs as threatening the US way of life.

Notably, we see in Dominican and Puerto Rican Spanish the borrowing of African words. Puerto Rican Spanish belongs to the Antillean/Caribbean zone, sharing many similarities with the Spanish of the Dominican Republic. And, we see, as John Lipski writes,

> The generally low level of literacy of Spanish of Dominican immigrants, their predominantly rural background, and the lack of strong normative influences on Spanish in the U.S. setting, combine to accentuate variable phenomena found in Dominican Spanish and to skew the language in the direction of rural and regional variants unchecked by pressures to adhere to an educated standard speech.
>
> (p. 138)

Puerto Rico also has a mixed history of institutionally sanctioned language practices. For instance, in 1903 English was made the official language of learning in schools, in 1948, the Puerto Rican legislature declared Spanish its official language, and, today English persists as the dominant language in advertising, TV, and film.

The Brown Power Movements of the 1960s and 1970s actively embraced Latinx identities as expressed through bilingual Spanish/English fluency as well as all variety of Spanish–English admixture; what's become known as code-switching or Spanglish. In addition to hearing the use of Spanish and English in activist marches, many Latinx creators of culture used Spanglish-isms as both an aesthetic shaping device and a way to embrace Latinx identities that were neither embraced by the US mainstream nor by those back in their countries of origin. Poet activists such as Alurista and Corky González used English, Spanish, and indigenous languages such as **Nahuatl** to give shape to their politicized verse lines that celebrated non-assimilated, in-between (Mexican and US American) identities.

Studies focused on the Chicano/a communities have identified this synthesis of languages as **caló**. In *Chicano Discourse: Socio-Historic Perspectives* Rosaura Sánchez defines

> Caló as an urban code [that] is a synthesis of the different varieties spoken by Chicanos in the Southwest, for it incorporates standard Spanish, popular Spanish varieties, loanwords from English, and even code-switching. It is primarily characterized by its penchant for innovativeness in its expansion of the lexicon to produce an argot, the slang of young Chicanos, primarily male.
>
> (p. 128)

Caló is filled with neologisms, all variety of idiomatic expression, and newly combined lexical units. It was used as a way to identify one's membership within the Chicano/a community—one that was politically charged and oriented. It's also identified with language and speech of **pachucos**/zoot suiters of the 1940s. Along with a distinctive dress code for Chicanos and Chicanas, what makes up *pachuquismo* includes language: caló, or pachuco slang. In "Saying 'Nothin'" Catherine S. Ramírez identifies caló as a "product of the Old and New Worlds, as it borrows from indigenous American languages, such as Nahuatl, and from zincaló, the idiom of the Spanish gypsies" (p. 3). She identifies how caló with its Spanish/English lexical crosspollinations and working-class roots was embraced in the '60s/'70s Chicano movement. This "distinctly racialized, working-class, urban youth style" (p. 2) was the language that announced one's "refusal to conform to the status quo" (p. 2). And, when used by Chicanas who were forbidden from using caló (if they did they were considered whores), it was a form of affirming ones' Latinidad as well as resisting the heteropatriarchy prevalent within the Chicano community. Notably, Lipski writes,

> rarely if ever does one hear Spanglish used in conjunction with expatriates from Spain or Southern Cone nations, whose population is perceived as 'white,' thus suggesting an element of racism coupled with the xenophobia that deplores any sort of linguistic and cultural hybridity.
>
> (p. 39)

This period of affirming Spanish (and indigenous languages) as part of the Latinx identity saw the push to create bilingual education programs for K-12. The aim of bilingual activists: not only to provide knowledge access to Spanish-language monolingual learners (Spanish-language learners could learn the main subjects such as reading, writing, and mathematics in Spanish then transition over to learning these subjects in English once a certain amount of fluency was gained)—but also a form of cultural affirmation, and this for all K-12 learners. This led to the Bilingual Education Act of 1968.

Since the 1960s, the push for bilingual education in the US has been difficult. While advocates during the Brown Power Movements made lots of progress, nationally and locally schools were not given the resources and teachers were denied the training for bilingual education to succeed. Often, teachers were deemed competent with little or no cultural training and linguistic preparation; they were not trained to understand the interdependence of Spanish and English languages and cultures (emphasizing syntax and grammar over language function in cultural context) nor were they given adequate and appropriate textbooks for the students to use; many teachers had to translate in their own time the English textbooks into Spanish. As Kip Téllez writes, "bilingual preservice teachers were, by and large, simply told to teach their students in Spanish without much regard for the inevitable transition to English" (p. 49).

Set up to fail because of the lack of resources, by the time of the 1980s bilingual education curricula was being dismissed at the national and local levels. Reagan in 1980 (and this followed through 1990s) appointed William J. Bennett, an avid opponent of bilingual education, to head the Department of Education and to redirect federal funds and support for bilingual/bicultural education into monolingual, English only programs. Congressional legislation also introduced legislation aimed at rolling back federal bilingual education funding and support. As Guadalupe San Miguel Jr. sums up,

> Two key changes were made. One of these placed limits on the number of years ELLs could participate in bilingual programs (two to three years), on the number of English-speaking children eligible to participate (from 40% of total to none), and on the amount of non-English languages one could use in bilingual education (less than half a day; less than one hour per day).

> (p. 104)

This was also a period when we saw an increase in Central American migrations into US because of civil war and economics (usually at the hand of US foreign policy making) and settling into cities/areas where Spanish is spoken. This is the beginning of propaganda that some have identified as the Latinx Threat Narrative: that somehow Latinxs are taking jobs and moving across the border in hordes. In the first half of the 1990s Clinton was a big supporter of bilingual education. However, during the second half with a Republican controlled congress came anti-bilingual initiatives in California and Arizona and the English-only movement leading up to the election in 2000 of George W. Bush, redirecting bilingual education funds into No Child Left Behind; pushing for immersion that would lead to fluency within 3 years. Republicans and anti-bilingual education educators interest groups pushed against bilingual education; monolingual English immersion and Second Language approaches were pushed. They claimed that bilingual communities were not supportive of bilingual education and that those in bilingual programs were low achievers. This was a proassimilationism that was ideologically driven.

Many scholars of language and education have shown that bilingual education, when done well and with adequate resources, does provide a space of learning where students can and do excel academically and where they also feel affirmed in their cultural identities. Many studies have shown that rather than see bilingual education as a move from Spanish to English, it should be thought of as a fluency in both languages that is empowering for Latinxs and non-Latinxs alike. In spite of such positive results, the US continues to debate language use in the classroom and beyond. To this day, we continue to see the to-and-fro struggles between political groups, some aligning Spanish as anti-American while others consider English-only classrooms as yet another way of structural gatekeeping that disallows Latinxs from having access to full education and therefore disallowing the full realization of their potentialities, ultimately leading to political and cultural disenfranchisement in the US. In the end bilingual education fosters academic achievement, cultural and linguistic pluralism, and ethnic minority political empowerment.

As mentioned earlier, no matter the political agenda, Spanish is heard and seen everywhere in the US. As a result of the constant contact with Spanish within Latinx communities, in everyday life on the ground many Latinxs speak Spanglish. Spanglish is the intertwining of the Spanish from a given Latinx language community (and the inter-mixing of regional varieties within urban centers of Spanish contact) such as Cuban Spanish or Puerto Rican Spanish, etc. with English; these differences extend to how one pronounces key consonants along with vocabulary variations as well as the use of the second person familiar pronoun vos (Central America) instead of tú (Mexico, the Caribbean, South America). (See Lipski, *Varieties of Spanish in the United States*.)

Instead of telling someone to park their truck we might hear parquear your trocke, for instance. And, even before the blending of Spanish with English many scholars have already recognized that Spanish itself is a blend. Not only does it borrow from romance languages and Arabic but also indigenous languages such as Nahuatl, Quechua, **Carib, Arawak**, and even Guaraní. For instance, we see this in words like such as tomate (tomato); chocolate; huracán (hurricane); canoa (canoe); barbacoa (barbecue); tiburón (shark); poncho; cóndor; and ñandú (rhea). We're more likely to hear lonche or lonchera instead of lunch or comida. Finally, scholars have also identified how in the mainstream, such as films (hasta la vista, baby), music, street signs, or with Chipotle and Taco Bell we hear Spanglish-isms. Some have termed these uses as "junk Spanish" to identify the kind of Spanish you'd find on a Mexican food menu, in jokes, and stereotypes found in mass media.

Scholars of Latinx Studies have been interested in understanding the nuances of everyday multilingual practices. In addition to Spanglish neologisms, there's been a concerted effort to understand code-switching and its systematic movement (words and lexical shifts) between Spanish and English in conversation. Paul Allatson defines "code switching" as: "the interlingual capacity to shift in and between two or more language communities" (p. 73). It is "a bilingual reality for many Latinxs who move back and forth, creatively and daily between English and Spanish in their daily lives" (p. 73). He identifies this as common among first gen

Latinxs and those living in multilingual communities. For Allatson and others, code-switching within the Latinx community is informed by one's class, gender, age, and contact with Spanish and English that share basic syntactic patterns. Latinx communities in constant contact with Spanish and English experience several phases of code-switching fluency. John Lipski sums this up as requiring:

- "only a minimal amount of fluency in the second language—is borrowing of words, with or without modification, to fit the phonetics of the borrowing language" (p. 223);
- "a higher level of bilingual proficiency, and it consists of transfer of translated idiomatic expressions (calques) as well as tilting word order patterns in a fashion as to make patterns in both languages more convergent—usually by expanding or contracting already available options in one or both languages, and rarely by violating grammatical rules in either language" (p. 223);
- bilingual fluency that allows the speakers to "switch between languages within the confines of a single conversation" (p. 223).

For Latinx Studies scholars and for Latinxs in the US, there's no doubt that Spanish, Spanglish-isms, and code-switching have been tied to identity. It is also a linguistic practice that has increasingly been used as a way to give shape to Latinx fiction. In addition to Junot Díaz, Ilan Stavans, Ana Castillo, Alurista, Rolando Hinojosa, Tomás Rivera, Corky González, Juan Felipe Herrera, and many others, in the writing of *Long Stories Cut Short: Fictions from the Borderlands*, Aldama chose to write across Spanish and English. Aldama writes how "bilingualism and bilingual identities throughout the Americas are the air we breathe" (p. 189). Moreover, the moving back and forth between languages can and does give vital shape to Latinx narrative fictions in ways that "give a unique stylistic stamp and rhythm to our stories" (p. 189).

Bilingualism and bilingual identities throughout the Americas are the air we breathe. By including the stories in Spanish, Aldama wanted to create additional layers of texture in our experience of shaping this art-prose flash fiction. Like many of our community who imagine, think, speak, and act in and across two languages, Aldama wanted the collection to exist in the world as such: as English and Spanish. But never as a one-to-one, line-by-line academic exercise—rather, as infinitely interlocking tesseracts in English and Spanish. Language is a key ingredient in US Latinx and Latin American narrative fiction creation. We are as used to ingesting stories that are monolingual Spanish or English as we are those that code-switch between Spanish and English or Spanish and other indigenous tongues. In each case, language doesn't act just to convey information; it is a shaper of the story. The interplay of English, Spanish, and other tongues offers shaping devices for us Latinx authors to give a unique stylistic stamp and rhythm to our stories; a taste of the resplendent cross-pollination of rhythms, sounds, sights, and smells that breath in and through these storyworlds. A chance for one to experience the Latinx borderlands as multilingual and multisensorial.

The long history of discrimination of Latinxs based on language led to the embracing of Spanish, Spanglish, and code-switching as a way of affirming one's Latinidad. There's no doubt that language has been intertwined with the exclusionary practices for Latinxs in the US. As Ana Celia Zentella discusses, often it's language that has become the object of discrimination, and not one's skin color, facial features, or hair texture. Indeed, the history of discrimination of Latinxs can be mapped just as well through the history of racist stereotyping of language as good and pure (English) versus bad and dirty (non-Spaniard Spanish). As Zentella sums up,

> this remapping is facilitated by notions of purity, hierarchy, and boundaries in the construction of both race and language: both are deemed to consist of superior and inferior varieties and as having inherent qualities that require strict separation, or boundary patrolling, to prevent pollution.
>
> (*Keywords* 210)

And, as briefly discussed, Latinxs have embraced Spanish and English as well as all of its translanguaging variants to wake others to how language has been used to discriminate and disenfranchise Latinxs historically. Strategic uses of Spanglish, code-switching, and caló work to draw awareness to how the surveillance of language is also the surveillance of people. It shows us how borderlands of language for Latinxs evolves as a strategy of survival as well as tools for communicating larger political struggles against discrimination in the US. They are a reminder, as Lipski sums up, that "the Spanish-speaking communities of the United States are dynamic entities, whose language is continually evolving through immigration, sociolinguistic modifications, interaction with English and other varieties of Spanish, and language-internal factors" (p. 13).

Works Cited

Aldama, Frederick Luis. *Long Stories Cut Short: Fictions from the Borderland.* Tucson, AZ: University of Arizona Press, 2017.

Allatson, Paul. *Key Terms in Latino/a Cultural and Literary Studies.* Malden, MA: Blackwell Press, 2007.

Lipski, John M. *Varieties of Spanish in the United States.* Washington, DC: Georgetown University Press, 2008.

Nieto-Phillips, John. "Language." In *Keywords in Latina/o Studies,* edited by Deborah R. Vargas, Lawrence La Fountain-Stokes, Nancy Raquel Mirabal. New York: New York University Press, 2017, pp. 109–113.

Ramírez, Catherine S. "Saying 'Nothin': Pachucas and the Languages of Resistance." *Frontiers: A Journal of Women Studies,* vol. 27, no. 3, 2006, pp. 1–33.

San Miguel, Guadalupe Jr. *Contested Policy: The Rise and Fall of Federal Bilingual Education in the United States, 1960–2001.* Denton, TX: University of North Texas Press, 2004.

Sánchez, Rosuara. *Chicano Discourse: Socio-Historic Perspectives.* Arte Público Press, 1994.

Téllez, Kip. "Preparing Teachers for Latino Children and Youth: Policies and Practice." *The High School Journal,* vol. 88, no. 2, 2004/2005, pp. 43–54.

Zentella, Ana Celia. "Spanglish." In *Keywords in Latina/o Studies,* edited by Deborah R. Vargas, Lawrence La Fountain-Stokes, Nancy Raquel Mirabal. New York: New York University Press, 2017, pp. 209–212.

LATINIDAD/ES

Latinxs in the US have a rich variety of ancestral and cultural roots, including deep ties to Mexico, Central and South America, the Dominican Republic, Puerto Rico, and Cuba, among others. There are important cultural, historical, and political legacies and contexts that differentiate these groups. For example, the various groups that inform the umbrella concept of Latinidad have different histories and experiences with migration. For instance, because of US immigration policies that wanted to put a good face on the US in contrast with the bad face of Cuba, those migrating from Cuba in the 1980s had a different experience to those migrating from Central America and Mexico; today, Puerto Ricans can move freely between the US mainland and Puerto Rico. However, there's also a sense of commonality: long histories of conquest, colonization, and today's **neoliberal** policies that continue to discriminate and oppress Latinxs of all ancestral origins. Latinx Studies scholars seek to at once acknowledge the differences as well as the commonalities. The umbrella term used to identify this sense of a shared history and inter-ethnic belonging is Latinidad.

For Latinx Studies scholars, the concept of Latinidad recognizes the need to overcome inter-group differences as a survival tactic within regions and communities where Latinxs are underrepresented. For instance, Mario T. García's ethnographic work at UC Santa Barbara (2002–2010) determined that ancestrally different Latinx groups forged bonds on campus, leading to cross-cultural influences and the forging of a pan Latinidad. Indeed, already in 1971 Wayne State University established The Center for Chicano-Boricua Studies to clear a space for the forming of a translatinidad among students. And, Felix Padilla's ethnographic work in Chicago (1965–1975) determined that to gain "access to American urban systems" (p. 64), Latinx workers put aside differences of national origin to form pan-Latinx coalitions and a pan-ethnic consciousness. Thus Latinidad (or what Padilla identifies as *Latinismo*) grew from a need to stand in solidarity against racial discrimination and exploitation in the work place.

For other Latinx Studies scholars, the concept recognizes inter-group commonalities based on shared conquest and colonial legacies (Euro-Spanish genocides of indigenous peoples and slavery) as well as decolonial histories, origin languages, and cultural practices. For these scholars, identifying shared experiences across the different Latinx groups (Mexican, Central American, Dominican, Cuban, Puerto Rican, and so on) of racialized violence—slavery, exploitation, surveillance, incarceral practices, linguistic discrimination—is important for the emergence of a resistant pan-Latinx identity and political solidarity. The use of the concept stands against other models for understanding US ethnoracial configurations, including the melting pot and assimilationist ones that seek to erase racial and ethno-cultural differences into a dominant, homogenous monolithic US culture and people. The melting pot and assimilationist ideologies assume Latinxs offer only a deficient, primitive culture in need of erasure for the full realization of a better "American" (mainstream) life. It's this ideology constantly pressuring Latinxs in all parts of daily existence that leads author and critic Richard Rodriguez to characterizes his sense of self as "mixed, confused, lumped, impure, unpasteurized" (*Brown* 197).

For some Latinx Studies scholars and creators, the concept of Latinidad (what we will hereby identify as a strategic Latinidad) clears the space for critiquing the colonial and neoliberal ideologies and contradictory practices that *racialize* Latinxs as brown, primitive—*Other*. So, while Latinxs are not as distinct a racial category as African Americans are with Caucasians, the everyday racism that Latinxs face in effect *racialize* Latinxs in the US. Richard Rodriguez enacts a kind of strategic Latinidad when he embraces and affirms the contradictory ideologies that inform his brown identity; or, as he states, "the gringo I became, the Mexican I remain [and who] violates straight narrative lines, again and again" (p. 276). For scholar Juana María Rodríguez, if one conceives of Latinidad as a constructed concept and space filled with contradictions, cross pollinations, **translations**, and transformations it can be used to intervene and move against monolithic ideologies (*Queer Latinidad* 22–23).

As an appendage to colonial legacies of exploitation and oppression and today's neoliberalism, the mainstream media plays an important role in this racializing of Latinxs. It does so through stereotypes seen with African Americans such as replicating Latinxs as at once dangerous and consumable objects, or mindless bodies to be more precise. The mainstream collapses and erases the different Latinx cultures—say, Puerto Rican with Mexican or Cuban—and reconstructs this as a homogenized whole for easy consumption. Latina media scholars such as Mary Beltrán, William Nericcio, Deborah Paredez, and Isabel Molina-Guzman, among others, critique the mainstream media's fusion of Latinx differences. They consider how mainstream film, TV, media, music, and dance reproduce stereotypes of Latinidad: from buffoon and bandido to eroticized brown bodies. They also consider how Latinxs actors and performers use a kind of strategic Latinidad to trouble and resist this mainstream homogenizing and racializing impulse.

Latinx Studies scholars have introduced important additions and correctives to what we identify as a strategic Latinidad. This includes the affirmation of other ancestries, including African, Asian, and indigenous native ancestral roots.

In terms of the inclusion of African legacies, Latinx Studies scholars have identified how in the US the mainstream media and dominant ideologies make race visible as black vs. white, neglecting the complex African and Latinx ancestral histories of cultural and biological crossings. For instance, Juana María Rodríguez critiques how the casting in mainstream media in the US *and* Central and South America perpetuates this white vs. black binary by erasing the intertwined histories of indigenous and African slavery as well as the intermixing with EuroIberian bloodlines; she's critical of the mainstream's elevating of whiteness (the casting of light-skinned, European looking Latinxs as heroes and protagonists) and denigrating those who look darker, more indigenous or African; she identifies how Afrolatinos are often only cast as **santeras** and

curanderas, functioning as dark, exotic, mystical, and impure figures who emphasize the purity of the light-skinned heroes and protagonists (*Queer Latinidad* 19). Other scholars identify how the black vs. white racialized schemas not only erase the complex biological mixtures that shape *Latinidad* but also how these schemas limit how Afrolatinos (or Blatinos) can represent themselves. The actress Zoe Saldana is a case in point. She's rarely (possibly only in the film *Colombiana*) given a role where she's identified squarely as Afrolatina. With black vs. white racial schemas permeating the US way of life, this often leads to people such as the author and poet Piri Thomas to delink identification with his Latinx heritage and community. (See also Claudia Milian's *Latining America*, Miriam Jiménez Román and Juan Flores' *The Afro-Latino Reader*, and I. P. Godreau's *Scripts of Blackness*.)

In terms of expanding the concept of Latinidad to include Asian ancestry, scholars such as Rudy Guevara and Camilla Fojas have identified how the history of EuroIberian conquest has led to a translatinidad formed out of the inter-ethnic relationship between the Filipinos and hemispheric American Latinxs. For instance, in *Becoming Mexipino*, Rudy Guevara traces the history of the making of this translatinidad to the Acapulco–Manila Galleon Trade (1565 to 1815) routes that created contact zones between indigenous peoples (slaves, servants, prostitutes, soldiers) in the Philippines and Mexico. Many of those forcibly removed from homelands and transported would escape upon arriving in Manila and Acapulco respectively; they would then blend in to the local indio and mixed-race communities. Along with trade routes that transported people in both directions for over 250 years (what Guevara refers to as resulting in Filipinized Mexicans in the Philippines, and Mexicanized Filipinos in Mexico) there was the shared indoctrination of Catholicism with its practices of *compadrazgo* (godparent-hood), religious festivals such as *Día de los Muertos*, and the coming-of-age ceremonies such as the quinceañera that continue to create common cultural ground between Mexicans and Filipinos and that continue to inform this expansive sense of a pan-Pacific Americas translatinidad.

In terms of the indigeneity, there's a long history of Latinx Studies scholars identifying and affirming ancestral ties to indigenous peoples. This along with the acknowledgment of the violence, murder, rape, and torture of indigenous ancestors becomes a way of Latinxs standing in solidarity with indigenous peoples today. Maylei Blackwell charts histories of colonization of indigenous peoples as a way "to articulate a diplomatic and legal framework for their survivance, self-determination, and territorial integrity in relation to colonial powers and settler states" (*Keywords* 100). An indigenous informed Latinidad was a way of affirming indigenous ancestry as well as recognizing the trauma of a shared history of genocide, **epistemic** violence, and trauma.

We see this impulse in the Brown Power Movements (Chicano and Nuyorican) of the 1960s and 1970s. For instance, El Plan Espiritual de Aztlán proclaimed the reclamation of expropriated lands (the Southwest) and symbolic and cultural recuperation of indigenous practices: community-based reclamations known as indianismo as opposed to state-sanctioned practices of **indigenismo** that preserved a commodified version of indigenous cultures all while committing acts of genocide. (See Josephina Saldaña-Portillo's *The Revolutionary Imagination in the Americas* and *Indian Given*.) This was also a way of affirming a Latinidad whereby ancestral indigenous roots transcend nation-state-imposed borders and policies that declared those who moved across these artificially imposed borders without government approval as illegal—as criminals. The embrace of indigenous roots (and with Nuyoricans this was with Taíno and Arawak Carib peoples) during the 1960s and 1970s allowed for the articulation of a Latinidad that was anticolonial and anticapitalist. It's a way of recognizing, too, that today our Latinidad is shaped daily by migrations of Oaxans, Mixtec, Triqui, and Zapotecs from Mexico and Central America to the US. (See Rafael Pérez-Torres's *Movements in Chicano Poetry* and *Mestizaje*, Dylan Minor's *Creating Aztlán*, and Arturo Aldama et al.'s *Comparative Indigeneities of the Américas*.)

In another important corrective move, Latinx Studies scholars have added to the concept of Latinidad the identity category of non-heteronormative sexualities. Building on the foundational work of scholar-creators such as Cherríe Moraga and Gloria Anzaldúa, Latinx scholars today such as Alicia Arrizón, Michael Hames-García, Ernesto Javier Martínez, Richard T. Rodríguez, Juana María Rodríguez, and Ramón H. Rivera-Servera, among many others have identified how significant sexuality is in the shaping of Latinidad. For some, non-heteronormative sexualities create a common, coalitional base for Latinxs with disparate ancestral heritages (Puerto Rican, Mexican, Dominican, Central American, and so on) to struggle in solidarity against straight and Anglo structural and ideological dominance. For instance, in *Performing Queer Latinidad* Ramón H. Rivera-Servera conceives of queer Latinidad as a counterpublic, an action, and "a model of social engagement" not necessarily defined through identity, but "more open to improvisational, at times accidental, routes to the formation of community and home" (p. 69). For Rivera-Servera the Latinx Pride Picnic clears a space for the articulation of a queer latinidad that materializes "pan-Latina/o queer social networks"

(p. 3). It's the space where "nonnormative sex practitioners of Latin American descent with greatly differing cultures, histories of migration or annexation to the United States, and contemporary living conditions encounter each other and build social, cultural, and political bonds" (p. 6).

Given the presence of undocumented LGBTQ Latinxs in the US, these counterpublic spaces provide a refuge for those who navigate homophobia and anti-immigration bodily violations. And, Juana María Rodríguez identifies "spastic contradictions and wild paradoxes of bodies and sites" as contradictory, where different discourses of histories, geographies, and "language practices collide" (*Queer Latinidad* 9–10). It's a Latinidad that undoes itself by constantly asking: "Who is Latina? Is latinidad in the blood, in a certain geographic space? Is it about language, history, and culture, or is it a certain set of experiences?" (pp. 9–10). In Juana María Rodríguez's *Sexual Futures*, she formulates a "theory of queer gesture" through kinship practices and sexual couplings that transcend identity groups and that push against straight-only nation-state sanctioned ways of existing. For Rodríguez, it's the Latinx queer club that provides a glimpse into a coalitional and contestatory space of Latinidad. The space of nonnormative sexual expression allows for the interconnecting of different Latinx groups in the affirmation of a queer pan-Latinidad.

Whether in the recent reshaping of the concept as a translatinidad or a queer pan-Latinidad, Latinx Studies scholars are constantly working to refine and expand the concept so that it continues to at once embrace a coalitional identity (economic, political, and intersectional) *and* acknowledge important differences within and across US Latinx communities. It's why Karen Christian identifies the concept as reflecting "ethnic identity as process" (p. 4). It's why Paul Allatson defines Latinidad as "**panethnic** Latinx identifications, imaginaries, or community affiliations that encompass, but do not supersede, diminish, or destroy, national origin or historical minority identifications" (p. 138). It's why Frances R. Aparicio identifies Latinidad as "the condition of being Latina/o" *and* as anchored in the "social, everyday realities of our diasporic communities and in the spaces populated by Latinas/os of various nationalities, generations, immigrant statuses, and racial and gender identities" (p. 113). The concept has importantly also been expanded to include those who are undocumented, DAPA (Deferred Action for Parents of Americans), and DACA (Deferred Action for Childhood Arrivals) within our Latinx communities. In this expansive sense, Caminero-Santangelo wants us to keep our eyes wide open to ways that we can imagine Latinidad not as "a single, monolithic" category but rather one that contains, in her words, "multiple Utinidades [sic]" (p. 214). Latinidad in all its powerful expansions and refinements provides an important conceptual framework for scholars and activists to recognize differences as well as join arms to push against forces of oppression and exploitation.

Works Cited

Aldama, Arturo J., M. Bianet Castellanos, and Lourdes Gutiérrez Nájera, eds. *Comparative Indigeneities of the Américas: Toward a Hemispheric Approach.* Tucson, AZ: University of Arizona Press, 2012.

Allatson, Paul. *Key Terms in Latinx Cultural and Literary Studies.* Malden, MA: Blackwell, 2007.

Aparicio, Frances R. "Latinidad." In *Keywords for Latina/o Studies*, edited by Deborah R. Vargas, Lawrence La Fountain-Stokes, and Nancy Raquel Mirabal. New York: New York University Press, 2017, pp. 113–117.

Blackwell, Maylei. "Indigeneity." *Keywords for Latina/o Studies*, edited by Deborah R. Vargas, Lawrence La Fountain-Stokes, and Nancy Raquel Mirabal. New York: New York University Press, 2017, pp. 100–104.

Caminero-Santangelo, Marta. *On Latinidad: US Literature and the Construction of Ethnicity.* Gainsville, FL: University Press of Florida, 2007.

Christian, Karen. *Show and Tell: Identity as Performance in U.S. Latina/o Fiction.* Albuquerque, NM: University of New Mexico Press, 1997.

García, Mario T. *The Latino Generation: Voices of the New America.* Chapel Hill, NC: University of North Carolina Press, 2014.

Godreau, I. P. *Scripts of Blackness: Race, Cultural Nationalism, and U.S. Colonialism in Puerto Rico.* Urbana, IL: University of Illinois Press, 2015.

Guevara, Rudy. *Becoming Mexipino: Multiethnic Identities and Communities in San Diego.* New Brunswick, NJ: Rutgers University Press, 2012.

Hames-García, Michael, and Ernesto Javier Martínez, eds. *Gay Latino Studies: A Critical Reader.* Durham, NC: Duke University Press, 2011.

Jiménez Román, Miriam, and Juan Flores, eds. *The Afro-Latino Reader: History and Culture of the United States.* Durham, NC: Duke University Press, 2010.

Milian, Claudia. *Latining America: Black-Brown Passages and the Coloring of Latinx Studies.* Athens, GA: University of Georgia Press, 2013.

Miner, Dylan. *Creating Aztlán: Chicano Art, Indigenous Sovereignty, and Lowriding Across Turtle Island.* Tucson, AZ: University of Arizona Press, 2014.

Padilla, Felix M. *Latino Ethnic Consciousness: The Case of Mexican Americans and Puerto Ricans in Chicago.* Notre Dame, IN: University of Notre Dame Press, 1985.

Pérez-Torres, R. *Mestizaje: Critical Uses of Race in Chicano Culture.* Minneapolis, MN: University of Minnesota Press, 2006.

——. *Movements in Chicano Poetry: Against Myths, Against Margins.* Cambridge, UK: Cambridge University Press, 1995.

Rivera-Servera, Ramón H. *Performing Queer Latinidad: Dance, Sexuality, Politics.* Ann Arbor, MI: University of Michigan Press, 2012.

Rodríguez, Juana María. *Queer Latinidad: Identity Practices, Discursive Spaces.* New York: New York University Press, 2003.

———. *Sexual Futures, Queer Gestures, and Other Latina Longings*. New York: New York University Press, 2014.

Rodriguez, Richard. *Brown: The Last Discovery of American*. New York: Penguin, 2002.

Saldaña-Portillo, María Josefina. *The Revolutionary Imagination in the Americas and the Age of Development*. Durham, NC: Duke University Press, 2003.

———. *Indian Given: Racial Geographies across Mexico and the United States*. Durham, NC: Duke University Press, 2016.

LATINOFUTURISM

Latinofuturism in fiction and popular media reveals the presence of Latinxs in imagined future-spaces. Borrowing heavily from the related concept of Afrofuturism, Latinofuturism is a growing but still nascent area of creativity concerning Latinxs. A similar term, "astrofuturism," concerns bursting through the limits of "terrestrial history" (Kilgore and Douglas, 1), and so in some respect it has an affinity with Latinofuturism—which is concerned with imagining Latinxs in alternate spaces. In addition, Latinofuturism argues for the importance of narratives of speculation and so-called "altermundos"—alternative worlds that mirror our own (Merla-Watson and Olguín). Frederick Luis Aldama emphasizes this key aspect of Latinxs and science fiction:

> Creators of narrative fictions with a so-called scientific explanation (hard or soft) distill from, then reconstruct the building blocks of reality. Today, and yesterday, these building blocks of reality in the US have been increasingly made up of Latinos and Latinas. Today, as the majority minority in this country (and in many states the majority), our existence, actions, and products are undeniably visible. Yet, we're still oddly absent from mainstream SciFi narrative fictions.
> (Goodwin, p. 14)

As such, Latinofuturism merges two historically marginalized domains of American culture: creative works by and about Latinxs, and genre fiction. This kind of double marginalization, however, has the power to reframe understandings of the position of Latinxs in American society as well as how the larger, mainstream society is affected and influenced by the addition or absence of Latinxs. Charles Ramírez Berg has noted the power of pernicious stereotypes of Latinxs in film: "A 'vicious cycle' aspect to repeated stereotyping arises because expressing learned stereotypes reinforces and to that extent validates and perpetuates them. Stereotypes are false to history, but conform to another historical tradition—namely, the history of movies and movie stereotyping" (p. 21).

Consider, for example, the crucial role Latinxs play in agribusiness and other labor-intensive industries that require skilled and unskilled labor. Such efforts are paradoxical because, on the one hand, these industries cannot function without this Latinx labor force. On the other hand, many of the Latinxs who work in these industries are undocumented, so they must remain a kind of invisible force. They are there, and they are not there. Filmmakers such as Alex Rivera and Sergio Arau take this very real problem and project them onto speculative storytelling modes. Rivera's *Sleep Dealer* imagines a near-future when the United States has militarized the US–Mexico border with drones and remote-controlled automatic weapons, effectively keeping Latinxs out of the country. Ironically, technology has allowed for the exportation of Mexican labor, essentially distilling the labor capacity from its humanity (González). Mexicans can remotely plug in and control construction or janitorial robots in the United States. In Arau's film *A Day Without a Mexican*, an unknown fog envelopes California and causes all Mexicans to disappear. Major industries are directly affected, and so many Latinxs who were taken for granted, exploited, or otherwise invisible are now "seen" through their absence. These films are examples of Latinofuturism because they take on the speculative genre and use it as a vehicle to propound how necessary Latinxs are to the United States while also magnifying their exploitation and the threat under which so many Latinxs live. (See also Curtis Marez's *Farm Worker Futurism* and Aldama's "Toward a Transfrontera-LatinX Aesthetic.")

One might wonder why it is so important to have Latinxs create and appear in speculative fiction and films. The historical disregarding of science fiction and fantasy as a genre within literary circles and academia is an entrenched obstacle and prejudice that has taken much time and effort to begin to remove. Speculative genres are often discussed as escapist and unserious. But it should be made clear that genre fiction is simply a recognizable mode of storytelling. And within these recognizable storytelling types, readers will find stories that remain pedestrian and forgettable, while others may take on the form of meaningful and lasting narrative world-building. Further, all speculative fiction, despite its fantastical trappings, always remains recognizable to us, as Aldama maintains in the quote above. Put another way, if speculative narratives were too far flung from human experience, they would be unrecognizable. This feature of speculative storytelling explains why alien species in well-known science fiction shows and films have all-too-human characteristics, even when they appear at first blush to be unlike humans. So, rather than think of science fiction as escapist fantasy that has nothing to do with our society or culture or world, science fiction that rises to the level of meaningful literature always reflects or refracts some crucial issue within society. The entire sub-genre of speculative fiction known as dystopian fiction is premised on exactly this issue of extrapolating a key issue within society and imagining the consequences of that issue pushed in extremis.

It follows that if speculative storytelling has the capacity to reorient our view of the world and of our society, then having Latinxs create and appear in such fiction is a crucial and necessary feature and not just an afterthought. Worse, a lack of Latinxs in speculative fiction seems to indicate the very sort of invisibility mentioned above, the sort of invisibility that occurs when the efforts of Latinxs in areas of society where they are needed but not necessarily seen. If Latinxs are kept from speculative fiction, it indicates that they are already unseen in the present. In fact, stories of the future without Latinxs do not square with the realities of the present. Of all demographics in the United States in the early twenty-first century, the Latinx demographic clearly outpaces all others. If anything, stories set in the future should prominently feature Latinxs.

Fortunately, there are filmmakers and storytellers—many who identify as Latinx and others who do not—who recognize the presence of Latinxs in the present enough to conceive of them in the future. Part of this not only has to do with the increased Latinx demographic but also the increased purchasing power of Latinxs in the United States. Both of these issues influence one another. One wonders, then, why up until the early twenty-first century, Latinxs were absent in these speculative spaces.

If we think beyond US Latinxs for the moment, we do find Latin American writers and artists working in speculative genres, as Bell and Gavilán have shown in *Cosmos Latinos*. One of the great speculative writers of all time, and one of the all-time great writers, period, was Argentinian Jorge Luis Borges, with his mind-bending realities in such stories as "The Garden of Forking Paths," "The Library of Babel," "The Book of Sand," and "Pierre Menard, Author of the *Quixote*." In Borges's fictions, often the banalities of reality suddenly become unfixed by an alternate reality or imagined universe that is just different enough to cause discomfort with our reality as a result of how the possible world illuminates it.

Other Latin American writers invested in speculative genres include Nobel laureate and Colombia author Gabriel García Márquez, whose forays into the speculative reside squarely within a genre called "**magical realism**," where banal events of the everyday are juxtaposed with the extraordinary, with a result that treats this mixture as perfectly normal. Such narratives as "A Very Old Man with Enormous Wings" and *One Hundred Years of Solitude* cast new light on very real but all too ignored realities of the contemporary world. In Guatemala (but Honduran by birth), Augusto Monterroso specialized in insightful, koan-like short-stories (or so-called flash fiction) that adopted a speculative aspect. He is often credited with writing one of, if not *the* shortest story, which reads in full, "When he awoke, the dinosaur was still there." And still more Latin American authors have written in this specific mode: Juan Rulfo, Carlos Fuentes, Roberto Bolaños, and Julio Cortázar used speculative fiction in nuanced and creative ways.

Indeed, Argentina has produced many excellent purveyors of speculative fiction, authors whose works have been consumed by global audiences. Héctor Germán Oesterheld, an Argentine writer and journalist, is perhaps best known today for his masterwork of graphic narrative, *El Eternauta*, a science fiction comic that takes on authoritarianism and the politics of the Argentine government at the time he was writing. With artwork by Francisco Solano López, *El Eternauta*, first published in the late 1950s, merges the post-apocalyptic, alien science fiction, and dystopian genres in a masterful and meaningful way. Like all excellent speculative fiction, *El Eternauta* highlights social shortcomings and raises the specter of what consequences might arise if those current conditions continue unchecked. Though Oesterheld went missing and is presumed dead—he was kidnapped and "disappeared" in 1977—he remains a visionary as a Latin American critic of dictatorship and imperialism as well as a giant in the visual-verbal mode of storytelling known colloquially as comics.

Another luminary of speculative visual storytelling is the Chilean writer and filmmaker Alejandro Jodorowsky, who is best known for his "acid film" *El Topo* (1970), which is credited with launching the "midnight movie" fad in the United States, *The Holy Mountain* (1973), comic *The Incal*, drawn by the French comics legend Jean Giraud, aka Mœbius, and infamously, his failed attempt to bring Frank Herbert's *Dune* to the screen. As detailed in the documentary, *Alejandro Jodorowsky's Dune*, Jodorowsky assembled a team of artists and writers to adapt *Dune*. Most notable of all, much of the work put into the project paved the way for the now-classic film *Alien* (1979), including a script by Dan O'Bannon and the iconic visual stylings of H. R. Giger, both of whom were handpicked by Jodorowsky to work on *Dune*.

This brief foray into Latin American speculative storytelling is really a reminder that, despite the dearth of Latinx science fiction in the United

States, relatively speaking, there is a long and trans American tradition of this type of narrative worldmaking—really going back as far as the nineteenth century in the Americas. In the US, speculative fiction by Latinxs has generally followed the precedent set by the Latin American "Boom" writers such as García Márquez and Juan Rulfo—that is, the magical realist mode, rather than the time- and dimension-bending worlds of Borges. Rarer still are the hard science fiction stories by Latinxs, the kind that involve technical, and often theoretical, science as the basis for their storytelling. Put another way, there are no Latinx Gene Roddenberrys, Robert Heinleins, or Philip K. Dicks—visionaries within the genre. One must speculate as to why, but there is clear enough evidence to support the contention that Latinxs have the capacity to imagine hard science fiction because we have begun to see the advent of that very thing in the late-twentieth and early twenty-first centuries. Thus, a rationale for such a lack has more to do with exclusion and opportunity than interest or ability by Latinx writers.

Writers such as Sandra Cisneros, Ana Castillo, Rudolfo Anaya, and others have infused their storyworlds with Latinx cultural traditions along with magical realist tendencies. Still others such as Salvador Plascencia, Junot Díaz, Carmen María Machado, Manuel Gonzales, Daniel José Older, and other emerging Latinx writers are going the route of acknowledging the roots of the golden age of science fiction— the kind Ray Bradbury, Isaac Asimov, Ursula K. LeGuin, and Arthur C. Clarke made a sensation in the mid-twentieth century. And Latinx filmmakers, too, are making a lasting impression in science fiction films. Alejandro Iñárritu, Alfonso Cuarón, and Guillermo del Toro, all Mexican-born directors and writers that have had tremendous success in Hollywood, combined with Robert Rodriguez's self-made Trouble-maker studios and his notable entries such as his "Grindhouse" film *Planet Terror*, have incidentally made such speculative filmmaking by independent Latinx filmmakers such as Alex Rivera and his *Sleep Dealer* a reality. And perhaps the most breathtaking example of Latinx speculative storytelling in a major US film is *Coco* (2017), the Disney Pixar smash hit that has been described as a "love letter to Mexico" in its carefully researched and consulted film about family and the Latinx holiday known as "*Día de los Muertos.*"

Yet another vital component in the continuing emergence of Latinofuturism lies in the realm of the comic book. As with speculative literature written by Latinxs, Latinx speculative comics, such as Oesterheld's *El Eternauta*, serve as a confluence of imagination and our current lived reality. Mario Hernandez, Gilbert Hernandez, and Jaime Hernandez—known collectively as "Los Bros Hernandez," have each contributed science fiction alternative comics. Frank Espinosa's stunning *Rocketo* depicts a far flung future rife with "mappers" who navigate a world filled with anthropomorphic animal/human hybrids. And Javier Hernandez (no relation to Los Bros) has created the successful independent comic *El Muerto* about a young Latinx man who is killed and is resurrected as a crime fighter. Such is the similar storyline in Marvel Comic's *All-New Ghost Rider*. DC Comics also featured a Latinx incarnation of Blue Beetle, while Marvel has continued to develop an alternative Spider-Man whose identity is a young Blatino named Miles Morales.

Though it has taken far too long, Latinxs are now finding the opportunity to write and create speculative stories for willing audiences. Junot Díaz's *The Brief Wondrous Life of Oscar Wao* literally opens with an epigraph from Marvel Comics's *The Fantastic Four*, and he only dives deeper into speculative fiction the further the novel progresses. We are continuing to see the expansion of a Latinx speculative universe of storytelling that bolsters the further formulation of Latinofuturism, even (and especially) in YA novels such as *Shadowhouse Fall* by Daniel José Older. Latinxs must be seen to appear in stories of alternate worlds, and especially, stories of the future. Even if Latinxs appear in stories that are dystopian such as Neill Blomkamp's *Elysium* (2013), it still indicates that Latinxs have survived into the future. To see futures imperfect and without Latinxs in them, indicates their invisibility in the now and the importance of such stories and the storytellers who tell them.

Works Cited

Aldama, Frederick Luis. "Toward a Transfrontera-LatinX Aesthetic: An interview with filmmaker Alex Rivera." *Latino Studies*, vol. 15, no. 50, 2017, pp. 373–380.

Bell, Andrea L., and Gavilán Y. Molina. *Cosmos Latinos: An Anthology of Science Fiction from Latin America and Spain.* Middletown, CT: Wesleyan University Press, 2003.

Berg, Charles Ramírez. *Latino Images in Film: Stereotypes, Subversion, and Resistance.* Austin, TX: University of Texas Press, 2002.

Díaz, Junot. *The Brief Wondrous Life of Oscar Wao.* New York: Riverhead, 2007.

González, Christopher. "Latino Sci-Fi: Cognition and Narrative Design in Alex Rivera's *Sleep Dealer.*" In *Latinos and Narrative Media: Participation and Portrayal*, edited by Frederick Luis Aldama. New York: Palgrave Macmillan, 2013, pp. 211–223.

Goodwin, Matthew D. *Latin@ Rising: An Anthology of Latin@ Science Fiction and Fantasy.* San Antonio, TX: Wings Press, 2017.

Kilgore, De, and Witt Douglas. *Astrofuturism: Science, Race, and Visions of Utopia in Space.* Philadelphia, PN: University of Pennsylvania Press, 2003.

Marez, Curtis. *Farm Worker Futurism: Speculative Technologies of Resistance.* Minneapolis: University of Minnesota Press, 2016.

Merla-Watson, Cathryn J., and Ben V. Olguín. *Altermundos: Latin@ Speculative Literature, Film, and Popular Culture.* Los Angeles, CA: UCLA, Chicano Research Center Press, 2017.

Oesterheld, H. G., and López F. Solano. *The Eternaut.* Seattle, WA: Fantagraphics Books, 2016.

Older, Daniel José. *Shadowhouse Fall.* New York: Arthur A. Levine Books, 2017.

MEDIA

Latinxs in the media, and media for Latinxs, has mirrored the growing demographic and noticeability of Latinxs. As Latinxs have increased as a significant sector of the population in the United States, the more that increase has been reflected in media. Here we will focus on these two notable aspects of Latinxs and media. And, reflected in this relationship is the undeniable fact that, as Latinxs continue to arise as a size of the nation's buying power that can no longer be ignored, so too do we see the emergence of media with Latinxs in mind. As Otto Santa Ana maintains regarding the shaping power of media,

> Media power is constituted in the ability to characterize the evets of the day and the social structure of society in a particular way. [...] Media owners attempt to bend the characterization of the world that their employees shape to their advantage at the expense of other social groups, so reinforcing a particular view of the structure of U.S. society is conscious, to a degree.
>
> (pp. 51–52)

It is precisely the power of the media and its ability to bend discourse, attitudes, and worldviews to its will—and the absence of marginalized groups such as Latinxs—that makes this such a relevant and defining issue for Latinxs. And, according to a Pew Research Center report,

> A study of more than 34,000 news stories that appeared in major media outlets finds that most of what the public learns about Hispanics comes not through focused coverage of the life and times of this population group but through event-driven news stories in which Hispanics are one of many elements.
>
> (*Hispanics in the News*)

In other words, Latinxs must "do" something newsworthy in order to gain coverage in the media. And, since news stories often focus on what are perceived to be negative stories, it is easy to see how this coverage is detrimental to Latinx communities.

First, what does "media" mean? Broadly speaking, media can be anything from news and journalistic services and the forms in which we encounter them (news reporting, newspapers, network, local, and cable news, websites, etc.), but it might also refer to the plethora of forms in which such information is disseminated. Here we would list television, social media, cinematic narratives such as documentaries, radio, podcasts, and even conventional venues for print. So, not only is it the information that is to be consumed by audiences, it is the form in which that information is conveyed. It is crucial to make this clarification and to understand that the concept of "media" is multifaceted, and thus the implications of media are also more encompassing than one might think at first pass.

Unlike what we have in the twenty-first century, Latinxs were not often represented in media, nor were there always media outlets that operated with Latinxs explicitly in mind or in their programming, and so they resorted to importing content from other nations—Spanish-speaking nations. G. Cristina Mora encapsulates this history:

> In the 1960s, there were no television networks or media firms connecting Mexican American, Puerto Rican, and Cuban American audiences across the country. Instead, Mexican American television entrepreneurs in cities like San Antonio and Los Angeles purchased programming from Mexico and broadcast it to audiences in the Southwest. At the same time, media entrepreneurs in New York traveled to San Juan to buy Puerto Rican variety shows for New York's Puerto Rican audiences. And because Cuban Americans could not return to Havana to purchase Cuban programming, they rented production studios in Miami and created their own news shows.
>
> (p. 3)

Mora further reveals how media enterprises had to contend with the multifaceted nature, rather than the commonly conceived homogeneity, of Latinxs.

As the twentieth century drew to a close, many Latinxs in the United States turned and literally tuned into Spanish-language television networks, radio stations, and movie production studios. Networks such as

Galavision, Univision, TV Azteca, and Telemundo provided Spanish-language programming to US Latinxs for decades, long before there was even a viable opportunity to have US-based networks who would feature programming for Spanish- and English-speaking Latinxs. Univision and Telemundo, in particular, learned to tap into the US Latinx television market. These networks did not concentrate on the Latin American audience. Rather, they focused on Latinxs in the United States all the while keeping the focus on the Spanish language. As a reflection of this, Univision's global headquarters is in New York City, and Telemundo is headquartered in the Miami suburb of Hialeah, Florida. NBC Universal, seeing the potential in programming for Latinxs, purchased Telemundo on October 11, 2001. Univision and Telemundo broadcast to Latinxs and Hispanics all over the world, but their primary audience is comprised of Latinxs in the US. All of this is confronted, problematically, by "the essentialized ideas about language that continue to be promoted by most 'Latino-oriented' media, a situation that the rise of English-language and bilingual choices for Latin@s has not challenged" (Dávila 5–6).

Nonetheless, the success of these two networks helped pave the way for the advent of more opportunities to concentrate programming for Latinxs, and it made perfect sense. Latinxs are as diverse a group, with all nature of niche interests, as any in the United States. In January of 2007, ABC-Walt Disney launched a Spanish-language version of their signature sports network, ESPN. Called ESPN Deportes, the network did not simply feature what are, in effect, Spanish language translations of their programming. Rather, ESPN Deportes has original programming in Spanish, featuring Spanish-speaking on-air talent. There are more shows and segments, for example, on fútbol (soccer), because the sport tends to be quite popular with Latinxs. Fox also has a similar network called Fox Deportes. Telemundo and Univision already had robust sports programming, and their ratings tend to skyrocket during years of major soccer tournaments.

In major US journalistic media, Latinxs have not comprised a significant portion of news reportage itself. According to Stephanie Greco Larson,

> Although Hispanics are the largest growing minority in the United States, their news coverage remains small. Studies of 1990s coverage consistently found that 1 percent of the news dealt with Hispanics, which is less than blacks and Asian Americans receive. This neglect was true of leading newspapers and network television news. [...] Even though they received four times more *New York Times*

coverage in the 1990s than in any other decade, they still only got a meager nineteen column inches a year.

(p. 119)

Not only were Latinxs absent in the new content generated daily by national and local media outlets, they have been historically invisible on screen as well.

Perhaps the most tragic and memorialized event when thinking of Latinxs and journalism is the case of Rubén Salazar. As a reporter for the *Los Angeles Times* and correspondent for KMEX, Salazar was killed in 1970 during a political rally for the Chicano Moratorium that protested the Vietnam War. The Moratorium itself called attention to the inordinate numbers of Latinxs who were being killed in Vietnam, and the protest also simultaneously was a criticism of the lack of the Latinx perspective in the news coverage of the war. Salazar and others had gathered at the Silver Dollar Cafe, which was soon surrounded by law enforcement. Salazar was killed when the police fired a volley of tear gas rounds into the Silver Dollar Cafe, one of which struck Salazar in the head.

Not all Latinx journalists and news figures have aspired to such heights of martyrdom. Geraldo Rivera (born Gerald Michael Rivera), whose father was Puerto Rican, ultimately adopted the Spanish version of his given name. He and his brother, Craig, have appeared on news shows and networks such as *Inside Edition*, Fox News, and, for a time, Geraldo had his own talk show and shows on ostensible news events. Infamously, on April 21, 1986, Geraldo made a newsworthy attempt in his claim to find a lost vault that belonged to Al Capone. At the moment of truth in the two-hour live television event, when the safe was opened, nothing more than an empty liquor bottle and some paper were found, and Geraldo endured this on live television. The event has become irresistible fodder for parody. Yet the issue of Latinx journalists is a real one, as América Rodriguez observes:

This process of making news by Latino journalists for Latino audiences—the mapping and disseminating of a common social, political, and cultural space, and of an imagined community of shared interests—is an element of the social processes that make up Latino ethnoracial identity.

(p. 6)

There have been crossover successes in Latinx media—those who began in Spanish-language programming and soon became a success in

English-language media. Cristina Saralegui, known simply as Cristina, began as a Spanish-language talk show host (in the style of *Donahue* and *Oprah*, as opposed to *Jerry Springer* or *Maury*) out of Miami. In time, she crossed over into English media with some success. Her *El show de Cristina* on Univision, was a success for over two decades. While she has had some success in English-language media, she appears to excel more in Spanish-language programming.

But the most notable crossover success in media has been with Jorge Ramos. A newsman in the mold of Edward R. Murrow or Walter Cronkite, Ramos is the most respected Spanish-language news person. Because he is fluent in English, he has become more well known to English-speaking audiences, appearing occasionally as a town hall or presidential debate moderator. Notably, he is known for asking tough questions, and was once ejected from a then-candidate Donald Trump campaign event (Cillizza). He was literally grabbed, roughed up, and forcibly removed for confronting the presidential candidate. That act was seen by the Latinx community as an act of defiance against the Trump agenda, while simultaneously becoming yet another media antagonist against Trump.

Latinxs have become an impactful presence on social media such as Facebook and Twitter. Interestingly, one of President Trump's biggest critics is former president of Mexico, Vicente Fox. Other Latinx social media personalities include Tony Díaz, the activist who goes by the name "El Librotraficante" (The Book Trafficker), CNN conservative political commentator Ana Navarro, and Lalo Alcaraz, political cartoonist and author of the syndicated comic strip "La Cucaracha." Incidentally, Alcaraz is a force behind the Latinx-themed satirical website, Pocho.com, which pokes as much fun at itself as it does American culture in general. Another news website dedicated to Latinx news is Remezcla.com. Ranging from the silly to the serious, Remezcla reports on an impressive range of topics, following the model of other news organizations that have a Latinx audience in mind. But Remezcla differs by presenting its content primarily in English.

Indeed, Remezcla is representative of a relatively recent development in media for Latinxs. Rather than presenting the content in Spanish, the target audience are English-speaking Latinxs. Now there are several media outlets that cater to the Latinx demographic. MiTú, Fusion TV, and El Rey Network (to some extent) recognize the potential gain in growing and cultivating a Latinx audience. And they are thriving.

What does it say that it has taken so many years to reach a point where the news and media industries of the US actually took the Latinx segment of the population seriously? Well, the implications are quite clear. Latinxs have been seen as an unimportant part of the public. Media has thought of its audience as white, as the group with the greatest purchasing power, and so, by default, the media is also white in its foundation. This further means that it will continue to take extra-ordinary effort, investment, and patience to bring demographic equity in media matters. Though this may be true, it does not exonerate the fact that these conditions exist.

We can be proud that there are Latinx faces on national evening news and in media entertainment. María Hinojosa, Soledad O'Brien, Natalie Morales, María Menunos, Mario Lopez, Alicia Menendez, Elizabeth Vargas, Ray Suarez, and others have shown that Latinxs should be prominent pieces of the American media landscape. What we see in media should approximate the general demographic of all of the US. And we are finally seeing it happen. But even despite of the triumphs Latinxs have had in the media, Latinxs still only constitute a modicum of the percentage of on-air talent and other prominent positions. Latinxs in the media, as well as the ones who watch them, celebrate their success and progress, but they also continue to understand that there is much further to go in this central part of the national identity. For the United States is and always has been forged, in large measure, by its own media. A media industry absent of a prominent and collective Latinx voice is only telling one side of the story, and thus falls short of its promise and potential.

Works Cited

Cillizza, Chris. "Donald Trump's Jorge Ramos News Conference, Annotated." *The Washington Post*, WP Company, 26 August 2015, www.washingtonpost.com/news/the-fix/wp/2015/08/26/donald-trumps-iowa-news-conference-annotated/?utm_term=.929bfa0f4bb8

Dávila, Arlene M., and Yeidy M. Rivero. *Contemporary Latina/o Media: Production, Circulation, Politics.* New York: New York University Press, 2014.

Hispanics in the News: Events Drive the Narrative. Washington, DC: Pew, 2009. Published online by the Pew Research Center, www.journalism.org/2009/12/07/hispanics-news/

Larson, Stephanie G. *Media & Minorities: The Politics of Race in News and Entertainment.* Lanham, MD: Rowman & Littlefield, 2006.

Mora, G. C. *Making Hispanics: How Activists, Bureaucrats, and Media Constructed a New American.* Chicago, IL: University of Chicago Press, 2014.

Rodriguez, América. *Making Latino News: Race, Language, Class.* Thousand Oaks, CA: Sage Publications, 1999.

Santa, Ana Otto. *Brown Tide Rising: Metaphors of Latinos in Contemporary American Public Discourse.* Austin, TX: University of Texas Press, 2007.

MYTHS AND MONSTERS

In his acceptance speech for the "Best Director" award for his film *The Shape of Water* at the 2018 Golden Globes, Mexican director Guillermo del Toro said,

> Since childhood, I've been faithful to monsters. I have been saved and absolved by them because monsters, I believe, are patron saints of our blissful imperfection. And they allow and embody the possibility of failing, and live. For twenty-five years, I have hand crafted very strange little tales made of motion, color, light, and shadow. And in many of these instances—in three precise instances—these strange stories, these fables, have saved my life.
>
> ("Guillermo del Toro wins")

The director spoke of monsters in a metaphorical yet personal way. His comments also reflect the relationship Latinx cultures have with the mythical and the monstrous.

This entry focuses on the longstanding myths and monsters in many Latinx subgroups. Often these topics fall into other related areas such as folklore, religion, superstition, and history. These areas converge into readily identifiable concepts that carry great significance in Latinx lore and history. Latinx myths and monsters are characteristics of Latinx culture as much as food or history. *Día de los Muertos* and the figure of the chupacabra have crossed over into the larger American consciousness, though they and other Latinx myths are often misconstrued or lampooned in the United States. They are also finding more accurate and authentic exposure as the years go on.

Further, it is important to reinforce the statement, as in this entire book of key concepts, that Latinx subcultures have variations on a theme. The Latinx version of the boogeyman, *El Cucuy* as it is known in Mexican culture, goes by different variant names and may have slight differences depending on nation of origin and other regional influences. Of course, all of these differences matter, and they are meaningful to the peoples in question who hold strongly to these myths and mythical figures. However, they may appear conflated and homogenized here due to space constraints.

To begin with, many Latinxs, and especially Mexican Americans, hold fast to the myth of **Aztlán**. Derived from the Nahuatl language, Aztlán refers to the homeland of the **Aztecs** from time immemorial. As with many myths, the myth of Aztlán has roots in historical fact, but it is not completely verifiable. As a result, it becomes representative of a larger idea or metaphor for the grandeur of a people—a bit like a lost kingdom. Scholars and historians tend to locate Aztlán from present-day northern Mexico to the US Southwest. It is thought of as an ancestral homeland, and thus carries with it tremendous significance for reasons that will be explained shortly. But the nature of Aztlán is open to interpretation. Some legends characterize Aztlán as a kind of paradise or Shangri-La that carried with it the qualities of a utopia. Other interpretations cast Aztlán as a dictatorship, rife with violence and brutality.

As Rudolfo Anaya and Francisco Lomelí write,

> For Chicanos the concept of Aztlán signaled a unifying point of cohesion through which they could define the foundations of identity. Aztlán brought together a culture that had been somewhat disjointed and dispersed, allowing it, for the first time, a framework within which to understand itself.

(p. ii)

Whatever the facts may be, as Anaya and Lomelí note, the myth of Aztlán symbolizes a deep-rooted sense of belonging and place within the North American continent and contributes to a cohering of identity. During the civil rights movements of the 1960s and 1970s in the United States, the Mexican American community, politicized as "Chicanos," appropriated the myth of Aztlán to symbolize their struggle and their identity. The writer and self-proclaimed "Chicano Lawyer" Oscar "Zeta" Acosta and other activists in the Chicano movement used the term Aztlán to refer to the American Southwestern states as a means of asserting their sense of ownership to the land, which cast them as natives while Anglo Americans were viewed as the interlopers and outsiders. In effect, the evocation of Aztlán was a powerful decolonizing movement that continues to resonate with many Latinxs into the twenty-first century. Aztlán became an idea of reclaiming the land from people who sought to marginalize Chicanos and minimize their importance to a nation and a government that had illegally taken land from Mexico. This was the result of the **Treaty of Guadalupe Hidalgo in 1848**. The myth of Aztlán, then, has become a symbol of resistance against the vilification and shaming of Latinxs as being foreigners with no home. A rallying cry, which has appeared in film and social media, goes "We didn't cross the border. The border crossed us!"

Related to the myth of Aztlán is the mythical figure known as **Quetzalcoatl**, or the "feathered serpent." He appears as a god in

Aztec and Mayan mythology, and he is a key entity to the history and downfall of these Mesoamerican civilizations. Quetzalcoatl was prophesied to return at a time when the Spanish conquistadores came to the Americas. There is some uncertainty as to whether or not this coincidence of timing affected how the Aztecs dealt with the threat of the Spanish colonizers. He is a key deity, along with Mixcoatl (his mother), though some myths have it that Coatlicue gave birth to Quetzalcoatl. Coatlicue represents the mother goddess figure and is central to Aztec mythology. **Huitzilopochtli**, another notable mythological figure, is the god of war and brother of Quetzalcoatl. Key here is Read and González's assertion that, "Mesoamerican myths cannot be defined simply as false stories. [. . .] Mesoamerican myths are actually true stories, because they describe either explicitly or metaphorically the way people think the actual world is" (p. 4).

Another figure, this time an actual person of antiquity, has come to bear the vilifying stain that often accompanies certain women in cultural myths, women such as Pandora and Eve. Like these women, an Aztec woman known as **La Malinche** has come to be associated with betrayal and faithlessness. She is generally regarded as an interpreter and mistress for **Hernán Cortés**, and thus seen as a key figure in the downfall of the Aztec Empire and the colonization and dispossession of the indigenous peoples of the Americas. Her name has become synonymous in Mexican culture as someone—and specifically, a woman—who will turn to traitorous schemes when it best suits her. Yet the archival work in reconstruction, *Malinche*, reveals that she "was a woman of consequence; intelligent and persuasive, she was a woman who warranted respect on both sides of the cultural divide" (Jager 54). Her alignment with the Spanish and the resulting conquest casts Malinche into a Latinx version of Benedict Arnold to the lore of the United States. She is now a metonym for a traitor, despite scholarship that has worked to counter this understanding of her.

Indeed, Mexican history specifically has had the penchant for exhalting certain key women figures to the level of the monstrous or the beatified. Another of these women who has moved down a tragic path is a figure simply known as La Llorona, or the Weeping Woman. La Llorona is essentially a ghost figure whose legend is shared by many Latinx cultures, not just Mexican. Domino Renee Perez characterizes her thus,

> From a pre-conquest portent, which consisted of a woman howling in the night months before Cortés' arrival, to the Houston mother from Mexico accused of murdering her children, who stated in an

interview, 'Yo soy La Llorona,' the Weeping Woman has permeated
the consciousness of her folk community.

(p. 2)

There are many variations on the story of La Llorona, but they generally
follow a similar narrative pattern. La Llorona is weeping for her lost
children—here "lost" often means "dead"—and she can be seen and
heard near bodies of water such as rivers. Ostensibly, her children have
drowned; some versions have La Llorona lamenting that her children have
drowned by her own hand for some reason. Because of her crime, she is
condemned to roam the landscape at night, a harbinger of doom for any
who see and hear her. The figure of La Llorona has much in common with
the kinds of Classical Greek figures who transgressed against the gods and
were forced to repeat action for eternity, a figure such as Sisyphus. La
Llorona also has much in common with the figure of the banshee, whose
defining characteristic is that she is the spirit of a howling woman. La
Llorona is a symbol of unrest and haunting retribution.

A creature akin to the boogeyman has also loomed large within the
recesses of the darkness in many Latinx cultures. He (though sometimes
it is a she) is known variously as El Coco, El Cucuy, and El Cuco, and
is a supernatural creature with malevolent intent. (Here we use the
variant names and refuse to settle on one.) El Coco is a creature that is
an especial menace for children, and is frequently used as a means of
scaring children into appropriate behavior.

The history of El Coco traces as far back as Portugal and Spain before
those nations set forth to colonize the Americas. It has proven to be a
durable legend, perhaps because it is effective within the imaginations of
children. El Cucuy is a bit like the German legend of the Krampus, who
punishes and kidnaps disobedient children during the Christmas season.
One key difference is that El Cuco is lurking all the time, not just
during a particular holiday season. While all children are susceptible to
El Coco, disobedient children are particularly vulnerable. If El Cucuy
gets you, kidnaps you, a horrible fate awaits—one in which you will
never be found or seen again. More perplexing, and perhaps why it has
such a primal power to conjure fright within children, is that El Coco
does not have a distinctive appearance or form. It is a monster of the
unconscious, and the unknown aspects of such a monster is precisely
what gives it such a fearful aspect.

A monster of Latinx culture that has effectively crossed over into
mainstream US culture is known as el chupacabra (*Celebrating Latino
Folklore*, pp. 324–325). Translated literally as "goat sucker," the

chupacabra falls within a category of monsters known as "cryptids," creatures that are believed to exist yet whose existence cannot be scientifically denied or confirmed. Famous cryptids include Bigfoot and the Loch Ness Monster. Because the chupacabra's defining trait is that of a blood sucker, it has connections to other vampiric beings in other mythologies. Unlike El Coco, the chupacabra has a characteristic form, in this case, it is smaller than a human adult and may appear with prominent fangs, claws, may be lizard-like in appearance, and may be adorned with spikes along its spine. Like many cryptid creatures, there have been eyewitness accounts of the chupacabra, but tangible, verifiable evidence remains typically elusive. The creature was first claimed to have attacked in Puerto Rico (Radford 1), as the dead bodies of several livestock were found. Other unexplained livestock killings have continued to give credence to the existence of the chupacabra, and the figure has appeared in popular culture within the United States, typically for humorous effect.

But perhaps one of the most prominent yet, ironically, the least understood Latinx myth in the United States is the Mexican holiday known as *Día de los Muertos* (or, more accurately, *Día de Muertos*) (Brandes 7–8). Day of the Dead, as it is known in English, occurs over several days (October 31 to November 2). Because it falls precisely on the more well-known holiday (in the United States) Halloween and features images associated with death, the two holidays are sometimes conflated. While Halloween emphasizes fright and ghoulishness in kid-friendly celebrations, *Día de los Muertos* is rooted in family members who have passed on and the memorialization in the land of the living that keeps the memories of those dearly departed alive. It is a deeply-felt and personal holiday, and its difference from Halloween reflects how Latinx cultures view death with less fear.

Día de los Muertos has been traced back to the Aztec empire of antiquity, and it has evolved over the centuries. However, as Regina M. Marchi observes, "Although assumed to be a timeless ritual that has been seamlessly passed down within Mexican families since precolonial times, it is actually a relatively recent tradition for many Mexicans" (p. 1). But its emphasis on keeping the dead alive and relevant by memorializing them once a year has not changed. Some traditions that are a part of the celebration include *calaveras* or decorated skulls and confectionary skulls made of sugar, and other *ofrendas* or offerings to the departed. Traditionally, family members create small shrines to honor the deceased relatives and ancestors. Often family members make treats and foods the departed enjoyed in life. The holiday foregoes the sadness of losing loved ones and emphasizes the love and devotion associated with the life of those now gone. In effect, they remain alive by being remembered.

Though some films and television shows have incorporated the holiday into parts of their narratives (e.g., the opening sequence to the 2015 James Bond film *Spectre*), understandings of *Día de los Muertos* in the United States have been helped immeasurably, and specifically, by two animated films: *The Book of Life* (2014) and *Coco* (2017). Though *The Book of Life* was a modest success by Hollywood standards, Disney Pixar's *Coco*, which has nothing to do with the boogeyman figure El Coco, was an unqualified critical and commercial success. The film's critical acceptance came, in large measure, as a result of the careful research and consultation the studio and producers committed to during the film's production. Some of Disney's most vocal and vociferous critics, including political cartoonist and cultural commentator Lalo Alcaraz, were invited to be a part of the making of *Coco* to ensure its respect to Mexican culture. Such accuracy in a global blockbuster will only help *Día de los Muertos* become a more well-understood holiday and potentially deepen an appreciation for Mexican culture in the United States.

Guillermo del Toro's reflection about the meaningfulness of monsters, that they are "patron saints of our blissful imperfection," is an excellent encapsulation of how myths and monsters form such a substantive part of Latinx culture. They are indicative of lost history and the trauma of colonization. They resound in the insecurities of Latinxs and the hidden terrors of what lies in the unknown. And they also remain a significant and vital part of Latinx identity, reminding of the central place family—and ancestors—hold within the Latinx identity.

Whether it is in the fear of El Cucuy, or in the heartfelt memorials Mexican-descended peoples create for family members they have lost, Latinx engagements with the supernatural, with the unknown, and with that which cannot be seen or easily proven, Latinxs have a rich heritage of myth making and folkloric beliefs.

Works Cited

Anaya, Rudolfo A., and Francisco Lomelí, eds. *Aztlán Essays on the Chicano Homeland*. Albuquerque, NM: University of New Mexico Press, 2017.

Brandes, Stanley. *Skulls to the Living, Bread to the Dead: The Day of the Dead in Mexico and Beyond*. Oxford: Blackwell Publishing, 2007.

"Guillermo del Toro wins best director at Golden Globes." *EW.com*, ew.com/awards/2018/01/07/guillermo-del-toro-golden-globes-win/

Herrera-Sobek, María, ed. *Celebrating Latino Folklore: An Encyclopedia of Cultural Traditions.* Santa Barbara, CA: ABC-CLIO, 2012.

Jager, Rebecca K. *Malinche, Pocahontas, and Sacagawea: Indian Women as Cultural Intermediaries and National Symbols.* Norman, OK: University of Oklahoma Press, 2015.

Marchi, Regina M. *Day of the Dead in the USA: The Migration and Transformation of a Cultural Phenomenon.* Brunswick, NJ: Rutgers University Press, 2009.

Perez, Domino Renee. *There Was a Woman: La Llorona from Folklore to Popular Culture.* Austin, TX: University of Texas Press, 2008.

Radford, Benjamin. *Tracking the Chupacabra: The Vampire Beast in Fact, Fiction, and Folklore.* Albuquerque, NM: University of New Mexico Press, 2011.

Read, Kay Almere, and Jason J. González. *Mesoamerican Mythology: A Guide to the Gods, Heroes, Rituals, and Beliefs of Mexico and Central America.* Oxford: Oxford University Press, 2002.

MUSIC

Latinx culture has a rich tradition of musical and lyrical creativity and entertainment. Latinx music ranges from early folk ballads to newer innovations such as *tropikeo* and everything in between—from "El corrido de Gregorio Cortez" to the 2017 phenomenon that was "Despacito." These creative efforts, like many musical traditions, bring together history, current events, dance, expression, and other aspects of culture. Music and dance within the Latinx community has been a commodity within the United States, and such crossover success has allowed many Latinx musicians to gain mainstream success and even parlay these breakthroughs into other notable enterprises and business. Indeed, by the end of the twentieth century and the advent of the twenty-first century, Latinx music had strongly shaped and influenced the American music industry, becoming a financial powerhouse. *Billboard* coined the phrase the "Despacito Effect," its description of the phenomenal confluence of the current Latin American music zeitgeist and the power of streaming music. As *Billboard* noted, "Earlier in August, 'Despacito' became YouTube's most-seen video of all time, but there were four other Spanish-language videos among the top 10 and 27 among the top 100 for the week of August 4." ("'Despacito' Effect"). Latinx artists such as Pitbull, Daddy Yankee, Luis Fonsi, J Balvin, JLo, and Cardi B have become household names and global superstars.

To understand the Latinx music of the US, one has to understand the history and development of music in Latin America, where music has always been a process of borrowing and synthesizing music styles and rhythms as groups came into contact with one another. The Spanish and Portuguese colonists brought with them the music of their countries, and these were brought to bear on the indigenous ritual soundscapes of the Américas. This early fusion would lead to a truly diverse range of music styles and tradition throughout Latin America.

While all music traditions that have emanated from Latin America have their own distinctiveness, there are commonalities between many of them. From rhythmic, instrumental, and thematic similarities, Latinx music has definite characteristics that make it readily identifiable. The use of specific instruments helps to give this defining quality, and one of those instruments is the simple yet invaluable percussive music maker known as the maraca. The maraca is native to the Americas and appears in the history of present-day Puerto Rico, Mexico, and many other Latin American countries. Puerto Rican music history is particularly rich, with its salsa and danza, "a particular dance form that evolved from English and European country dance (contradanza) and became trans-culturated in the Caribbean" (Aparicio 8).

Continuing a quick survey of other percussive instruments, various sorts of drums are strongly identified with Latinx music. The conga drum from Cuba, a descendent of the African drums that made their way to the Caribbean due to the importation of slaves, has proven to be the heart-beat of many Cuban styles of music—even Puerto Rican—including Bomba (Flores 15). Another similar drum known as the bongo has become characteristic of much of the Latinx-Caribbean music styles. Indeed, music from Latin America has many percussive instruments, many of which are of simple yet elegant design and function. Such instruments include the claves, timbales, cencerro, güiro, and certainly many others. This array of percussive instruments is proportional to their importance in the music itself. Rather than have the percussion move beneath the music, it often takes the center of the stage in Latinx music.

Some instruments that feature in Latin American music originated with Spanish colonizers. The guitar is the most prominent example of such an instrument, and other stringed instruments such as the Mexican *bajo sexto* provide distinctive sounds to Latin American music. And, because the guitar can be played by a single musician and can be played while singing, the guitar allowed musical narratives called **corridos** that became a mainstay for balladeers in Latin America and especially in Mexico. Also in Mexico is the featured use of brass instruments such as trumpets and tubas. And as the dawn of the twenty-first century neared,

Latin American music began to take on innovations from American Hip-Hop, including the use of sampling and turn-tabling.

In terms of musical styles, Latin America has a myriad of lasting and popular ones that have influenced music in the United States and in nations around the world. One of the most potent and mobile music forms originated in and first grew in popularity in the Caribbean near Colombia, morphing into variants in far-reaching locations around the globe. Characteristic of cumbia is its recognizable and rhythmic dancing. Traditional cumbia now resides mostly in the purview of folkloric celebrations. Cumbia has much in common with música tropical, and they both remain very much connected to Colombian identity. Cumbia is an exemplar of a musical form that the Spanish brought with them and, when united with indigenous music traditions, became a key aspect of Colombia's musical identity (Fernández, L'Hoeste, and Vila 3–5). In time, the spread of cumbia became a force unto itself. When it arrived in Mexico, it would in time become a much-vaunted musical style in that country as well. Cumbia as a dance has an easy point of entry, and it eschews intricate and complex dance moves. It is an efficient and inviting dance and music. Other nations welcomed cumbia, including Peru, Argentina, and the United States. Within the US specifically, cumbia has been adapted by such mainstream artists as Charles Mingus, Los Lobos, and Macklemore.

In Mexico, there was a flowering of many distinct music genres. These include the corrido, mariachi, norteño, duranguense, ranchera, and Mexico has adopted musical styles born elsewhere, such as pop and rock, and has shaped them into its own distinct iteration of these imported genres. Many of these native Mexican music genres have made their way into Latinx communities in the US. Of these, the corrido deserves special attention here.

Conceived of as a form of ballad, the corrido has a very specific structure and has its roots in folkloric tradition. Because it is a ballad form, it tends to have a high degree of narrativity about it. Simply put, it tells a story that is often inspired by real life events or cultural myths. The subjects of these ballads are often outlaw figures—characters who have done heroic deeds or have broken the law for what they see as a purpose that transcends manmade law. Corridos have no chorus intervals, and so each verse flows right into the next one. Hence its name, which indicates continuous motion or running.

Perhaps one of the most significant corridos is "The Corrido of Gregorio Cortez," a song that recounts two brothers who were confronted by a white sheriff. Gregorio's brother was shot and killed by the sheriff, and Gregorio did the same to the sheriff. A police chase ensued, and the corrido is much concerned with showing Gregorio's bravery as well as the injustice of the nominal representative of justice. The corrido is the subject of a brilliant and discipline-altering study by Américo Paredes titled, *With His Pistol in His Hand: A Border Ballad and Its Hero*. The corrido form continues to be a popular form in Mexican American communities specifically.

In popular culture within the United States, it is notable that one of the first and biggest stars on television of Latinx heritage was the musician and actor Desi Arnaz. The Cuban-born singer and husband of Lucille Ball brought his orchestra's music into America's home for years. Indeed, for six years *I Love Lucy* was the number one on television. His signature song "Babalú," is about an Afro-Cuban deity from the Santeria religion. For a mostly white American audience, many of whom had not encountered Latinx music in any substantive way, it did not matter what the songs were about nor whether Arnaz was not as talented a percussionist as he seemed on television. Carrying on the tradition of bandleader Xavier Cugat, and helping establish a televisual presence that would help Tito Puente and Celia Cruz, Arnaz immeasurably helped Latinx music work its way into the mainstream consciousness of the United States.

Moving directly from Arnaz, who was less a force in the music industry than he was in the television industry (he and Ball would co-found Desilu studios, which was directly responsible for *I Love Lucy, Star Trek, The Untouchables, Mission: Impossible*, and other iconic television shows), there were other Latinxs in the US who influenced the music industry and the music enjoyed by millions of Americans. Though the many genres of Latin American music that have and continue to be consumed in US aid in Latinxs maintaining strong bonds to nations of ancestral origin, Latinxs in the United States have significantly influenced the music industry.

No other Latinx in the mid-twentieth century did more to shape music in the US than Ricard Steven Valenzuela, who is remembered by his stage name Ritchie Valens. Not only did Valens become one of the founding generation of rock and roll in the US, he is the fountainhead for what would be later known as Chicano rock. It is almost unbelievable that Valens was so impactful when one considers he was really only a "star" for less than a year, his life and career cut tragically short when he, Buddy Holly, and J.P. "The Big Bopper" Richardson were killed in a plane crash in Iowa on February 3, 1959. American singer and songwriter Don McClean immortalized this event in his song, "The Day the Music Died."

Valens may have died three months shy of his eighteenth birthday, but his legacy soon became larger than even he might have imagined. In this much-too-abbreviated career, he managed to generate the hit songs "Come On, Let's Go," "Donna," and perhaps most significantly, "La Bamba." The song, of Mexican folk origin, is about a folkloric dance that accompanies festivals and celebrations. Though many artists have recorded "La Bamba," the Valens version is especially notable. Not only was it a Top-40 hit for Valens, thanks to him it soon became a rock and roll classic. What is more, it is sung entirely in Spanish, a rarity in US popular music at the time, which makes it especially remarkable. It is arguably the greatest rock and roll song not to be sung in English. Others would continue to cover what now is seen as Valens's song, including the Chicano rock band Los Lobos, who provided the vocals for the song in Luis Valdez's 1988 biopic of Valens, titled *La Bamba*. The film and the cover by Los Lobos put new vitality into the song and the importance of this pioneering US-born Latinx musician.

Yet another tragic story concerning the trajectory of Latinxs in US music must surely be that of Selena Quintanilla Perez, known by her stage name Selena. In 1995, Selena, who was already overwhelmingly successful in Spanish-language music outlets, and had just begun to crossover into the US music industry with English-language songs, was murdered by the former president of her fan club. Like Valens, Selena received the Hollywood biopic treatment in a film of her life and death, with Jennifer Lopez in the title role. Lopez herself, who would become known to the world more familiarly as J-Lo, would go on to have a successful music, film, and entrepreneurial career of her own.

In the years after the death of Ritchie Valens, more Latinx musicians (here we refer to Latinxs of US origin rather than Latin American musicians who have crossed over into the US music scene) have made their name in American music. Some of those not yet identified in this entry include the innovative and iconic rock guitarist Carlos Santana, Gloria Estefan, her husband Emilio Estefan and their band the Miami Sound Machine, the actor and singer Ruben Blades, Ricky Martin, Jon Secada, Marc Anthony, Pitbull, Selena Gomez, and many more.

In a land that has often been inhospitable to Latinxs throughout its history, the music of Spanish-speaking peoples of the Américas has proven to be a highly mobile and dominant force for culture and entertainment. While there are instances of cultural appropriation of music by Latinxs in the US, as there are in many facets of Latinx culture, Latinxs have often been at the bleeding edge of the music industry. Josh Kun puts it this way:

> Music can't topple regimes, break chains, or stop bullets. But it can keep us alive. Music can always surprise us, be unpredictable, refuse to submit to what is put upon it. Music can always sound different from one listening moment to another, and mean radically different things to all who hear it.

(p. 17)

So too with Latinx music in the US. The rhythms, the instrumentation, the passion of Latinx music is often one of the more acceptable aspects of Latinx culture that tends to work its way past prejudice and questionable borders. It is one of the defining features of Latinx culture, and its transformative power often proves irresistible.

Works Cited

Aparicio, Frances R. *Listening to Salsa: Gender, Latin Popular Music, and Puerto Rican Cultures.* Middletown, CT: Wesleyan University Press, 1998.

"'Despacito' Effect: Behind This Year's Latin Music Revolution." *Billboard*, www.billboard.com/articles/columns/latin/7897123/latin-music-takeover-despacito-mi-gente-charts

Fernández, L'Hoeste H. D., and Pablo S. Vila. *Cumbia! Scenes of a Migrant Latin American Music Genre.* Durham, NC: Duke University Press, 2013.

Flores, Juan. *From Bomba to Hip-Hop: Puerto Rican Culture and Latino Identity.* New York: Columbia University Press, 2000.

Kun, Josh. *Audiotopia: Music, Race, and America.* Berkeley, CA: University of California Press, 2005.

Paredes, Américo. *"With His Pistol in His Hand": A Border Ballad and Its Hero.* Austin, TX: University of Texas Press, 2010.

NARRATIVE

Storytelling, or the creation and reception of narrative, is a part of human history and existence. Narrative, whether created as a means to relate experience or to entertain or provide insight into human experience, is an understandably vital function—whether it be as a repository of knowledge or as a means of expression to others. Latinxs are no different from other demographics in the United States in that they have engaged in narrative form in particular and meaningful ways. Speaking of narratives by Chicanos, Ramón Saldívar writes,

> The task of Chicano narrative is thus not simply to illustrate, represent, or translate a particular exotic reality, nor even a certain conception of reality—this epistemological theory of reflection is theoretically sterile. Instead, it serves to realize the agency of thematic figures in the process of demystifying the old world and producing a new one.
>
> (p. 7)

Chicano narrative, and by extension, Latinx narrative, is transformative, not simply a document of the world.

Latinx authors and writers have also adapted other forms—from within the United States as well as from other global traditions such as the Latin American form of the *testimonio*, a kind of personal narrative that puts personal experience against oppressive ideological structures—and have made notable contributions to the understanding of Latinx identity and the form and function, as well as the limits, of narrative. And, as Frederick Luis Aldama argues,

> The multitude of media forms created by and that feature Latinos in the twenty-first century is a radically different landscape than earlier epochs. This proliferation of diverse media formats by and about Latinos extends into film, television, animated cartoons, comic books, and Internet, among many others.
>
> (*Latinos and Narrative Media* 1)

Thus, narrative styles and modes are constantly in flux.

First, a quick word about the term "narrative." Narrative theorists have worked to find an effective yet comprehensive definition for the term, and it has proven to be a difficult endeavor because narratives are so multivalent. H. Porter Abbott provides one of the most efficient definitions for narrative: "Simply put, narrative is *the representation of an event or a series of* events" (13). As one can see, Abbott does not make a distinction for *how* the events are represented, nor does he make exceptions for whether or not the events are rooted in fact or in fiction. Thus, one sees the capaciousness of that which we call "narrative."

The term, as it applies to extended writing or literature, often came to be associated with memoir or other forms of life writing. Some

famous examples include *The Narrative of the Life of Frederick Douglass.*
Indeed, the term narrative has become associated with the genre of one-
time American slaves who, through trial and tribulation, managed to
extricate themselves from bondage. These "slave narratives," as they came
to be identified, create a corpus of texts that speak to the brutality of that
historical period in the US, as well as to be exalted as tangible proof of
the equal capacity for intelligence of enslaved blacks. These texts have the
air of truthfulness and authenticity, and so in time, "narratives" came to
signify someone's true account of something they personally experienced
or witnessed. Within the context of Latinx culture, a close synonym for
this sort of narrative would be the *testimonio.*

Since then, the idea of what a narrative is, and what it can do, has
undergone significant expansion. In contemporary parlance, especially
when applied to politics, a narrative suggests a particular emphasis on
what is being talked about in the media at any given time. If, say, a
politician is hounded by a particular scandal, pundits may recommend
that the politician work hard to "change the narrative." That is, the focus
of what is being emphasized when people speak of that politician. But
this, too, is a limited connotation for a term as expansive as narrative.

In literary studies, there is a subfield known as narrative theory
(formerly narratology). This field is devoted to the understanding of
how an author designs a narrative, how it manifests in different media
forms, and how readers engage and interact with narrative. Of specific
use to this entry on Latinx narrative is what we mean when we say
narrative. It is not simply fiction or nonfiction; it can be both. It can
occur in prose form, in graphic form such as a comic book, in a filmic
mode such as cinema, in televisual venues such as cable, network, or
streaming apps, and even in face-to-face social interactions.

Yet there is a particular issue that dogged, and in many ways,
continues to dog Latinx narrative. If it is a given that the experiences
of Latinxs in the United States are substantively different than that of
mainstream white culture, we should expect a potential difference in
how that experience is captured and conveyed in narrative form. But
sometimes difference does not meet with the expectations of those
gatekeepers of the publishing, television, and film industries. As
Christopher González argues,

> Since its inception Latino/a literature has faced publication
> challenges born from matters of audience and reader expectation.
> This fact correlates with the viable narrative forms available to a
> Latino/a author's desire to have his or her work published by a

major publisher with the distribution power to increase visibility and marketability of those works.

(p. 11)

Put simply, Latinxs' goal of publishing narratives of their own creation, narratives that suit their own creative whims rather than the narrow notions of what they are *expected* to write has hindered Latinx writers until relatively late in the twentieth century.

With this particular hindrance in mind, we can better understand the development and evolution of Latinx narrative. To begin with, what do we say is the first US Latinx novel—the first novel written by a Latinx author about an identifiably Latinx experience? Some say it is María Amparo Ruíz de Burton, who wrote sophisticated novels in the mid-nineteenth century in California. But we run into the problem of definition here. Ruíz de Burton was actually Mexican born, when California still was a part of Mexico. But after the Treaty of Guadalupe Hidalgo in 1848, California and much of the present-day American Southwest changed hands from Mexican to US control. Her novels mostly dealt with the interaction between Mexicans and Americans, and is surely a different type of novel than narratives written by Sandra Cisneros or Oscar "Zeta" Acosta.

If we are to look for a published narrative by a Latinx born in the US and one that deals with the experience of being a US Latinx in some significant measure, then the first written narrative as a novel by a Latinx in the US must be José Antonio Villarreal's *Pocho*, published in 1959. **Pocho** is symbolic of many of the barriers to publishing Latinxs faced. It was published literally centuries after the first American novels and it revealed an uncertainty in how to incorporate the bilingualism that is often present in Latinx communities in the US. *Pocho* was modestly successful, which revealed another obstacle to later works through no fault of its own. Successful novels, especially in specialized markets such as ethnic fiction, often create the desire for their clones in the publishing world. The early Latinx novels that engaged with the issues of their times—of being Latinx, of being born and raised in an impoverished environment, of working hard to avoid prison (or to become a well-adjusted person *after* a stint in prison), unwittingly limited the potential variety in Latinx narratives. It has taken many decades since the advent of *Pocho* for Latinx literature to move beyond such restricted types of storytelling.

Subsequent to Villarreal's novel, other Latinx writers made important contributions to Latinx letters, both in fiction and in nonfiction. Latinx writers of the 1960s and 1970s quickly established a foundation of Latinx narrative in the United States that continues to resonate into the twenty-first century. In 1968, Piri Thomas, a Puerto Rican from New York, published an **autobiography** titled *Down These Mean Streets*. In it, Thomas chronicled his early years trying to come to terms with his Latinx heritage, his African lineage, his parents, and with the streets in which he received an education of criminality and drug use. In the second half of the book, Thomas unfurls his prison experiences as well as his determination to become a writer and put down his lived experiences into print. It is a tour de force narrative, and it helped initiate a long tradition of Latinx life narratives that aimed to shed light on the struggles and plight of this specific marginalized community. Such books would come to include the not-quite-factual *Autobiography of a Brown Buffalo* by Oscar "Zeta" Acosta and his follow up, *The Revolt of the Cockroach People*, Ernesto Galarza's *Barrio Boy*, Richard Rodriguez's *The Hunger of Memory*, the philosophical, meditative, poetic *Borderlands: La Frontera: The New Mestiza* by Gloria Anzaldúa, Jesus Colón's *A Puerto Rican in New York and Other Sketches, The Distance Between Us* by Reyna Grande, and many more. This specific kind of narrative—generally about the Latinx growing up within the United States, has dominated Latinx letters. There is good reason for this. Not only are the authors of these books beyond talented, the narratives help give an insider's perspective to Latinx culture that has not always been accurately or authentically represented in the American imagination. On the other hand, as mentioned above, the success of these kinds of books created a market in which publishers wanted more of these sorts of narratives. While this helped establish the viability and visibility of such narratives, it has tended to limit other types of life narratives from Latinx authors. This is to say nothing of the struggles that Latinx LGBTQ writers face when breaking past entrenched paradigms of what structures their narratives must take (Cortés).

Latinx works of fiction also became a viable yet niche market with books such as the classic *Bless Me, Ultima* by Rudolfo Anaya. Published in 1972, *Bless Me, Ultima* became one of the most notable and widely read novels by a Latinx in the twentieth century. It has never been out of print, and it often appears in university and high school classrooms as the representative work by a Latinx. Sandra Cisneros's *The House on Mango Street* also continues to be required reading in schools. Since the publication of these two books, many works by Latinxs have begun to flourish within the publishing world. It also helps to gain exposure by winning significant prizes. Oscar Hijuelos and Junot Díaz have both won a Pulitzer Prize for novels that center on the Latinx communities both in the United States and in the Caribbean—Cuba for Hijuelos; Dominican Republic for Díaz. These two authors, however, are the only Latinxs to win the vaunted literary prize in its entire history.

In terms of the narrative forms Latinx novels have employed, early novels were more straightforwardly told in linear time and without many narrative characteristics that asked a high demand of the reader. These novels were often examples of literary realism, and in time, with the advent of the use of "magical realism" by Latin American authors such as Gabriel García Márquez, Julio Cortázar, Carlos Fuentes, and others, Latinxs began to incorporate this literary mode within their own fiction. Yet it has taken many decades for Latinx writers to write fictional narratives that reach beyond what has now become a kind of stereotype—the magical realist novel about getting out of your hardcore neighborhood to get educated enough to write a book about it. It has only been within the first decade or two of the twenty-first century where fictional narratives by Latinxs have begun to break into areas long a part of the fictional worlds and modes of white, male American writers such as postmodernist forms of fiction. (See also Aldama's *Postethnic Narrative Criticism*.)

Unfortunately, the same holds true for filmic narratives. In the history of filmmaking, the number of US-born filmmakers and directors is infinitesimal and statistically insignificant. We do not need sophisticated statistical measures to determine this. A majority of their names appear right here: George Romero, Luis Valdez, Edward James Olmos, Robert Rodriguez, and Alex Rivera. To make up for the dearth of US Latinx filmmakers, discussion of Latinx filmmakers and directors must be expanded to include Latin American filmmakers who have made films in the United States or for American audiences. Such directors include Alfonso Cuarón, Alejandro Iñárritu, Guillermo del Toro, Jorge Gutierrez and his wife, Sandra Equihua, and others. It makes one wonder where all of the US Latinx directors are.

Perhaps the most prominent of the US Latinx directors is the Austin, Texas-based Robert Rodriguez, known for such films as *El Mariachi, Desperado*, and the *Spy Kids* tetralogy. Whereas Olmos and Valdez have focused their efforts on telling traditional and realist stories of Latinx struggle and triumph, Rodriguez is very much cut from a similar cloth as Quentin Tarantino. Because Rodriguez is independent minded, not wanting to be restricted by studio expectations, he established his own independent filmmaking enterprise called "Troublemaker Studios," where he really works to live up to the auteur filmmaker designation by scripting, shooting, directing, editing, and scoring his own films. Rodriguez is a rarity in Latinx filmmaking, and perhaps his very existence reveals just how difficult it is for Latinxs to break into filmmaking (Aldama, *The Cinema of Robert Rodriguez*). Not many have the talent or serendipity to establish their own movie studio as Rodriguez has.

Finally, Latinxs have blazed a trail in the graphic narrative form, also colloquially known as comics. No discussion of Latinx comics can really begin without invoking the overwhelming importance of three brothers from Oxnard, California. Known collectively as "Los Bros Hernandez," Mario, Gilbert, and Jaime Hernandez have created so-called "alternative comics" for over 30 years. What began as an independently-created and distributed comic called *Love and Rockets*, was taken on by Gary Groth and his newly-launched comics publishing house, Fantagraphics Books. The partnership has been mutually beneficial to both parties, and issues of *Love and Rockets* continue to be enjoyed and appreciated by adoring fans. The brothers, and specifically Gilbert and Jaime, are among the leading comics artists working in the industry today.

Other Latinx cartoonists are gaining more attention, thanks in large measure to the ever-expanding Latino Comics Expo, held yearly in California since 2011, which has highlighted the work of Javier Hernandez, J. Gonzo, Liz Mayorga, Jules Rivera, Lalo Alcaraz, Raul the Third, and many more. This independent wave of Latinx cartoonists and comics artists, in direct response to the relative indifference of major mainstream comics publishers such as DC Comics and Marvel Comics, are breathing new life into a such a long-existing form as the visual-verbal narrative.

After centuries of being kept out of major publishing houses in the United States, Latinxs have now begun to claim narrative spaces as their own. As such, scholars such as William Orchard and Yolanda Padilla are taking stock and attempting to understand what Latinx narratives are now in contrast to what they were. And they are finding receptive audiences that are both Latinx and non-Latinx. The stories Latinxs tell reflect to a large degree how they view themselves within a national context that both invites and repels. As such, Latinx narratives, in their varied forms, are an invaluable aspect of Latinx culture, as well as a vital part of what it means to be an inextricable component of the United States.

Works Cited

Abbott, H. Porter. *The Cambridge Introduction to Narrative.* New York: Cambridge University Press, 2015.

Aldama, Frederick L. *Postethnic Narrative Criticism: Magicorealism in Ana Castillo, Hanif Kureishi, Julie Dash, Oscar "Zeta" Acosta, and Salman Rushdie.* Austin: University of Texas Press, 2003.

——. *Latinos and Narrative Media: Participation and Portrayal.* New York: Palgrave Macmillan, 2013.

Aldama, Frederick L. *Latinos and Narrative Media: Participation and Portrayal.* New York: Palgrave Macmillan, 2013.

——. *The Cinema of Robert Rodríguez.* Austin, TX: University of Texas Press, 2014.

Cortés, Jason. *Macho Ethics: Masculinity and Self-Representation in Latino-Caribbean Narrative.* Lewisburg, PA: Bucknell University Press, 2015.

González, Christopher. *Permissible Narratives: The Promise of Latino/a Literature.* Columbus, OH: Ohio State University Press, 2017.

Orchard, William, and Yolanda Padilla. *Bridges, Borders, and Breaks: History, Narrative, and Nation in Twenty-First-Century Chicana/o Literary Criticism.* Pittsburgh, PA: University of Pittsburgh Press, 2016.

Saldívar, Ramón. *Chicano Narrative: The Dialectics of Difference.* Madison, WI: University of Wisconsin Press, 1990.

NARCO CULTURA

Latinx Studies scholars have begun to delve into the difficult topic of the culture that has grown in and around cartel drug trade and human trafficking (*narcotráficante*) along the US/Mexico border. Scholars understand the violent, murderous reality. Since the beginning of the twenty-first century, over two hundred thousand civilians have been murdered, and usually in horrific and ghastly sensationalized ways: smartphone recordings and Internet postings of decapitations, hangings, and death by dynamite, among others. At the same time, these scholars seek to understand the cultural phenomena that have grown from *narco* life within the US/Mexico borderlands. While *narcotráficante* and *Narco Cultura* are in many ways inseparable for scholarly study, the culture doesn't just reflect the murderous reality, in a feedback loop-like system—as already forewarned by Luis Astorga's seminal 1995 study *Mitología de narcotraficante en México*—it grows the reality it describes. *Narco Cultura* is a billion-dollar industry grown from a rule of law economic system that, as Ryan Rashotte sums up, "annually destroys thousands of lives" ("*Narco Cultura*" 395).

There's an important cadre of scholars of *Narco Cultura* that seek to nuance understanding of *narco* operations. This includes identifying hierarchies within the *narcotráficante* scene. For instance, Kendra McSweeney et al. identify at the top of the hierarchy a *narco*-bourgeoisie that uses drug and human trafficking profits to expropriate lands historically protected for and sustained by indigenous groups. Capitalism in its most barbarous form, the *narco*-bourgeoisie (and these exist across the

Américas) use their vast wealth to take control of public and farm lands (para. 16). To effectively expropriate lands, the *narco*-bourgeoisie often endorse politicians at the local and national levels; this system is known as *narcopolítica*. Lower on the rung in this hierarchy are the petty *narcos* and the soldiers. The petty *narcos* are those who extort monies ($50 to $100 per person) from the coyotes (or polleros) who guide groups of people across borders; in so doing, these petty *narcos* make upwards of $2,000 a month—an exponentially huge increase in salary for those otherwise working at a minimum wage in places such as Mexico. Given that *narcotráficante* exercise power through a rule of law system, this requires soldiers. For instance, the Mexican cartel known as the Zetas use ex-special-forces commandos to terrorize communities with their signature brutal mutilations and beheadings. Often, the soldiering and control of the movement of peoples across borders by coyotes and polleros go hand in hand; the petty *narcos* and cartel soldiers preying on the innocent, kidnapping and raping women to assert territorial dominance *and* to make money by enslaving women in sex-traffic rings. (For more on this, see Jeremy Slack and Howard Campbell's field research based in Nogales, Sonora, published in their article, "On Narco-coyotaje.") At the bottom of this hierarchy are the ad hoc and disorganized burreros (marijuana smugglers) as well as border residents and migrants paid (cash, women, or death-threats) by the cartels to guard US/Mexico crossing points such as along the Rio Grande.

The *narcotráficante* economy has also transformed the coyote and pollero system for transporting people (pollos) across the border. In the past, coyotes formed local networks grown from hometowns and communities. With the rise of *narcotráficante* systems, the coyotes work for the cartels and are detached from hometowns and communities; they operate along the borders with no connection to the people they are transporting—and increasingly kidnapping for human trafficking. (See Díaz and Swecker, *No Boundaries: Transnational Latino Gangs and American Law Enforcement.*)

Within this very real and horrific context, scholars have sought to understand a culture that at once sensationalizes, heroizes, and normalizes it. For instance, *narcos* in the state of Sinaloa sport cowboy styles with their boots, buckles, and sombreros. They seek to replicate the cowboy/*charro*-outlaw figure in sartorial wear as well as in lifestyle—pickup trucks, horses, and ranch ownership. As Natalia Mendoza Rockwell interprets, this is *narco*-traffickers' attempt to "legitimize themselves as the heirs of the local genealogy of Indian attacks, contraband, cattle rustling, shoot-outs, and territorial controls" (NACLA Report on the Americas, May/June 2011, 27).

There are other ways that *narcos* seek to construct a façade of the outlaw-hero that naturalizes their daily terrorizing and exploiting of civilians. This includes bank-rolling careers of *narcocorridodistas*—singers who specialize in creating songs that glorify the *narco* life. As Curtis Marez sums up in *Drug Wars*, these songs often aim to lionize the traffickers as Robin Hood-like figures all while demonizing the police and establishment (p. x). Singers like Edgar Quintero and Alfredo Ríos (El Komander) use the bandas (brass bands especially prevalent in north-western Mexico) or norteños (accordion based and known in the north of Mexico) soundscapes to give shape to songs (first- or third-person) that recount the blood battles of drug kingpins and their acts of bravery, and this with some of the bloodiest murderers, for instance, Manuel Torres Félix, a top lieutenant in the Sinaloa Cartel, infamously known for torturing and decapitating over 200 people in one week. The lyrics also include code-words such as *gallo* for marijuana, *chiva* for heroin, *perico* for cocaine.

These and other *narcocorridodistas* do not appear ex nihilo. Scholars have traced their lineage to the border balladeers of earlier epochs that celebrated the heroic acts of Latinxs who defended families and communities against unlawful violence; one such *corrido*, "The Ballad of Gregorio Cortéz," celebrates his heroic defense against racist Texas Rangers. Other scholars have traced the origins of the *narcocorrido* as far back as seventeenth-century Spain and its tradition of the *jácara*—comic ballads that recount the life of underdogs. (See Ted L. L. Bergman's "*Jácaras* and *Narcocorridos* in Context.")

Nor are *narcocorridodistas* part of a niche music marketplace. They are extremely popular on both sides of the US/Mexico border. Alfredo Ríos fills stadiums in Mexico and Central America; his fans fill huge ten-thousand-plus-person arenas in places such as Fresno and Bakersfield. His YouTube distributed music videos have over one-hundred-million-plus views. As Chris Muniz argues, the more performances by Grupo Exterminador, Explosion Norteña, or Movimiento Alterado include details of torture and murder, the more satisfied the audiences are. Muniz suggests that these *narcocorridos* that perpetuate "frontier fantasies" function like a coping mechanism for those living in constant fear. For Muniz, the community externalizes this fear through the music (pp. 66–67). (See also Josh Kun's "Minstrels in the Court of the Kingpin.")

This is not without cost to the balladeers. These singers might profit financially (concerts, albums, professional studios, and cartels) but they also live in constant fear. It is commonly known that if their lyrics fail to please a respective *narco* kingpin, they risk being attacked and murdered. For instance, in "*Narco Cultura*" Ryan Rashotte identifies how the

32-year-old *narco* balladeer for the Sinaloa cartel, Chalino Sánchez, was murdered for precisely this reason.

In addition to clothes (the *charro*-look and labels like Antrax and El Cartel Clothing and tees with fake bullet holes) and music, there's also a thriving *narco* film industry that lionizes cartel kingpins and life. This includes direct-to-video films, made with relatively small budgets ($20,000 to $50,000) and distributed at flea markets in Mexico and the US. In *Narco Cinema* Ryan Rashotte analyzes the cartel-financed films of director José Luis Urquieta such as *Tres veces mojado* (Three Times a Wetback, 1988) and *La camioneta gris* (The Gray Truck, 1989) that glamorize "a sexy, well-remunerative narco-lifestyle in such a way that may seem attractive to impoverished youth" (p. 22). And, there's the more commercially polished *narco* films and TV series produced by companies such as Netflix with their hugely popular serialized shows: *El Chapo, Reina del Sur*, and *Narcos*. Notably, standing in sharp contrast to *narcopeliculas* that heroize *narco* violence, there is Shaul Schwarz's *Narco Cultura* (2013). Schwarz shows the reality of *narcoculture* along the El Paso/Juárez border: the violence of the cartels hunting down and murdering innocent victims stands in sharp contrast with the pop cultural phenomenon that continues to heroize *narcos* as romantic outlaws; one stunning scene shows a music-going audience who has committed all the lines of a *narco* ballad to memory.

We can add literature to the list of cultural phenomena that make up *Narco Cultura*. *Narco* biographies such as *Joaquin "El Chapo" Guzman, Amando a Pablo, odiando a Escobar* (2007), and *La bella y el narco* (2011), along with *narco* journalism, *narconovelas*, and oral storytelling practices within the community also distill and reconstruct the *narco* life—uncritically and critically. The *narco* stories often follow formulaic plotlines that included beginnings (initiation), middles (the confessions, and ends/horrors). While some authors choose to turn the *narco* life into a consumable, glamorous narrative, usually in the form of the fairytale or heroic journey, others choose to critique it. For instance, Amanda L. Matousek analyzes the important creation of a female protagonist in *Perra brava* that "inverts the image of the macho male trafficker" (p. 119). For Matousek, *narconovelas* can provide a space to denounce *narco* violence and potentially inspire readers to think "dynamically about how to solve real-life problems" (p. 136). She concludes of *narconovelas*: "When the newspaper article is too often just a list of statistics, a novel can recreate names and stories and fill in the blanks" (p. 136). In addition to *narco* narratives appearing in literature they have also become a fact of everyday social events such as birthday parties and quinceañeras. For instance, in *Narrating*

Narcos Gabriela Polit Dueñas presents her field research based in Culiacán, Mexico, and Medellín, Colombia where she discovered traditions of storytelling within the community. She remarks on how "people tended to remember not the events but how they were told. In other words, they remember not what they witnessed, but what they read, recognizing themselves in the words of others" (p. 5). She identifies the locally created *narco* storytelling (including local gossip) grown from communities directly affected by the presence of cartels as a "collective process of recognition and identification" (p. 5) with the codes, social and economic networks, language, memories, and shared physical space with the *narcos* (p. 10). In *When I Wear My Alligator Boots* Shaylih Muehlmann identifies the mothers, wives, and daughters and their active roles within the *narco* economy to counter the media's perpetuation of a myth that this is a strictly male-dominated murderous phenomenon.

In closing, it is worth noting two additional cultural phenomena that have grown in and around the *narco* way of life. One is the preservation and exhibition of all things *narco* in the form of museums. For instance, in Mexico City there is now the Museum of Drugs (Museo de Enervantes) that includes pictures, dioramas, drug paraphernalia, and weapons, including gold-plated guns. And, with murder becoming a near everyday occurrence, there's been an upsurge in worshipping Santa Muerte, both by civilians and *narco* traffickers; the latter pray to Santa Muerte to ensure safe passage of drugs and as self-protection.

Latinx Studies scholars have sought to understand better the inter-relationship between the violence of the *narco* economy alongside the rise of *narco* cultural phenomena that sentimentalizes and heroizes its violence, exploitation, and oppression of regular, common people. Indeed, the real heroes of this are the daughters, sisters, mothers, cousins, and friends who struggle to survive from day to day in an Americas increasingly controlled by the cartel's rule of law.

Works Cited

Bergman, Ted L. L. "*Jácaras* and *Narcocorridos* in Context: What Early Modern Spain Can Tell Us about Today's Narco-culture." *Romance Notes*, vol. 55, no. 2, 2015, pp. 241–252.

Campbell, Howard. "Drug Trafficking Stories: Everyday Forms of Narco-folklore on the U.S.–Mexico Border." *International Journal of Drug Policy*, vol. 16, 2005, pp. 326–333.

Diaz, Tom, and Chris Swecker. *No Boundaries: Transnational Latino Gangs and American Law Enforcement.* Ann Arbor, MI: University of Michigan Press, 2009.

Dueñas, Gabriela Polit. *Narrating Narcos: Culiacán and Medellín*. Pittsburgh, PA: University of Pittsburgh Press, 2013.

Kun, Josh. "Minstrels in the Court of the Kingpin." *New York Times*, March 5, 2010. www.nytimes.com/2010/03/07/arts/music/07narcocorrido.html

Marez, Curtis. *Drug Wars: The Political Economy of Narcotics*. Minneapolis, MN: University of Minnesota Press, 2004.

Matousek, Amanda L. "Shades of the Borderland Narconovela from Pastel to Sanguine: Orfa Alarcón's Perra brava as Anti-Novela." *Frontiers: A Journal of Women Studies*, vol. 35, no. 2, 2014, pp. 118–142.

McSweeney, Kendra, Nazih Richani, Zoe Pearson, Jennifer Devine, and David J. Wrathall. "Why Do Narcos Invest in Rural Land?" *Journal of Latin American Geography*, vol. 16, no. 2, 2017, pp. 3–29.

Muehlmann, Shaylih. *When I Wear My Alligator Boots*. Berkeley, CA: University of California Press, 2013.

Muniz, Chris. "Narcocorridos and the Nostalgia of Violence: Postmodern Resistance en la Frontera." *Western American Literature*, vol. 48, no. 1 & 2, 2013, pp. 56–69.

Mendoza Natalia Rockwell. "Boots, Belt Buckles, Sombreros: Narco Culture in the Altar Desert." *NACLA Report on the Americas*, vol. 44, 2011, pp. 27–30.

Rashotte, Ryan. "Narco Cultura." In *The Routledge Companion to Latino/a Pop Culture*, edited by Frederick Luis Aldama. New York: Routledge, 2016, pp. 394–411.

Slack, Jeremy, and Howard Campbell. "On Narco-coyotaje: Illicit Regimes and Their Impacts on the US–Mexico Border." *Antipode*, vol. 48, no. 5, 2016, pp. 1380–1399.

PERFORMANCE

Latinx Studies scholars have theorized performance in two main ways: the study of the theatre, dance, music, spoken word, and performance arts as well as rituals and festivities; and, the study of the performance of intersectional (gender, race, ethnicity, class, sexuality) identities. In both cases, Latinx Studies scholars have been largely interested in how Latinx performance resists, challenges, and transforms otherwise restrictive material and ideological spaces.

The decades of the 1960s through the 1970s marks a **renaissance** in Latinx arts and activism. The establishing of the Latinx INTAR Theatre in New York and the galvanizing work of artists and activists with the *teatro campesino* in California, among others, proved to be important, long-lasting spaces for affirming Latinx identity and experience through performance. Along with the growth of resistant performance art spaces came the formulation of a more flexible understanding of Latinx identity. As Ramón H. Rivera-Servera sums up of the Latinx Studies formulation of the concept of performance: it "unsettles the assumed certainty of cultural and social coordinates by highlighting them as effects of performative enactment and thus dependent on continuous repetition to sustain their force and apparent constancy" ("Performance" p. 155). This was especially important within the Latina and Third World feminist creative and activist work of Cherríe Moraga and Gloria Anzaldúa, among others. As the Latinx performing arts developed so too did the critical understanding of a Latinx identity as performing a more complex and fully realized intersectional identity.

We see this focus on the performing arts *and* performing intersectional identities (without using this more contemporary concept) in the early work of Américo Paredes, Jovita González, José E. Limón, Richard Flores, Tey Diana Rebolledo, and Maria Herrera-Sobek, along with creator-scholars such as Norma Cantú. These scholars sought to provide a creative and theoretical formulation to Latinx identity as "iterative" and not a "stable truth," as Ramón H. Rivera-Servera states ("Performance" p. 152).

This impulse to analyze performance as cultural phenomena *and* as identity has grown into the significant theoretical contributions of Latinx scholars such as Alicia Arrizón, José Esteban Muñoz, Juana María Rodríguez, Larry La Fountain-Stokes, and Ricardo Ortiz, among others. Not only was this an important correction to a mainstream seeking to essentialize Latinx identities, but it proved a cornerstone to the interrogation of the straight-male dominated Chicano nationalism of the 1970s. Indeed, as Alicia Arrizón identifies, this radically altered the *el movimiento*'s impulse and direction, leading to an expansion and liberation inclusive of the "Chicana-mestiza body" and complex understandings of *mestizaje* and "the intercultural body" ("Mythical Performativity" p. 24). By using the concept of performativity, Arrizón seeks to "expose the ways in which Aztlán secures the formation of identity in the gap between the real and the representational" (p. 24). The Chicano performances together with the Latinx activist theatre on the East Coast exposed the heterosexual and patriarchal impulse to the various movements: Chicano, Cuban, Nuyorican especially. Latina theatre and performance artists across the nation brought a Latina feminist, lesbian, and Third World women's struggle worldview to the shaping of activist art that sought to critique and resist restrictive straight, Anglo, and Latinx cultural mores.

While Luis Valdez used the **carpa** to enact a theatre of resistance, it wasn't till self-identified queer Latinx playwrights and performance artists such as Cherríe Moraga and Luis Alfaro created performances that we began to see a more complex creative activism. Moraga and Alfaro, among others, used their performances to: (a) destabilize mainstream identity norms and combat racism; and (b) shake up and complicate restrictive gender, sexuality, and ethnoracial roles imposed within the Latinx kin and community networks. Moraga and Alfaro's affirming of their queer mestizaje functioned as a **decolonial** act of resistance that sought to also transform material and ideologically restrictive mainstream and Latinx spaces.

Performance as a decolonial act becomes the central theoretical thread for Latinx Studies scholars seeking to identify intercultural and transactional identities and experiences. For instance, in Arturo Aldama et al.'s *Performing the US Latina and Latino Borderlands*, the concept of a "decolonizing performatics" (p. 1) is used to uncover how US Latinx *testimonio*, theatre, ceremony, ritual, storytelling, music, dance, improvisation, play, spoken-word, dance, and other embodied enactments create a politically progressive performative borderland space. This decolonizing performatics identifies how the different intersectional identities (gender, sexuality, race, class, ethnicity) function in Latinx performances to "exceed all oppressive and criminalizing social orders" (p. 19). And, in an analysis of Chicana Monica Palacios' *Amor y Revolución*, Marivel Danielson analyzes how she decolonizes normative sexualities and language practices by performing the "written word in motion" (*Homecoming Queers* 191).

Here, too, we have Latinx Studies scholars who seek to identify how the Latinx performance arts can be taught in classrooms. For instance, William Orchard not only teaches students the history of Latinx theatre production and the nuts and bolts concepts for analyzing it, but also enlists "the creative energies of students" by having them imagine how any given play might be staged. His approach is interactive and collective. By having the students examine the choices made in the realizing of a play Orchard shows us how students learn first hand how different technical devices can and do have dramatic consequences in the realization of a play from print to stage production. ("Theater in the Latino/a Literature Classroom"). Paloma Martínez-Cruz articulates an approach to teaching the Latinx performance art La Pocha Nostra. Using as her primary texts the videos of live performances along with their in-print performances, she creates a series of performance-based assignments for her students. This allows Martínez-Cruz to grow through her students' critical insights into how Latinx performance art can be a space for interrogating restrictive identity categories. (See Martínez-Cruz's "Teaching Americas-based Performance Studies through La Pocha Nostra Guillermo.") And, we see something similar with Marivel Danielson's pedagogy of Latinx performance arts. In "Teaching US Latino/a Performance" Danielson discusses how she creates a learning environment where concepts learned (orchestrations of gesture, posture, gait, spinal alignment, and gaze) enable students to reflect on the creating of their own activist performance pieces.

Not only have Latinx Studies scholars excavated performance arts grown from West Coast and Southwest soils (and largely informed by Mexican and Central American ancestral heritages), but also those grown from Eastern US soils (largely informed by Puerto Rican, Cuban, and Dominican ancestral heritages). During this same period of the 1980s, several significant Cuban Americans and Nuyoricans arrived on the scene, identifying feminist dramaturges. They include María Irene Fornés, Ana María Simo (1943–), Caridad Svich, and Dolores Prida (1943–). In each we see different techniques and styles used to convey issues of bilinguality, sexual identity, and their respective forms of Latinidad.

Latinx Studies scholars have attended to this performance work grown on Eastern US soils. In the work of José Esteban Muñoz we learn how Latinx LGBTQ performances by Carmelita Tropicana and Marga Gomez, among others, *disidentify* (his concept to identify the strategic practice of exaggeratedly recycling mainstream sanctioned techniques, styles, and genres to critique **heteronormative** conventions) to clear room for the expression of a complex Latinx body, desire, and experience. Tropicana's "disidentificatory" performances such as vogue-ing Ricky Ricardo-style or reenacting mainstream media stereotypes forces traditionally restrictive images and genres to cross over into a queer performance space. And, when Vaginal Creme Davis performs a kind of terrorist drag, Davis's **disidentification** strategy demands that a queer Latinx phobic audience imagine themselves in radically different ways. (See Muñoz's *Disidentifications: Queers of Color and the Performance of Politics*.) And, Larry La Fountain-Stokes identifies the Jorge Merced performances as "transloca" because they put under the limelight a lived, diasporic Latinx transvestism that *troubles* mainstream conceptions of how one can be nationally, ethnoracially, and sexually in the world. (See La Fountain-Stokes's "Trans/Bolero/Drag/Migration.") And, in *Queer Ricans* La Fountain-Stokes analyzes the performance art of Bronx-based creators, Arthur Aviles and Elizabeth Marrero. Here he demonstrates how "sexuality has been a constitutive element in shaping Puerto Rican migration principally (but not exclusively) to the United States, and how different artists have represented or publicly articulated this issue" (p. xii). These and other scholars seek to shed light on how queer Latinx performance artists foreground non-normative sexual identities that intersect importantly with diasporic migratory experiences.

Latinx Studies scholars have turned their analytical gaze to Latinx dance as also clearing a space of everyday affirmation of intersectional identities and resistance to normative ideologies and practices. For instance, in *Performing Queer Latinidad* Ramón Rivera-Servera identifies generally how the queer body is at once constrained by urban, heteronormative actions and ideologies (the queer Latinx taunted and assaulted outside the local bodega) and whose strategically choreographed body can become a site of resistance. He

> proposes a model that privileges the body and its actions and conduits of knowledge about the world. It is in the acts of performance that I situate both theory and the potential interventions queer latinidad can make in the public sphere at large.
>
> (p. 18)

Queer dance club spaces become, for Rivera-Servera, spaces to "re-hearse strategies of survival and interconnected-ness that might enable the emergence of queer pan-Latina/o communities beyond it" (p. 150).

Latinx Studies scholars have analyzed the work of Luis Alfaro, Migdalia Cruz, Nilo Cruz, Coco Fusco and Nao Bustamante, Marga Gomez, Ricardo Bracho, Naomi Iizuka, Oliver Mayer, Pedro Monge-Rafuls, Cherríe Moraga, Monica Palacios, Caridad Svich, and Alina Troyano, among many others, as performances that decolonize minds, desires, and bodies; that reverse the colonial/colonizing heterosexual gaze that seeks to consume and contain the Latinx pleasurable, pleasuring body.

In addition to theatre and performance art, Latinx Studies scholars have formulated spoken word poetry as an important resistant performative space. In the introduction to his book, *Formal Matters*, Aldama talks about some of today's poets whose poetic lines rely on public performance—or as recorded for YouTube—in order to convey the full complexity of their message; when one reads silently and in isolation, for instance *Hi-Density Politics, Public Domain,* or *Collapsible Poetics Theater for Sustainable Aircraft* one misses a great deal of the phatic energy and charge that can potentially lead to political action (2009). In addition to the work done to analyze Nuyorican spoken word poets in *In Visible Movement*, Urayoán Noel also articulates a method for teaching this poetry. In "Teaching U.S. Latino/a poetry in the age of social media" Noel formulates a "performalist pedagogy" that can be used to teach students not only a grammar for close-reading poetry (figures of speech, sound, and tone) but also an understanding of how meaning is generated by performance. For Noel, the formal matters that give shape to any given poem (or corrido) and its performance form an inseparable unit of meaning.

Latinx Studies scholars have used the concept of the performative when analyzing other cultural phenomena such as music, film, and TV. For instance, scholars such as María Elena Cepeda, Deborah Parédez, and Deborah Pacini Hernandez analyze how Latinx popular music such as **merengue, bachata**, and **reggaeton** perform a resistant Latinidad. (See respectively *Musical ImagiNation, Selenidad,* and *OYE COMO VA!*). They variously show how Latinx musicscapes are not only transcultural and syncretic but also offer performance spaces that rupture mainstream and national impulses to flatten out and purify musical expression—and with this Latinx identities. And scholars such as Isabel Molina-Guzman, Camilla Fojas, Charles Ramírez Berg, Chon Noriega, Ana Lopez, and Mary Beltrán, among others, have set their sights on how Latinx film and TV stars such as Jennifer Lopez, America Ferrera, Salma Hayek, Jessica Alba, among others *perform* (body movement, language, and phenotype) a Latinidad that pushes against mainstream media's stereotypes that package for the consumption of Latinas as exotic: dangerous *and* desirable. To different degrees, Latina media figures perform identities in order to wake audiences to a complex, non-consumable Latinx identity. As Molina-Guzman sums up, Latinas in the media can and do perform in ways that disrupt "particular ways of understanding the intersections of gender, sexuality, ethnicity, race, and class" (p. 8).

In Latinx Studies scholarship, performance is at once that which is created by Latinxs to be presented in front of audiences and at the same time a conceptual term used to identify how Latinx creators disrupt and resist normative conventions of existing.

Works Cited

Aldama, Frederick Luis. *Formal Matters in Contemporary Latino Poetry*. New York: Palgrave Macmillan, 2013.

Aldama, Arturo, Chela Sandoval, and Peter J. García, eds. *Performing the US Latina and Latino Borderlands*. Bloomington, IN: Indiana University Press, 2012.

Arrizón, Alicia. "Mythical Performativity: Relocating Aztlán in Chicana Feminist Cultural Productions." *Theatre Journal*, vol. 52, no. 1, 2000, pp. 23–49.

Danielson, Marivel. *Homecoming Queers: Desire and Difference in Chicana Latina Cultural Production*. Brunswick, NJ: Rutgers University Press, 2009.

Cepeda, Elena María. *Musical ImagiNation: US-Colombian Identity and the Latin Music Boom*. New York: New York University Press, 2010.

Danielson, Marivel. "Teaching US Latino/a Performance." *Latino/a Literature in the Classroom: Twenty-First-Century Approaches to Teaching*, edited by Frederick Luis Aldama. New York and London: Routledge, 2015, pp. 150–158.

La Fountain-Stokes, Lawrence. "Trans/Bolero/Drag/Migration: Music, Cultural Translation, and Diasporic Puerto Rican Theatricalities." *WSQ: Women's Studies Quarterly*, vol. 36, no. 3 & 4, 2008, pp. 190–209.

———. *Queer Ricans: Cultures and Sexualities in the Diaspora*. Minneapolis, MN: University of Minnesota Press, 2009.

Martínez-Cruz, Paloma. "Teaching Americas-based Performance Studies through La Pocha Nostra Guillermo." *Latino/a Literature in the Classroom: Twenty-First-Century Approaches to Teaching*, edited by Frederick Luis Aldama. New York and London: Routledge, 2015, pp. 159–168.

Molina-Guzmán, Isabel. *Dangerous Curves: Latina Bodies in the Media*. New York: New York University Press, 2010.

Noel, Urayoán. "Teaching U.S. Latino/a Poetry in the Age of Social Media." *Latino/a Literature in the Classroom: Twenty-First-Century Approaches to Teaching*, edited by Frederick Luis Aldama. New York and London: Routledge, 2015, pp. 131–140.

Orchard, William. "Theater in the Latino/a Literature Classroom." *Latino/a Literature in the Classroom: Twenty-First-Century Approaches to Teaching*, edited by Frederick Luis Aldama. New York and London: Routledge, 2015, pp. 141–149.

Pacini Hernandez, Deborah. *OYE COMO VA! Hybridity and Identity in Latino Popular Music*. Philadelphia, PA: Temple University Press, 2010.

Parédez, Deborah. *Selenidad: Selena, Latinos, and the Performance of Memory*. Durham, NC: Duke University Press, 2009.

Rivera-Servera, Ramón H. *Performing Queer Latinidad: Dance, Sexuality, Politics*. Ann Arbor, MI: University of Michigan Press, 2012.

———. "Performance." In *Keywords in Latina/o Studies*, edited by Deborah R. Vargas, Lawrence La Fountain-Stokes, Nancy Raquel Mirabal. New York: New York University Press, 2017, pp. 152–155.

POLITICS

As a demographic, Latinxs have only recently begun to have a significant influence on the political landscape of the United States. Cristina Beltrán notes how, "Latinos in the United States have long been characterized as subjects on the cusp of political power and influence" (p. 3). The reality, however, is much different. For much of their history within the US, the number of Latinx voting groups have trailed other minority groups, especially those of African American voters. Much of this has to do with the history of disenfranchising minority voters with poll taxes and literacy tests, and the outright threat of law enforcement at polling locations. In addition, voter apathy among Latinxs has traditionally been high, perhaps because Latinxs have not seen themselves reflected in either the politicians or the issues deemed important by the politicians running or in office. As a result, Latinxs were often regarded as an inconsequential voting block except at very local levels. In the twenty-first century, the seeming unimportance of Latinx voters has begun to dissipate, especially since Latinxs now form the majority minority in the United States. For Conservatives and right-wing political groups, the advent of the Latinx voting block is worrisome, as a majority of Latinxs identify with politicians and policies of the left wing of the US political spectrum. And yet, as Rodolfo Esposito and David L. Leal note, "This is an exciting time to study Latino politics" (p. 4), thanks to the surging demographic and growing interest in political issues. What makes this such a vexed issue is often something as basic as what a "Latinx" is, as Lisa Garcia Bedolla notes (pp. 2–4). Because identity is often at the heart of politics, this issue is one that requires careful consideration.

The Voting Rights Act of 1965 finally made the process of voting more accessible to Latinxs, and it is here that the slow but increased engagement in the US political process began for Latinxs. However, due to issues of language accessibility (many Latinxs spoke only Spanish and had to navigate an English-only process), Latinxs were not really able to significantly participate in the political process as a voting demographic until nearly a decade later, thanks to the efforts of the Mexican American Legal Defense Fund (MALDEF), who challenged the burdens and obstacles Latinxs, and pertinent to this topic, Latinx voters, faced. Formed in 1968, MALDEF and the League of United Latin American Citizens (LULAC), championed the push for civil rights for Latinxs. With the aid of the NAACP Legal Defense Fund, MALDEF recognized a need for Latinxs within the legal system. If the laws were to be changed for the common good of Latinxs in the US, Latinxs themselves would have to work toward becoming attorneys and judges. Incidentally, it is no small detail that a vast majority of politicians in the United States receive much of their knowledge and experience of the political system as lawyers first. Part of the push for more Latinx attorneys was the goal of having Latinxs as major players in the political system. In many ways, this endeavor has succeeded.

MALDEF also made history in filing suit in a case that was ultimately taken up by the Supreme Court, in a brief that was argued entirely by a group of Latinx lawyers. Never before had that happened in the United States. Over a series of cases in the late 1960s and the 1970s, MALDEF was instrumental in raising attention to the issues that disenfranchised Latinxs in the US, but also in garnering some noteworthy victories in the US Supreme Court. In 1975, the Voting Rights Act was expanded to include allowances for language issues, and this suddenly opened up voting opportunities for Spanish-speaking Latinxs. The implications of this are staggering. Despite Latinxs being a part of the United States for centuries, Latinxs as a voting block has only really existed for less than three generations, or around forty years. This makes Latinxs, in some sense, a young voting group.

When compared to young voters in general, who tend to turn out in lower numbers relative to other age groups, suddenly the lower voter participation by Latinxs makes some sense. Unlike African Americans, who have established efficient and effective community organizing efforts and have contested the historic unfairness of the US voting and political process, Latinxs have only had a scant few decades to develop similar political and legal efforts. Though the Latinx demographic is growing significantly in the US, the percent of Latinxs who participate in voting and other aspects of the political system is not growing at the same rate.

This fact makes the Latinx voting demographic, as a powerful force in recent elections, as somewhat of a myth. Again, as with the youngest group of voters in the United States, the trend is that Latinxs are not as reliable when it comes to voting. If Latinxs voted in percentages equivalent to, say, older voters or white voters, it would clearly alter the political landscape. And, since a majority of Latinx voters tend to vote Democrat, an increased turnout of Latinx voters signals doom for Conservatives in high Latinx population states such as Arizona and Texas. Indeed, Texas and its robust Latinx population is a holy grail of sorts for Democrats. With its second-highest number of electoral votes (38), turning Texas "blue" would make the election of another Republican president a near impossibility. In a sense, then, Latinxs are at once an invisible voting group, but their *potential* is extraordinarily enticing or nerve-wracking for all politicians. Yet there seems to be the idea that Latinxs as a substantive and irresistible political force, one that will come to fruition, is inevitable and only a matter of time.

As Mexican Americans comprise the greatest percentage of all Latinxs in the United States at over 70%, it is notable that a majority of Mexican Americans identify as Democrat in their politics. Attention and engagement during the Civil Rights movement from President John F. Kennedy, his brother Robert F. Kennedy, and later, President Lyndon B. Johnson created a lasting sense of loyalty to the Democrats. These politicians advocated for and actively sought the support of Latinxs, and specifically Mexican Americans in Texas and California. After the assassinations of both Kennedy brothers as well as the

Rev. Dr. Martin Luther King Jr., these political leaders achieved martyr status for many Latinxs who saw them literally killed while advocating for the rights of the disenfranchised and dispossessed.

While MALDEF and LULAC were fighting battles based out of their headquarters in Texas, other Latinx leaders and political organizations were fighting in California. The political battles for Latinxs were being waged on three fronts. The Latinx farmworkers who worked in pitiless conditions often had no recourse to better treatment and higher wages. The Latinx who ultimately became the face for Latinx labor rights was César Chávez. Chávez grew up as a farm laborer, and he was intimately familiar with the harsh conditions and treatment that were the common practices at the time. As an adult, Chávez would go on to organize and motivate Latinxs not just in California but all over the United States.

Chávez's greatest contribution was arguably his founding, along with Dolores Huerta, the National Farm Workers Association (NFWA) in 1962. This organization would later come to be known by a name more familiar to posterity, the United Farm Workers (UFA), and it would forever change the agricultural and labor laws of California and the United States, thanks in particular to one issue: a work stoppage that came to be known as the Delano grape strike in 1965. The strike was initiated by grape pickers, who were predominately Filipino American, who protested the low wages they received for such grueling work. Chávez and the NFWA came to the defense of the workers and led a month-long strike, raising it from a local or state level issue to an issue of national concern. Not only did the workers strike, there was a call for a national boycott of grapes. The strike continued for years, and Robert Kennedy publicly aligned himself with the strikers and Latinx farmworkers.

Notably, this initial and sustained strike set off a chain of similar farmworker protests across the United States. Chávez and Huerta also became involved in other political issues concerning Latinxs, including immigration, the Bracero program, and they became community organizers for politicians who aligned with Latinx issues. These politicians were almost always Democrats, and Chávez and Huerta became recognizable icons for Latinx civil rights whose efforts and reputation still resonate into the twenty-first century.

Despite the dominance of Democrats among Latinxs, the other side of the political spectrum in the United States has a significant group of Latinxs. Cuban Americans and Salvadoran Americans traditionally identify as more politically conservative, and nearly every Latinx who has been voted into elected office as a Conservative has come from Cuban ancestry (De La Torre). While Cubans comprise about one-third of all Latinxs in the US, they are a staunch and reliable voting block for Republican candidates. Just as Mexican Americans viewed John F. Kennedy with reverence and respect, Cuban Americans knew Kennedy best from the disastrous Bay of Pigs invasion. This unease with Kennedy also fell upon his party, the Democrats, and a kind of resentment made an indelible mark on the political views of all Cuban Americans who remembered or were affected (directly or indirectly) with the failed invasion.

Subsequent to and in contrast with President Kennedy, Cuban Americans held President Ronald Reagan in high esteem, mostly because of his perceived strong stances against Communist leaders. Many Cuban Americans have continued to maintain a strong allegiance to Republican policies and politicians. And though Cuban Americans appear as a significant percentage of the demographic in many states, it is Florida where their vote is most impactful. Florida, along with Ohio and a handful of other states, often determine the Presidential election because the general voting demographic is very evenly split. In recent elections, Cuban Americans have come close to splitting their vote, and they are not as reliably Conservative as they were in decades past.

Other Latinx demographics are not as solidly determined in their politics. Regionalism here may be as influential to their vote as is their Latinx heritage. In other words, a Mexican American living in Oklahoma may be more likely to vote Republican than a Cuban American in New Jersey is to vote Democrat. As such, it is important to remember that Latinx heritage is not voting destiny. Though there are certainly discernible trends for how Latinx subgroups vote, no single Latinx voter is bound to vote in a certain way. Couple that with the still unpredictable nature of Latinx voter turnout, and one can see why the Latinx voting demographic is highly desired.

In terms of politicians, there is a long but lean history of Latinxs in elected office at the national level. The first Latinx to serve in the US Senate was Octaviano Larrazolo of New Mexico, after he had served as governor of the state. Elected to the US Senate in 1928, he marks the first in a line of Latinxs in national politics. More recent Senators include Mel Martinez (Florida), Ken Salazar (Colorado), Bob Melendez (New Jersey), Marco Rubio (Florida), Ted Cruz (Texas), and Catherine Cortez Masto (Nevada). Latinxs have also helped shape the US House of Representatives. Such Congressmen and Congresswomen include Henry B. González (Texas), Manuel Lujan (New Mexico), Bill Richardson (New Mexico), Luis Gutiérrez (Illinois), Nydia Velázquez (New York), Rubén Hinojosa

(Texas), Raúl Grijalva (Arizona), Linda Sánchez (California), Joaquín Castro (Texas), Norma Torres (California), and many more.

Though there has still never been a Latinx elected US President or Vice President, this entry would be remiss without mention of the first person of Latinx heritage to become a US Supreme Court Justice, and being the first Latina to hold such a position. Nominated by President Barack Obama in May 2009, Sonia Sotomayor was confirmed later that year. Though her role of Supreme Court Justice is not overtly political, she is a member of one of the three branches of the US government, and her votes affect court decisions on matters of US legal policy, which are clearly of a political nature. During her nomination hearing, comments that she had once made concerning her identity as a "wise Latina" and how it might provide certain insights that non-Latinas might not have, was used against her in right-wing media and among Conservative politicians and pundits, calling it a racist remark. The backlash did not hinder her hearings much, and she was confirmed by an overwhelming majority.

Latinxs are relatively new to the process of voting and the ebbs and flows of the political landscape of the United States. John A. Garcia argues that the future of Latinx politics is connected "to community, shared interests, culture and organizations, and identity construction" (p. 12). As they continue to increase in size as a demographic, their power and potential may also swell as to no longer be ignorable (Barreto and Segura). Voters who identify as Latinx are not necessarily predictable in their choices for political office and laws, which makes it difficult for those who try to ascertain how they may best be courted. Nation of origin, historical events, changes to the laws, and activism have all molded the Latinx demographic as an idiosyncratic and vital voting group in the United States. They will continue to be impactful in the politics of the United States for the foreseeable future.

Works Cited

Barreto, Matt A., and Gary M. Segura. *Latino America: How America's most Dynamic Population Is Poised to Transform the Politics of the Nation.* New York: Public Affairs, 2014.

Beltrán, Cristina. *The Trouble with Unity: Latino Politics and the Creation of Identity.* Oxford: Oxford University Press, 2010.

De La Torre, Miguel A. *La Lucha for Cuba: Religion and Politics on the Streets of Miami.* Berkeley: University of California Press, 2003.

Esposito, Rodolfo, David L. Leal, and Kenneth J. Meier. *Latino Politics: Identity, Mobilization, and Representation.* Charlottesville, VA: University of Virginia Press, 2008.

Garcia Bedolla, Lisa. *Latino Politics*. Cambridge, UK: Wiley, 2014.
Garcia, John A. *Latino Politics in America: Community, Culture, and Interests*. New York: Rowman & Littlefield, 2017.

POPULAR CULTURE

Latinxs continue to shape and influence popular culture within the United States through a variety of media forms, fashion, music, popular narratives such as television, performance art, social media, dance, and more. According to Michelle Habell-Pallán and Mary Romero, "Images circulated through popular culture are an important part of the contested terrain in the struggle to define the place of Latinos in North America" (p. 2). So, popular culture can be contentious. But as Habell-Pallán and Romero suggest, Latinx pop culture does not exist within a vacuum. Latinx pop cultural production is an inextricable part of US popular culture, and vice versa: "Latina/os appear in all variety of today's pop culture: TV (web and otherwise), film, animation, comic books, video games, art, slam poetry, music, food, sartorial wear, and so much more" (*The Routledge Companion* 1). More and more, the two are becoming more integrated as the twenty-first century progresses. Indeed, we may think of popular culture as a sensorial process of cumulative and contemporaneous experience. Pop culture has become a kind of capital that is traded and exchanged within society, and Latinxs have become a larger aspect of this commodification of heritage and tradition. Latinxs, who are a multifaceted and diverse group themselves, affect and influence US popular culture in a variety of ways.

One way of thinking of how Latinx cultural traditions have helped US popular culture into what it is today is to evaluate and ascertain where the traces and evidence of Latinx culture appear within the everyday cultural practices of a majority of Americans. Where do Latinxs and Latinx culture appear in mainstream entertainment, artistic, and other areas of consumerism and consumption? Moreover, how are those artifacts of Latinx culture put into service or appropriation? Are those aspects of Latinx culture in the mainstream created by Latinxs themselves or are they created without their say? Indeed, how are Latinxs represented in all aspects of popular culture within the US. How do Latinxs in popular culture shape and influence not only the United States, but in a global perspective?

These questions necessitate capacious engagements of thought and examination, and they drive a great deal of how we proceed with Ethnic Studies and American Studies programs at the university level. In many ways, these pop cultural manifestations of Latinxs and Latinx culture are more readily consumed than the latest Academy Award-winning film by a Latinx director or a Pulitzer Prize-winning novel by a Latinx author. As such, it is an indication of the power and influence of popular culture on the US imagination writ large. The high visibility of popular culture and its ability to go viral also reminds one of the deleterious nature certain pernicious manifestations of Latinxs in popular culture can be.

In considering how and when Latinxs have appeared in popular culture, one can gain a sense of a starting point, the first few tremors that began the avalanche. Unfortunately, as is mentioned elsewhere in this book, most of the early representations of Latinxs in popular culture relied heavily on base stereotypes and ignorant conceptions of Latinx culture in the US. The figures of the *bandido*, the spicy bombshell, the lazy Mexican, the Latin lover, the dancing dynamo, and others have helped create these mental shortcuts for people who are confronted with what they know about Latinxs in the US. This history has been extensively written about by scholars of Latinx media and culture, especially by William Nericcio, who has notably excavated the value and costs of a character such as Speedy Gonzales from the Warner Brothers line up of Looney Tunes characters in *Tex[t]-mex: Seductive Hallucinations of the "Mexican" in America.*

Suffice it to say that Latinxs have had to constantly resist such limiting representations without their consent or allowed participation for much of the twentieth century. But rather than spend more time talking about those instances here, the rest of this entry will concentrate on those instances in popular culture in which Latinxs have played a significant part.

On the entry for "Music," the musician, television actor, and television producer Desi Arnaz, who starred in *I Love Lucy* alongside his real wife Lucille Ball, is discussed at length, and so he will only be mentioned here. But he is a crucial advent in the evolution of US popular culture with substantive contributions to Latinx culture. His culture, of Cuban origin, the character he portrayed, and his importance as a studio head and producer (he and Ball co-founded Desilu Studios), bestowed upon all Latinxs to come a prime example of the transformative power Latinxs might contribute to the American mainstream. Arnaz was not simply an actor playing a character. He himself was helping to shape the television landscape of the US. And, because television is such a medium of mass consumption, it is one venue where Latinxs have been able to make a noticeable impact on the popular culture of the United States.

Freddie Prinze played the redoubtable Chico Rodriguez in the television show titled *Chico and the Man*. Appearing on television nearly two decades after the premiere of *I Love Lucy*, *Chico and the Man* is notable for being a show whose setting is in a predominately and noticeably Latinx neighborhood in Los Angeles. With a theme song by José Feliciano, *Chico and the Man*, for the first time in mainstream US network television (NBC), presented Latinx culture and, unlike *I Love Lucy*, Mexican American culture, in a sustained and robust way. Though it, too, was a sitcom like the show that featured Arnaz and so seemed to revel in exploring Latinidad via humor, it still took television audiences into narrative spaces they had not seen heretofore. And, noticeably divergent from *I Love Lucy*, *Chico and the Man* had a consistent lineup of Latinx actors that appeared both in minor roles and those of more substance. The show takes the form of an odd couple—the older white man who resists the diversification of his neighborhood, and the good-natured, persistent, and noticeably younger Latinx, who ultimately become friends. The show ran for several seasons but was irrevocably shaken to its foundation when Freddie Prinze, suffering from depression and substance abuse, committed suicide at the age of 22. Though the show never recovered after this tragedy in terms of ratings, it remains a valuable contribution of Latinx heritage in US popular culture.

In the wake of *Chico and the Man*, there were several attempts to incorporate Latinx culture in the television landscape in the 1970s and 1980s, many of which did not last long enough to make a lasting impression. A show that had much in common with *Chico and the Man* but was arguably much more successful was *Sanford and Son*. While the show focused more on African American culture, there was a recurring Latinx character by the name of Julio Fuentes (Gregory Sierra), who moves in next to Sanford and becomes a recurring opportunity for Fred Sanford (Redd Foxx) to quip and insult Julio's Puerto Rican heritage.

Other less than successful shows focused on Latinx culture premiered and were cancelled almost before anyone took notice. *¿Que Pasa, USA?* was the first bilingual sitcom, and it ran on PBS for four seasons. It concerned the culture class experienced by a family of Cuban American heritage and the difficulties in navigating Cuban and "American" ways of being and thinking. ABC tried their hands at featuring Latinxs in sitcoms such as *Condo*, which aired only thirteen episodes in 1983, and a year later ABC tried again, this time with stand-up comedian Paul

Rodriguez as the star of a show called *a.k.a. Pablo*. The show did even worse despite the efforts of Rodriguez, Hector Elizondo, and Mario Lopez, lasting only six episodes. The failure of these shows reveals, in part, the unwillingness of audiences to watch a primetime sitcom that focused on Latinx characters, as well as a heavy reliance on stereotypes and insults as much of the source of its humor.

Televisual exposure of Latinxs tends to come, by and large, in the form of the sitcom. This was the case in the 1970s and 1980s, and this trend continues well into the twenty-first century. *Saved by the Bell*, *The George Lopez Show*, *That 70s Show*, *Ugly Betty*, *Jane the Virgin*, and *Modern Family* all showcase fully realized Latinx characters, even if it is always in the service of comedy. By contrast, when we examine similarly robust Latinx characters in television drama, we tend not to see as many. Erik Estrada became a '70s icon in *CHiPs*, while the next decade saw Edward James Olmos in *Miami Vice*, Rene Enriquez in *Hill Street Blues*, and Jimmy Smits in *L.A. Law*, both hit shows in the 1980s. Smits in particular has featured prominently in notable dramatic roles in television on such shows as *NYPD Blue*, *The West Wing*, and *Sons of Anarchy*, to list just a few. Olmos, who has appeared in many films, returned to television to helm the battleship *Galactica* as William Adama in the reboot of *Battlestar Galactica*. While there still appear many stereotypical Latinx characters in recent shows—typically legal or police dramas like *Blue Bloods* and *NCIS: New Orleans*, Latinxs are appearing as more complexly created characters.

In film, Latinxs have also begun to make inroads in an industry that has, for most of its history, either marginalized or stereotyped them. Some of this is addressed in the entry "Body" in this volume. Here it is worth mentioning that Cheech Marin, Edward James Olmos, Luis Valdez, Gregory Nava, Salma Hayek, and Robert Rodriguez have been some of the major arbiters of Latinx representation on the silver screen. Films such as *Born in East LA*, *American Me*, *La Bamba*, *Frida*, *El Mariachi*, and *Desperado* have been invaluable in disseminating Latinx cultural representation in Hollywood. Significant here is these film-makers' level of control and power in creating their films. All of these films were made in the years since 1987, when *Born in East LA* was released. This means that Latinxs have actually begun to be an unavoidable presence in Hollywood for only a little more than 30 years. This nascent film tradition by Latinxs mirrors how Latinxs in general have only appeared as an inexorable part of US popular culture, as authentic and deliberate representations, within the last few generations.

Comic books, as a medium of popular culture, have been a longtime purveyor and shaper of cultural understandings of the United States. As with many other forms, Latinxs have appeared as little more than back-ground characters and plot devices in comics made by comics artists and writers who not only identify as Latinx, but also take no deep interest in Latinx culture—interest enough to create substantive representations of them in their worlds (Aldama and González). Superhero comics and their massive avatars Marvel Comics and DC Comics, seemed to have beings of every shade of color other than brown. For a longer tradition of Latinxs in comics, one has to look to the Latinx independent comic book authors and artists who have been creating these stories for decades. The most prominent of these artists are known as Los Bros Hernandez: comprised of brothers Mario, Gilbert, and Jaime. The Latinx Comics Expo has helped nurture and gain exposure for many of these author/artists, including J Gonzo, Jules Rivera, Rhode Montijo, Javier Hernandez, Liz Mayorga, Lalo Alcaraz, Raul the Third, and many others. Not only have these independent artists begun to gain a wider audience, the major comics publishers have tried, through fits and starts, to create Latinx comic book characters, with mixed results.

Perhaps the most notable splash made by Latinxs in popular culture is the phenomenon of the musical *Hamilton*. With lyrics and music written by Lin-Manuel Miranda, *Hamilton* has been without argument the greatest and most successful Broadway show since it opened. Despite Miranda's success with *In the Heights*, his previous Broadway musical set in the mostly Latinx neighborhood in Washington Heights, *Hamilton* is an unqualified cultural phenomenon. This musical is what happens when Latinx culture shapes the broader US popular culture *par excellence*. It is the telling of Alexander Hamilton's biography, seemingly as white as white culture can get. Stories of the nation's Founding Fathers, despite their emphasis on independence from Britain, are quite Eurocentric. Only through efforts of historians and biographers to include the likes of Sally Hemings and William "Billy" Lee are we reminded that there were people of color who mattered.

Miranda's talents took the all-white cast of Founding Fathers, as posterity has rightly cast them, and featured actors of color in the roles of Jefferson, Hamilton, Burr, Madison, and Washington, as well as all of the cast except for King George III of England. Not only that, Miranda incorporated the rhythms and rhyming styles of hip-hop. Despite what seem to be obvious incongruities with his idea, audiences have been overwhelmed by the artistry and craft of *Hamilton*. It is arguably the greatest cultural phenomenon by a Latinx in the twenty-first century—based on how its influence has reached people who care little for Broadway musicals or stories featuring people of color. As a result,

Miranda's star continues to rise, and he must surely be one of the grand artistic icons of Latinx culture in the twenty-first century (*Hamilton: The Revolution*).

Popular culture is seemingly everywhere—from music to television to film to Broadway to comic books, as Frederick Luis Aldama tells us (*Latinx Superheroes*). Though it cannot all be referenced or mentioned in this brief entry, what should be emphasized is the lack of a substantive history in shaping US popular culture by Latinxs—due to lack of access or opportunity—and how Latinx cultural representation is very recent in the greater scope of US popular culture, relatively speaking. But as the twentieth century closed and the twenty-first century opened, we can now see the waxing influence of Latinx culture on our national understanding of who we are and how we are represented. The more Latinxs appear as substantive, vital parts of how American popular culture is created and represented, which makes sense thanks to an ever-growing demographic of Latinxs, the less the United States will be able to ignore them.

Works Cited

Aldama, Frederick L. *The Routledge Companion to Latina/o Popular Culture*. New York and London: Routledge, 2016.

——. *Latinx Superheroes in Mainstream Comics*. Tucson, AZ: University of Arizona Press, 2017.

Aldama, Frederick L., and Christopher González. *Graphic Borders: Latino Comic Books Past, Present, and Future*. Austin, TX: University of Texas Press, 2016.

Habell-Pallán, Michelle, and Mary Romero. *Latino/a Popular Culture*. New York: New York University Press, 2002.

Miranda, Lin-Manuel, and Jeremy McCarter. *Hamilton: The Revolution*. New York: Grand Central Publishing, 2016.

Nericcio, William A. *Tex[t]-mex: Seductive Hallucinations of the "Mexican" in America*. Austin, TX: University of Texas Press, 2007.

REGIONALISM

Throughout this volume, the fact that Latinxs are a highly diverse group has been emphasized, and here again it manifests when geographic clustering of Latinxs in the United States is under consideration. When one takes into account the historical migration patterns of immigrants from the multitude of Latin American nations that exists, it is clear that certain regions of the US have developed particular types of Latinx communities. These regions can be broadly identified as the Southwest, the Intermountain West, the South, the Mid-Atlantic, Florida, the Midwest, and Northeast Coast. Even within these regions, subregions manifest quite clearly. For instance, the Southwest includes Texas, New Mexico, Arizona, and California—each with its specific Latinx enclaves, subgroups, and cultural traditions. Further, within this rubric of Latinx regionalism, there is more to consider beyond just nation of origin. Foods, customs, religions, and even dialects create significance differences among Latinx groups.

To begin to understand Latinx regionalism, careful consideration of the history behind the decisions to migrate and settle into certain areas is a necessary task. Perhaps the most obvious of these migration patterns reveals the predominance of Mexican Americans in the American Southwest. One reason for this is rather obvious: citizens of Mexico were in this geographic area of the North American continent before the US–Mexico border, as we now know it, was defined and articulated. When over half of Mexico's territory was demanded by the United States as a result of the culmination of the Mexican–American War and the terms of the Treaty of Guadalupe Hidalgo in 1848, all of those Mexican citizens who had populated what are the current states of New Mexico, Arizona, and California, and other soon-to-be states of the US Southwest, were suddenly, literally overnight, within the United States. It was effectively an instant Latinx demographic, and the presence of Mexican Americans has been a consistent part of the US ever since.

The other factor that makes this particular Latinx demographic and region so robust is that the US–Mexico border is one of the longest contiguous borders between nations in the world. With nearly 2,000 miles of terrain to cover, much of it inhospitable during much of the year, it provides ample opportunity to cross. Also, it was only with the Immigration Act in 1929 that it became "illegal" to cross the border, a law that essentially sought to preserve the whiteness of America (i.e., too many Mexicans were coming into the US). Couple that with those instances when the US government invited Mexican laborers i.e., *braceros*, to work in the absence of the many soldiers who left home to fight in World War I and World War II, and it is little wonder that Mexican Americans comprise nearly three-quarters of all Latinxs in the United States.

Considering the American Southwest for a moment longer, we note that there are differences between Latinx groups that we can identify easily by the state within which they reside. Latinxs in Texas have cultivated a long history in the state as well as in the United States (Alonzo 1–3). Some of the earliest Mexican enclaves in the area were situated in the San Antonio region, which boasts some of the oldest sites west of the Mississippi River, such as the Cathedral of San Fernando. Built in 1738, it the oldest church in Texas and the oldest Roman Catholic cathedral in the United States. In time, the independent spirit of Texas would become a part of the Mexican American tradition in Texas. Calling themselves *Tejanos*, many of them only consider a tenuous affiliation with Mexico as something of the distant past. *Tejanos* have adopted many of the traditions characteristic of Texas, including work as farmers or with livestock. The *Tejano* identity goes as far back as the founding of the Republic of Texas, and its history includes interactions with such legendary figures as Stephen F. Austin, General Sam Houston, and Juan Seguín. It is important to note that *Tejanos*, many of them of elite status and with claims to large tracts of land given to them by Mexico, were already in the area when Anglo-Americans began their process of colonization. This fact puts the lie to the claim that all Latinxs in Texas are recent arrivals or that they should go back to their native lands. For many Latinxs in Texas and their ancestors, they are already home. Indeed, this is the case for many Latinxs throughout the Southwest.

Latinxs in the Southwest have historically been religious due to the long history of Catholicism in the area, and they have helped create their own variant of Catholicism that has conflated the tenets of the religion with the indigenous belief system. One example of this is seen in the reverence and devotion to the Virgen de Guadalupe, who, legend has it, appeared to a peasant named Juan Diego near Mexico City in the sixteenth century. In addition to religious practices, Latinxs from Texas also have established a cuisine that is heavily reliant on beef, which is logical for a state with so many heads of cattle. So much is wrapped up in imagined histories and stories told. Indeed, the myth of the American West has been dominated by stories that depicted "white men as courageous protagonists fighting savage Indians on the Plains or battling cowardly Mexicans in Texas, Arizona, or California" (Iber and DeLeón 2).

In New Mexico, however, many Latinxs there see their ancestry and heritage as directly linked, not to Mexico, but rather, to Spain. Since the late 1500s, Spain and its Catholic Church was in charge of the area now known as New Mexico. Indeed, it was the colonizing nation of Spain that bestowed the name of Nuevo México upon the land, significant because, contrary to common belief, New Mexico was given its name even before Mexico had its current-day designation. Of all regions with high populations of Latinxs, New Mexico bears the highest numbers of Hispanics (here a more proper term because of their ancestry to Spanish peoples) in the United States. Many Hispanics in New Mexico hold dearly to their Spanish lineage, and they go to great pains to clarify their distinction from Mexican Americans and other Latinx subgroups.

In the Southwest, the other large grouping of Latinxs must surely be in California. Even before California was a US state, it was well populated with people of Spanish and Mexican descent (Hayes-Bautista 1–3). As with other areas in the Southwest, Spanish colonizers established settlements and churches throughout *Califomio*, and as in Texas and New Mexico, California Latinxs have embraced and kept alive their connections in the region from long before the United States was a presence in the area. In the early twenty-first century, California had more Latinxs than in any other state, making them a significant political and cultural force in the state and in the nation. As with Latinxs in Texas, today California Latinxs are heavily influenced by the culture and climate of the state in which they reside—and to generalize either of these groups would be unhelpful. Politically, most Mexican-descended groups, regardless of the region in which they live, tend to align more with left-leaning causes than right-leaning. (Some issues, such as abortion, often find this group more right-leaning, often as a result of the influence of Catholicism.)

A significantly distinct group of Latinxs happens to reside in the state of Florida. There the dominant Latinx subgroup is that of Cuban origin, for clear geographical reasons. Famously, there is a scant 90 miles between Key West, Florida and Cuba, and so many Cubans made Florida their destination of choice because its climate and culture was so reminiscent of their own (Stepick et al.). But this small separation of water has historically limited Cuban immigration, relative to the Mexican Americans in Texas and California, and Spanish-Americans of New Mexico. Further, the history of Cuba, as an island nation in the Caribbean, as a one-time stronghold of the slave trade, and its relatively recent history with Communism, all work to position Cubans within a different political and cultural context within the United States than those Latinxs of Mexican heritage. Unlike most Latinxs in the Southwest, Cubans are politically conservative, aligning themselves with US Presidents such as Ronald Reagan, George H.W. Bush, and George W. Bush. The manner in which Cubans were able to emigrate to the US differed significantly from those of other Latin American nations. Because Cuba was the closest Communist nation to the US, the US government altered its immigration policies accordingly to allow more Cubans to enter with fewer bureaucratic obstacles than other Latinx groups.

As Cuban nation and its culture are very different from Mexican culture, the two relevant Latinx subgroups also bear similar differences. Cuban cuisine is heavily influenced by its Caribbean island geography. Rice and beans are staples of both Mexican American and Cuban American communities, but pinto beans characterize Mexican American cuisine while black beans are a staple of Cuban dishes. Similarly, plantains, plentiful in Cuba, comprise an important aspect of its food traditions. There is an abundance of pork and seafood in Cuban cuisine, and they help distinguish it from other Latinx demographics.

Another Caribbean island nation has long been a vital part of New York and New Jersey: Dominican Republic. Rather than emigrate to Florida as Cubans have done, Dominicans have historically settled in New Jersey and New York. A nation, like Cuba, heavily influenced by Catholicism, the slave trade, and dictators, the Dominican Republic revels in its Spanish ancestry. While the United States occupied the Dominican Republic twice from 1916–1924 and in 1965, and there were some Dominicans who began to come to the US, they did not really begin to emigrate to the United States in large numbers until the 1980s. Because of this, Dominicans have the feel of being more recently arrived than other Latinx subgroups in the United States, and their percentage within all Latinxs is relatively small. Though they may settle anywhere in the United States, as with any of these Latinx subgroups, Dominicans have a tendency to settle in New Jersey and New York.

One issue that affects Dominicans who come to live in the United States concerns the influence and consequence of race. Historically, many Dominicans have African heritage in their ancestry, and this is noted in such phenotype characteristics as darker skin color and coarse or "nappy" hair. What makes this issue so volatile and potentially troubling to Dominicans is that in their nation of origin, individuals may not see themselves, or be seen by others, as "black." Yet in the United States, a nation that obsesses over race and phenotype, these individuals may be categorized as black. This disorientation may often lead to a kind of identity crisis in Dominican immigrants, one that creates a doubly marginalized status. They are Latinx and may not speak much English, *and* they must deal with how the United States deals with blackness. In terms of Dominican cuisine, it has much in common with Cuban fare—plantains, black beans, pork, and seafood, though it has its own regional differences.

The final Latinx subgroup that makes up a significant percentage of Latinxs in the United States is that of Puerto Ricans, who are, unlike the rest of the subgroups, all US citizens. The island of Puerto

Rico, which lies in the Caribbean east of the Dominican Republic, has a rich tradition like many of its island neighbors. However, the fact that it remains an unincorporated territory of the United States bestows upon it singular characteristics not featured in other Latinx groups. Puerto Ricans are free to move back and forth between the island and the mainland (Soto-Crespo). When they do leave the island, New York tends to be where the greatest concentration of Puerto Ricans relocates. This group, often called nuyoricans, has thrived and helped give New York City some of its character throughout the years through music, poetry, writing, and art. Puerto Ricans have been emigrating to New York since the island was still under Spanish rule in the mid-1800s. In New York, Puerto Rican neighborhoods, *barrios*, emerged in Brooklyn and in East Harlem (later known as Spanish Harlem).

Latinxs that do not fall within the specific subgroups above are often in more rural areas of the United States. The Midwest, for example, has the large urban city of Chicago, the beneficiary of the postwar surge in Mexican- and Puerto Rican-descended peoples (Fernandez), which has a vital and enthusiastic demographic of Latinxs. Yet outside of Chicago, there are not major urban areas in the Midwest with high numbers of Latinxs, and so Latinxs thus appear in more rural communities and in lower concentrations in these areas.

In considering the many areas Latinxs have come to call home within the United States, it is important to remember that even in these specific regions, many different and distinct Latinx subgroups thrive. You will find Mexican Americans in New Jersey, Puerto Ricans in California, and Cuban Americans in Texas. What is key here is that the specific percentages of the groups tend to align with certain geographic locations. Such an understanding of the regional aspect of the Latinx demographic in the United States aids in conceiving of Latinxs not as a homogeneous block of culture, but rather as a highly nuanced and multi-storied collection of histories and communities that share as much in common as they stand out individually.

Works Cited

Alonzo, Armando C. *Tejano Legacy: Rancheros and Settlers in South Texas, 1734–1900*. Albuquerque, NM: University of New Mexico Press, 1998.

Fernandez, Lilia. *Brown in the Windy City: Mexicans and Puerto Ricans in Postwar Chicago*. Chicago, IL: University of Chicago Press, 2014.

Hayes-Bautista, David E. *La Nueva California: Latinos from Pioneers to Post-Millennials*. Berkeley, CA: University of California Press, 2017.

Iber, Jorge, and A. De León. *Hispanics in the American West*. Santa Barbara, CA:
ABC-CLIO, 2006.
Soto-Crespo, Ramón E. *Mainland Passage: The Cultural Anomaly of Puerto Rico*.
Minneapolis, MN: University of Minnesota Press, 2009.
Stepick, Alex. *This Land Is Our Land: Immigrants and Power in Miami*. Berkeley,
CA: University of California Press, 2003.

SPORTS

Though sports in the United States is a profit-driven behemoth, Latinxs have only relatively recently become a prominent, significant player and shaper of this industry. But as Jorge Iber et al. maintain, "The story of Latinos in U.S. sport history must take heritage into account" (17). The exclusionary history of sports in the US applied to Latinxs just as it did African American athletes during the majority of the twentieth century, resulting in the major professional sports organization having over-representation of white athletes. Not only did Latinxs encounter the typical obstacles all individuals who want to compete at elite levels face, they had the added burden of not being allowed to play alongside white athletes. With the advent of the civil rights movement and the consistent pressure applied to major sports organizations, Latinxs have begun to take a greater role in the development and evolution of the shape and color of sports in the United States. In sports where there were few Latinxs—sports such as professional football and basketball—we now see them on the national stage more frequently. Latinxs are literally changing the sports landscape of the United States.

Historically, people of Latin American cultures and traditions have seemingly always had more than a passing interest in sports. One of the earliest sports traditions in **Mesoamerica** was a game known as *ulama*. Appearing in the geographical area of present-day Mexico, *ulama* was a game of skill that featured the use of a rubber ball. Archeologists have dated artifacts of the game such as the ball and ballcourts as far back as 1200 BC, a clear indicator of its prominence and historical significance. Perhaps most surprisingly, the game is still played in some parts of Mexico. The ball was kept in play by striking it variously with the forearm and hip, and winners were determined by a point system. Despite its antiquity, *ulama*, in its basic principles, has much in common with many modern-day sports, such as the use of a rubber ball, a clearly delineated court, a system for scoring, and well-articulated rules. Indeed, for many in the United States who see Latinxs as not very visible in some sports, it may come as a shock to learn that Mesoamerican peoples were among the earliest to create athletic contests that bear a striking resemblance to what we think of as a sport today.

Within the United States, Latinxs were as segregated, or in this case prohibited, as they were in other spheres of life, until rather late in the twentieth century. The push for civil rights legislation helped in this regard, as well as the advent of the GI Bill many decades earlier. In 1944, the GI Bill, as it became known colloquially, allows soldiers to serve in the military and, as one of the benefits, would be able to attend college at a much more affordable rate. As a large part of the military demographic identifies with a marginalized community, the consequence was that the bill made college more affordable, and more accessible, to people of color. This also allowed those students, who heretofore could not access college, the opportunity to play sports at the collegiate level. Many Latinxs who served would go on to participate in collegiate sports. The opening up of the university to those historically marginalized groups, through the GI Bill and through other means such as Affirmative Action and more grant money, would have truly game changing effects to professional sports—especially basketball and football (Aldama and González).

Not all sports in Latinx culture involved direct contests in a person-to-person fashion. In many parts of Latin America there has been a tradition of sporting contests that prominently feature animals. Two of these have survived into the contemporary period, but not without its controversy: *pelea de gallos* and *toreo*. *Toreo*, or bullfighting, is certainly not a sport within the United States. However, it is a sport that has a long history in Spain and in Latin American countries such as Mexico, Peru, and Colombia. This affinity for bulls, in the United States, manifests in the sport known as rodeo. Indeed, many US Latinxs and Latin Americans participate in high level (and high stakes) bull riding and rodeo. The organization known as the Professional Bull Riders (PBR) is the major organization devoted to competitions featuring bulls in the United States.

On the other hand, *pelea de gallos*, or cockfighting, has a long and honored tradition in many parts of the world, including Latin America. Latinx culture tends to view *pelea de gallos* with pride and emblematic of national and regional pride. Songs, films, and television shows, especially in Mexico, have exalted this bloodsport, while in the United States, such contests are reviled as brutal and cruel. In Mexico, singers/actors such as Vicente Fernandez and Antonio Aguilar cultivated an image of the cockfighter in film and in their music. These performers and their art were and continue to be highly celebrated in the Mexican American community, despite the fact that cockfighting is now illegal in all 50 US states. The issue is fascinating because it reveals how cultural norms and practices are perceived differently. Cockfighting has been abolished in the United States, but proponents of the sport point to the seeming hypocrisy of a nation that raises livestock in what are often inhumane conditions in order to sate the appetites of American carnivores.

In more high-profile professional sports, Latinxs continue to be an integral piece that is no longer easily ignored. Latinxs in general have a passion for *fútbol* (soccer), and Latin American players are among the best in the world. In addition, "there is no more popular sport in the Americas" than *fútbol*" (Stavans ix). While Latinxs participate in soccer in the United States—from the leagues comprised of grade-school children all the way to the professional level—soccer itself still struggles to gain the kind of viewership like those amassed by the National Football League (NFL), the National Basketball Association (NBA), or Major League Baseball (MLB). Thus, we see a situation where a historically marginalized group (Latinxs) are excelling and have a passionate interest in a historically marginalized sport within the United States. Networks that broadcast sports are recognizing the potential audience boom for soccer, which currently reflects the growing numbers of Latinxs in the US. Soccer is rising in popularity, and it shows little sign of fading.

The one national sport where Latinx participation and sport prominence have meshed is baseball, though as one might expect, this was not always the case (Hermoso). Baseball notoriously refused to integrate, and Jackie Robinson's smashing of the color line in professional baseball forever altered both baseball and professional sport. Though Robinson's breakthrough was a revelation, Latinxs did not really have a place in America's pastime until the advent of the near mythic, near saint baseballer from Puerto Rico, Roberto Clemente. Like Robinson, Clemente endured racist attitudes and actions as he traveled throughout the United States, experiences he had never had to endure back in Puerto Rico. Unlike Robinson, Clemente had the added burden of not being fluent in the English language. Yet he persevered to become one of the greatest baseball players in baseball history. Not just in the United States, but among all baseball players on the global stage. But what makes Clemente a singular figure in MLB lore is his tragic death in a plane crash, on a mission to bring humanitarian aid to victims of an earthquake in Nicaragua. Still playing when he died at the age of

38 years old, Clemente's death has left many fans to wonder what might have been.

Since Clemente, MLB has seen a surge of players of Latinx ancestry (Burgos). Unlike most other major sports leagues in the United States that may have some significant Latinx players of note but in still relatively small percentages, MLB is dominated by Latinx players. It is no surprise to see players with Hispanic surnames such as Rodriguez, Hernandez, Fernandez, Gonzalez, Altuve, Romo, and so on. The Latinx professional baseball player is no longer a surprise or rarity, and they are such a vital aspect of the MLB that it is difficult to imagine how the league would function or even exist without them.

Another major professional league has also seen the number of Latinx players rise within the last few decades. The NBA, another sport, like baseball, that was developed and innovated in the United States, also followed the all-too-familiar path of exclusion and segregation trod by other US sports organizations. In time, however, African American players would be included in the college and professional ranks, soon becoming a large percentage of all players. And it stayed a majority-black sport for several decades, especially from the 1980s to the 2000s. But during the twenty-first century, more international players began to break into the professional ranks. Suddenly, players from Argentina, Spain, and even US colonies such as Puerto Rico, were now playing among the best basketball players in the world. The NBA, for its part, has embraced its more inclusive identity, and it specifically features a part of the season where it emphasizes Latinx culture. Likewise, Latinxs continue to be a larger segment of NBA viewership. As a result, we see a correlation between participation and audience/fan engagement.

But the gold standard for sports in the United States is the NFL. Football is neatly aligned with American culture writ large on a global scale. Unlike basketball, baseball, and soccer, which is enjoyed by a great many nations on the planet, football has had a difficult time in gaining an invested audience in nations other than Canada, Mexico, and Great Britain. It is the most popular sport in the US, and it has historically been a venue in which Latinxs have worked hard to leave their mark. Though their progress has been slow, especially compared with the MLB, Latinxs have made significant contributions to the NFL. Perhaps one of the earliest cases of successful Latinxs in the NFL must surely be that of Joe Kapp, Jim Plunkett, and Tom Flores. These players, who achieved their greatest on-field successes on either side of the advent of the Super Bowl era, were California Latinxs, and specifically, Chicanos, who helped set the stage for future Latinx players in the NFL.

Joe Kapp, who enjoyed great success as the quarterback of the Minnesota Vikings, leading them to an NFL championship over the Cleveland Browns in 1969, but would lose to the Kansas City Chiefs in Super Bowl IV. Kapp was proud of his Mexican ancestry, and would often play up his heritage on the sidelines and on the field. The cover of *Sports Illustrated* proclaimed Kapp as "The Toughest Chicano" in 1970.

Jim Plunkett, another Mexican American from California and Heisman trophy winner with Stanford University, would become a highly successful quarterback in the NFL with the Oakland Raiders, though his career would be characterized by crests of victory and valleys of injury. He remains the only Latinx quarterback to start in and win two Super Bowl victories, and in one of those victories, Super Bowl XV, he was named the MVP.

The third pioneer for Latinxs in the NFL was Tom Flores, yet another talented player in the state of California. Though he never reached the upper echelon of success as a player, he did have tremendous success as a head coach. In fact, Flores was Jim Plunkett's coach with the Raiders, and so Flores also has two Super Bowl victories as a head coach. He would go on to have a long and successful career in the NFL, and he and Plunkett often appear in discussions for Hall of Fame voting. As of 2018, neither Plunkett nor Flores have been inducted into the Pro Football Hall of Fame, an extreme oversight for many observers. Regardless, Latinxs have continued to be a steadfast and increasing presence on the professional gridiron.

In the early twenty-first century, Latinxs have continued to carve out a space for themselves in all manner of sports and athletic achievement in the United States. Professional tennis has seen the rise and fall of Ricardo Alonso Gonzalez, better known as Pancho Gonzales—a tremendous talent who was the target of racist behavior during his career. Professional golf has seen the likes of Chi Chi Rodriguez, Lee Trevino, and Lorena Ochoa to name just a trio. Boxing has seen the likes of Julio Cesar Chavez, Roberto Duran, Manny Pacquiao, Hector "Macho" Camacho, all competitive fighters at the highest level of their sport. Boxing's more electric cousin, Mixed Martial Arts (MMA) has been propelled by Latinx fighters such as Tito Ortiz and Cain Velasquez. And in 2018, even NASCAR has a Latinx driver, Aric Almirola, whose parents emigrated to the United States from Cuba. In short, Latinxs are changing the sports landscape of the United States. Though systematic and institutional obstacles have made this history a relatively short one, it is certainly not short lived. With the swell of the Latinx demographic in the twenty-first century in the US, the increased interested in sports and athletics by Latinxs, the accessibility of training facilities in communities, high schools, and universities, and the broadening of opportunities for sports excellence, there is really no reason why Latinxs should not continue to be a greater part of sports competition in the future.

Works Cited

Aldama, Frederick Luis, and Christopher Gonzalez. *Latinos in the End Zone: Conversations on the Brown Color Line in the NFL.* New York: Palgrave Macmillan, 2014.

Burgos, Adrian. *Playing America's Game: Baseball, Latinos, and the Color Line.* Berkeley, CA: University of California Press, 2007.

Hermoso, Rafael. *Speak English! The Rise of Latinos in Baseball.* Kent, OH: Kent State University Press, 2013.

Iber, Jorge, Samuel O. Regalado, José M. Alamillo, and Arnoldo De León. *Latinos in U.S. Sport: A History of Isolation, Cultural Identity, and Acceptance.* Champaign, IL: Human Kinetics, 2011.

Stavans, Ilan. *Fútbol.* Santa Barbara, CA: Greenwood, 2011.

YOUTH

Latinx Studies scholars approach the topic of youth from many different disciplinary directions, including family, education, health, and culture. Inevitably, these approaches interface with issues of language, migration, politics, citizenship, gender, and sexuality, among others. Given that each of these approaches could and does fill weighty tomes, we will simply provide an overview of the general scholarly trends.

The Latinxs are the fastest growing demographic in the US. This results largely from births, and not migration. In the Southwest Latinxs are already the majority population; and, in places such as the South and Midwest, Latinxs are growing exponentially—and with the majority under 18 years old. However, such demographic shifts have not led to better quality of life nor better access to good schools for Latinx youth. There continue to be systemic social structures along with a prevailing xenophobia that curtail the full realization of potentialities for Latinx youth across the country.

In many ways, for Latinx youth family is the alpha and omega of everyday life. No matter the culture of origin (Dominican, Puerto Rican, Cuban, Mexican, Central American, for instance), family continues to play an important role in the lives of Latinx youth. This includes meals together and the ritual of *reunions familiares y las conversaciones de sobremesa*. The vertical studies show that Latinx youth who grow up with these important rituals where speaking about one's day and life at dinner can and does offer them the coping skills for dealing with the stressors of being Latinx in the US. And, the family practice of *ser bien educado* is centrally about growing in Latinx youth, as Angela Valenzuela, "respect, reciprocity, and relation" (p. 52).

Within family life, Latinx youth grow a deep sense of their sense of self as part of a larger collective. However, within a US culture that emphasizes and rewards individualism, this can grow a collectivist sense of self among Latinx youth that can have a negative impact. Mainstream US culture's constant reinforcing and rewarding of self-promoting actions and an individualist **ethos** stands in sharp contrast with the collectivistic values that inform the shaping of Latinx youth. Within lower income Latinx families, this collectivism manifests itself also with Latinx teens working to help support the family. This can and does create tensions between Latinx family values and those promoted by the US mainstream culture at large, leading to anxiety, and even fear in Latinx children and teens. (See R. Enrique Varela and Lauren Hensley-Maloney's "The Influence of Culture on Anxiety in Latino Youth.")

Of course, there are other stressors within Latin families that exert themselves on Latinx youth. These include the continued reproduction of a *machista* culture whereby there is a distinctive difference in the social roles assigned to girls versus boys. Unlike for boys, gender roles for girls tend to be restrictive to the domestic sphere and conservative when it comes to sexuality and its exploration. And, with family life deeply informed by a culture of Catholicism, coming out as LGBTQ for Latinx youth can be and is incredibly painful, often leading to total ostracism.

In addition to issues of gender and sexuality, there are other social and political factors that shape the well-being of Latinx youth. One's undocumented/documented status (green card or citizen) in the US impacts profoundly the realization of a healthy sense of self. One's status impacts access to health care, education, and other important basic services. This can and does lead to daily stressors that lead to a general sense of anxiety and even psychological paralysis. And, it matters too whether one is a first generation Latinx, with and without visas and official documents. Latinx youth who physically cross borders (land or sea) experience a form of PTSD. The trauma of the crossing compounded by a post-migration experience of living in the US without adequate social, political, and educational systems in place to receive them and for them to acquire the skills (linguistic and cultural) for what Adrian J. Archuleta and Monica Lakhwani identify as an "environmental mastery" (p. 121). This is not the same as systems that push Latinxs toward assimilating to the dominant culture. Rather, this is the providing of resources and learning spaces for Latinx youth to develop skills to "actively seek out and change environmental conditions to support their psychological well-being" (p. 121).

As Latinx youth grow up, while family continues to play an important role, it is life at school that becomes increasingly important. As already mentioned, even in the twenty-first century access to education spaces is not equal. There are undocumented Latinx youth who continue to face unsurmountable obstacles in attaining an education. And, because of the linking of race with class in the US, most Latinx youth live in districts where public schools are underfunded, under resourced, and over enrolled. And, many Latinx youth experience the push-out then lock-out patterns of discrimination. That is, Latinx youth are not given the full access to the kinds of resources that would allow for the growing of their full potentialities. Instead, the poor quality of learning spaces leads to affective and anxiety disorders and the blocking of full and healthy emotional and cognitive development.

Many Latinx activists and educators have fought this system, even creating spaces that can provide Latinx youth with learning opportunities as well as spaces for community building. At the Ohio State University, for instance, Frederick Aldama created: LASER/Latinx Space for Enrichment & Research. Undergraduates and graduate students meet weekly with Latinx students at Columbus high schools, working with them to ensure that they have as full an access as possible to knowledge and creativity—and the tools for further refining and shaping for a better tomorrow. At Utah State University, Christopher González launched his Latinx Cultural Center that includes a LASER program education pipeline outreach component. In Atlanta, Georgia, there is the important Freedom University, also providing a space for Latinx youth (especially undocumented) to prepare for successful access to college. These and other programs provide spaces generally for the kind of "participatory action" necessary to equip Latinx youth "with the intellectual, scholarly, policy and political tools they need in order to become agents of change in their own respective contexts," as Angela Valenzuela states (p. 54).

These initiatives (and there are many others) stand on the shoulders of a long history in the US of discriminatory education policies that have long targeted Latinx youth. Beginning with the signing of the Treaty of Guadalupe Hidalgo in 1848, the US formally and informally instituted a type of two-tier system of education. In the southwest, for instance, this led to the non-funding of schools for Latinxs (non-English speakers) and state-funding for Anglos. The youth that informed the Chicano Movement of the late 1960s sought to put an end to this racist system. We see this with the 15,000 Latinx students that walked out of schools in LA, beginning with the famous Blowouts of Garfield High School (March 1–8, 1968). And, the writing of "El Plan Espiritual de Aztlán" in 1969 happened at the Chicano Youth Liberation Conference in Denver. Decades of discrimination and racist education policies led Latinx youth to stand up and fight to end centuries of discrimination. (See Michael Soldatenko's "Mexican Student Movements in Los Angeles and Mexico City, 1968" as well as Carlos Muñoz's *Youth, Identity, Power*.)

In the "Education" Key Concept, we discussed the Latinx youth who fall under the category known as DACA (Deferred Action for Childhood Arrivals). The DREAM Act allowed these Latinx youth to have access to education without the fear of being deported to countries where they either face death one way (economic) or another (violence of gangs). However, the current administration has put under duress and uncertainty Latinx youth who are part of the DACA program. While it is an especially uncertain and therefore stressful time for DACA, this simply extends and exaggerates what has always been the case for Latinx youth generally: policies that delimit full access to *all* of education in the US.

Latinx Studies scholars have also turned their attention to how Latinx youth interface with cultural phenomena such as music, literature, comic books, animation, and the like. Here we see a two-pronged approach: those that seek to identify how the reproduction of stereotypes in mainstream culture negatively impacts Latinx youth; and, those who seek to enrich our understanding of how Latinx youth have metabolized and made their own in empowering ways cultural phenomena such as music.

There's a long history of Latinx youth using music soundscapes to assert a unique identity and an empowered self, refusing the status quo both of the mainstream and their parent's Latinx culture. There were Latinx youth identified as the Zoot Suiters of the 1940s on the West Coast who not only distinguished themselves with their sartorial wear and *caló* but also in their embrace of the big band music soundscapes of boleros and corridos. (See the music of Eduardo "Lalo" Guerrero, for instance.) On the East Coast in the 1970s, Latinx youth embraced *salsa*. In their youth, musicians living in the Bronx and other *barrios* of New York (Willie Colon, Tito Puente, and Bobby Cruz, for instance) grew music soundscapes from the Afro-Cuban son, rumba, guaracha, cha cha cha as well as the Puerto Rican bomba and plena. For these young musicians and their young Latinx audiences, salsa became a space of cultural empowerment—and resistance to an Anglo-identified rock scene. More recently, we see Latinx youth embrace all kinds of different music soundscapes, including *rock en español*, punk, and reggaeton. For instance, East LA in 1990s saw the rise of Latinx fusion bands (Aztlán Underground, Blues Experiment, Ozomatli, Quetzal, Quinto Sol, Yeska, among others) that variously brought together sounds from Brazil (samba) with those of Caribbean (reggae) and the US (rap), clearing a space for young Latinxs to stand together and against dominant forces of oppression. As Victor Hugo Viesca remarks, these soundscapes functioned as a "form of political possibility [...] grounded in the new spatial and social relations generated in Los Angeles in the transnational era" (p. 720). We see with the popularity of N.O.R.E. and Daddy Yankee how reggaeton—grown from Jamaican, Panamanian, Puerto Rican, Dominican, Cuban, and the US (hip-hop) rhythmic soundspaces—has also been embraced by Latinx youth to express a unique identity. And, queer Latinx youth have embraced the hardcore rock/punk music known as Emo as a way to, in Marisa López's words, "resignify the body, to free it from heteronormative discourses of race and gender" (p. 899). Finally, we see with Latinx youth the making and embracing of different music genres to create what Josh Kun has identified as "audiotopias" whereby "the listener and/or musician new maps for re-imagining the present social world" (p. 23). (See also Pablo Vila's edited, *Music and Youth Culture in Latin America*.)

In literature Jaime Campbell Naidoo sums up the history: "they highlighted piñata parties and festivals, the plight of poorly educated Latinxs in need of a white savior, or outdated folktales used by well-meaning educators to represent Latinx daily life. Cultural outsiders wrote most of these books" (p. xi).

The domain of literature has proved to be an important space of self-affirmation for Latinx youth: children's and young adult fiction as well as comic books. For instance, there's Rhode Montijo's *Pablo's Inferno* and Javier Hernandez's *El Muerto* that take young readers on an adventure through Mictlan (the Aztec underworld), all while educating them about pre-Columbian history. There are comics by Ivan Velez Jr., Liz Mayorga, Breena Nuñez, Graciela Rodriguez, Crystal Gonzalez, Kat Fajardo, Vicko, and many others that clear positive spaces for LGBTQ Latinx youth to identify. (See Aldama's *Tales from la Vida*.) Along with the renaissance of Latinx comics aimed at Latinx youth there is also a flourishing of children's and young adult fiction. Authors such as Monica Brown, Angela Dominguez, Pat Mora, Julia Alvarez,

Daniel José Older, Xavier Garza, Maya Christina Gonzalez, Pam Muñoz Ryan, Jenny Torres Sanchez, Gabby Rivera, and so many others create young Latinx protagonists that affirm the experience of being a Latina girl, young woman, or LGBTQ Latinx teen. As Marilisa Jiménez García writes, this literature for Latinx youth "ask us to look at the breaks and switches, the spaces between cultures, the shelf of children's books that we divide by race, nation, and language" (p. 120). These authors along with the comic book creators mirror back at young Latinx readers Latinx complex subjectivities with worthwhile experiences: histories, cultures, languages. They affirm Latinx youth in ways that propel them forward toward engaging with and then transforming the world. (See Aldama's *Latino/a Children and Young Adult Writers on the Art of Storytelling*.)

Set against the work that seeks to enrich understanding of Latinx created cultural phenomena, we have scholars who attend to how Latinx youth are adversely affected by stereotypes circulating in mainstream TV. For instance, scholars such as Laura Fernández, Cristina Rivera, and Isabel Millán have critically analyzed shows such as *Dora the Explorer* (2000–), *Handy Manny* (2006–), *Mucha Lucha!* (2002–2005). For instance, that Dora only ever uses Spanish in a didactic way and only as a series of words outside of any cultural contexts tells children that Spanish is only a *tool*, much like Handy Manny is only useful to fix tires and the like for his Anglo neighbor, Mr. Lopart. These Latinx scholars and others demonstrate how TV shows for Latinx youth (and all others) actively unmoor important Latinx cultural signifiers as well as disempower Latinx youth audiences.

Latinx Studies scholars have also considered the negative impact on Latinx youth of the stereotypical representations of Latinxs in video games. Scholars such as Carlos Kelly, Osvaldo Cleger, and Frederick Luis Aldama have attended to representation as well as the emotive, cognitive, and physiological effects of playing video games. Playing video games where Latinxs are only represented as gangbangers or identified only as obstacles to be avoided, overcome, or destroyed solidifies exclusionary practices in the real world. Aldama has analyzed video games created by noncorporate-based teams such as *ICED* (2008) and also *Papo y Yo*. Conversely, Osvaldo Cleger determines that while 65% of video game players are Latinx youth, the companies deliberately either don't create playable Latinx characters or they create stereotypical Latinxs. For instance, there's Resistance Records's *Ethnic Cleansing* (2002) that requires its players to shoot and kill poncho-wearing Latinxs. Latinx scholars of video games have determined that stereotypical constructions of Latinxs in video games solidify in-group and out-group appraisal schemas. These and other Latinx scholars seek to clear a space for a Latinx ludology (the intersection of Latinx Studies and Game Studies) to study video games that construct negative and positive game experiences for Latinx youth.

Latinx youth continue to be embattled, at home, at school, and within the larger US society. However, they also continue to find pathways to grow, learn, and ultimately to discover and to create complex expressions of Latinidad through music, literature, comic books, video games, and much more. They continue to fight to create a level playing field where *all* Latinxs can realize their full potentialities in the world.

Works Cited

Aldama, Frederick Luis. *Tales from la Vida: A Latinx Comics Anthology.* Athens, OH: Ohio State University Press, 2018a.

Aldama, Frederick Luis. *Latino/a Children and Young Adult Writers on the Art of Storytelling.* Pittsburgh, PA: University of Pittsburgh Press, 2018b.

Archuleta, Adrian J., and Monica Lakhwani. "Posttraumatic Stress Disorder Symptoms among First-Generation Latino Youths in an ESL School." *Children & Schools*, vol. 38, no. 2, 2016, pp. 119–127.

Fernández, Laura Michelle. "Canta y no llores: Life & Latinidad in Children's Animation." In *The Routledge Companion to Latino/a Pop Culture*, edited by Frederick Luis Aldama. New York and London: Routledge, 2016, pp. 68–75.

García, Marilisa Jiménez. "Side-by-Side: At the Intersections of Latinx Studies and ChYALit." *The Lion and the Unicorn*, vol. 41, 2017, pp. 113–122.

Kun, Josh. *Audiotopia: Music, Race and America.* Berkeley, CA: University of California Press, 2005.

López, Marissa. "¿Soy Emo, Y Qué? Sad Kids, Punkera Dykes and the Latin@ Public Sphere." *Journal of American Studies*, vol. 46, 2012, pp. 895–918.

Millán, Isabel. "'¡Vámonos! Let's Go!': Latina/o Children's Television." In *The Routledge Companion to Latino/a Pop Culture*, edited by Frederick Luis Aldama. New York and London: Routledge, 2016, pp. 44–58.

Muñoz, Carlos. *Youth, Identity, Power: The Chicano Movement.* New York: Verso, 1989.

Naidoo, Jaime Campbell. "Foreword: Magical Encounters with Latino Children's Literature." *Latino/a Children and Young Adult Writers on the Art of Storytelling.* Pittsburgh, PA: University of Pittsburgh Press, 2018, pp. xi–xv.

Rivera, Cristina. "Branding 'Latinohood', Juan Bobo, and the Commodification of Dora the Explorer." *The Routledge Companion to Latino/a Pop Culture*, edited by Frederick Luis Aldama. New York and London: Routledge, 2016, pp. 60–67.

Soldatenko, Michael. "Mexican Student Movements in Los Angeles and Mexico City, 1968." *Latino Studies*, vol. 1, no. 2, 2003, pp. 284–300.

Valenzuela, Angela. "Education." In *Keywords in Latina/o Studies*, edited by Deborah R. Vargas, Lawrence La Fountain-Stokes, Nancy Raquel Mirabal. New York: New York University Press, 2017, pp. 51–54.

Varela, R. Enrique, and Lauren Hensley-Maloney "The Influence of Culture on Anxiety in Latino Youth: A Review." *Clinical Child Family Psychology Review*, vol. 12, 2009, pp. 217–233.

Viesca, Victor Hugo. "The Cultural Politics of Chicana/o Music in the Greater Eastside." *American Quarterly*, vol. 56, no. 3, 2004, pp. 719–739.

Vila, Pablo, ed. *Music and Youth Culture in Latin America: Identity Construction Processes from New York to Buenos Aires*. New York: Oxford University Press, 2014.

GLOSSARY

Arawak and Caribs Amerindians that inhabited the Caribbean archipelago before the European conquest that began in 1492. The Arawak were known as a peaceful tribe whereas the Carib were known to have been violent—possibly practitioners of cannibalism. See Philip Boucher's *Cannibal Encounters*. See also Yolanda Martínez-San Miguel's "Taino Warriors?"

Autobiography Latinx creators (prose, comics, film, among others) telling stories of their own life that includes social, political, historical, and personal facts. The autobiography establishes a pact or contract with the reader that it corresponds to facts. Autobiographies can and do include the use of devices one finds in narrative fiction such as voice, perspective, temporal play, and the like. See Norma Klahn's *Literary (re) Mappings*. See also Frederick Luis Aldama's *A User's Guide to Postcolonial and Latino Borderland Fiction*.

Aztecs Indigenous people who spoke Nahuatl and who inhabited central Mexico between the fourteenth and sixteenth centuries. See Paul Allatson's *Key terms in Latino/a Cultural and Literary Studies*.

Aztlán (Nahuatl) The term used in the Chicano Movement to identify the ancestral homelands of the Nahua peoples. Aztlán comprised the northern territories of Mexico we know as the Southwest. Chicanos sought to reclaim materially and symbolically this territory.

Bachata A type of music that grew from the African presence in the Dominican Republic. It solidified as a genre in the early twentieth century, spreading to other parts of the Hispanophone Caribbean and Latin America generally. See Juan Flores's "Oye Como Va! Hybridity and Identity in Latino Popular Music."

Barrio A district or neighborhood populated by Latinxs, typically grown in and around urban centers in the US. See Paul Allatson's *Key Terms in Latino/a Cultural and Literary Studies*. See also Raúl Villa's *Barrio-Logos*.

Borderlands American or Mexican culture, Chicana literature provides a voice to the people of the borderlands as reclaimed space of gender, class, race, sexuality, ambiguity, and space of multilingualism.

Elenes, C. Alejandra. "Reclaiming the borderlands: Chicana/o identity, difference, and critical pedagogy."

Boricua/Boricuan A person who was born in Puerto Rico or with Puerto Rican ancestry who might not have grown up in Puerto Rico. More than Puerto Rican, the term has a political connotation, recognizing its indigenous Native and African social, historical, and cultural roots. See Lisa Sánchez-González's *Boricua Literature*.

Bultos Carved figures of saints seen crafted in Latinx communities in the Southwest and the Midwest. See Manuel Martin-Rodríguez's "Aesthetic Concepts of Hispanics in the United States."

Caló Refers to the slang (or argot) used by Mexican Americans (or Chicanos) and is usually associated with urban *barrios*. It was first associated with pachucos (or zoot-suitors) of the 1940s. See Paul Allatson's *Key Terms in Latino/a Cultural and Literary Studies*.

Carpa Playwright Luis Valdez conceived of carpas as a tent theater that addresses sociopolitical issues faced by Latinxs. His tent theater sought to empower Chicanos in a symbolic recuperation of lands lost after 1848— lands that were the northern Mexican territories and mythologically known as Aztán. See Luis Valdez's *Early Works* and Nicolás Kanellos's *Hispanic Theatre in the United States*.

Central America The geographic region (subcontinent) of the Americas that connects the northern with southern Americas. It includes: Belize, Costa Rica, El Salvador, Guatemala, Honduras, Nicaragua. See Ana Patricia Rodríguez's "Refugees of the South."

Chicano Movement Known also as el movimiento, during the 1960s and early 1970s Chicanos throughout the Southwest stood in solidarity to fight for equal rights as citizens of the US; the movement solidified goals of achieving enfranchisement already seen in incipient form in the 1940s and before. See Carlos Muñoz's *Youth, Identity, Power*.

Classism A socioeconomic-based prejudice and discrimination against Latinxs. It includes all those attitudes and behavior as well as all variety of policies and practices that discriminate against Latinxs as a lower class to benefit the upper class. See Dolores Delgado Bernal's "Critical Race Theory, Latino Critical Theory, and Critical Raced-Gendered Epistemologies."

Code-switching The linguistic phenomenon of combining two linguistic codes (English and Spanish, typically) when moving back and forth between phrases. See Lourdes Torres's "In the Contact Zone."

Colonialism The establishment, exploitation, maintenance, acquisition, and expansion of colonies in the Americas by outsiders—the Europeans. Colonialism in the Americas used military and political procedures to set up unequal (racial, social, economic) relationships that at best disenfranchised the indigenous populations and at worst led to genocide. We are more familiar today with forms of neocolonialism whereby global capitalists assert influence over countries. Also known as imperialism and hegemony. See Paul Allatson's *Key Terms*.

Colonization The US, Mexico, Puerto Rico, Cuba, the Dominican Republic, Central and South America all experienced different histories of colonization as settler colonies, trading posts, mining centers, plantations, and so on. All in all, colonialism in the Americas resulted in the ruling of the existing indigenous peoples along with those uprooted in the slave trade. See Paul Allatson's *Key Terms*.

Conquest 1492 marks the year of the beginning of the conquest (and genocide of the indigenous) of the Americas. Christopher Columbus's arrival at Hispanola (Cuba today) soon led to the decimation of the indigenous population both from infectious diseases brought by the Europeans as well as the horrors of their enslavement. The genocide of the indigenous population led to the importing of Africans as slaves. The conquest continued with Hernan Cortes's slaughter of the Aztecs that led to his controlling of the territories that we know of today as Mexico and the Southwest US. See Ilan Stavan's *The Norton Anthology of Latino Literature*.

Corrido Refers to the popular ballads (narratives in song and poetry) that focus on themes of oppression and the daily life everyday heroes. This form of storytelling was popular in the Southwest in the early twentieth century and continues to be popular today in its modern, *narco-corrido* variant. *Narco-corridos* tell the stories of everyday heroes but are set within today's drug trafficking and culture. See Paul Allatson's *Key Terms*.

Curanderismo/curanderas Refers to the healing tradition commonly practiced in the Southwest and the Central and South Americas. This has been used as a central theme in novels such as Rudolfo A. Anaya's *Bless Me, Última*. See Melissa Pabón's "The Representation of Curanderismo in Selected Mexican American Works."

Decolonial Refers to Latinx creators, scholars, and activists taking control of frameworks of interpretation and knowledge making that have traditionally been controlled by the Euro-Anglo colonizer. See Walter Mignolo's *The Darker Side of Western Modernity*. Arturo J. Aldama et al.'s edited volume *Decolonial Voices* and see also Emma Pérez's *The Decolonial Imaginary*.

Diasporas Refers to the movement of people with common origins from their homelands across countries, continents, and the globe. See Lisa Sánchez-González's *Boricua Literature*. See also José L. Torres-Padilla's and Carmen Haydée Rivera's edited collection, *Writing off the Hyphen*.

Disidentification   This term coined by José Muñoz refers to how racial and sexual other survive by negotiating and transforming mainstream culture—and not aligning with it. See Muñoz's *Disidentification*.

Epistemic (episteme)   Refers to knowledge and degree of its validation. Latinx scholars can investigate the ways that Latinx culture critiques Western epistemes. See Román De la Campa's *Latin Americanism*.

Ethos (Greek for "character")   Refers to those guiding beliefs or ideals that characterize a community (and nation or ideology) in Latinx cultures. Scholars have explored how Latinx culture conveys a Latinx ethos that seeks validation and self-determination. See Juan Flores and George Yudice's "Living Borders/Buscando América".

Exile   Refers to the political or punitive prohibition of people from living in their native country. See Marta Caminero-Santangelo's "Contesting the Boundaries of 'Exile' Latino/A Literature."

LGBTQ   Is an acronym that refers to Lesbian, Gay, Bisexual, Transgender, and Queer people. It reflects the nuances of our LGBTQ community that earlier terms in use such as *gay* did not capture adequately. See Richard T. Rodríguez's *Next of Kin* and Lázaro Lima's *The Latino Body*.

Hegemony   Refers to the use of ideology and implied threat of force by a leader state (*hegemon*) to rule subordinate states. See Mary Alexandra Rojas's "An Examination of US Latino Identities as Constructed In/Through Curricular Materials."

Hernán Cortés de Monroy y Pizarro (1485–1547)   A Spanish conquistador who used brutal military tactics to bring about the fall of the Aztec Empire. See Earl Shorris's *Latinos: A Biography of the People*. See Dietrich Briesemeister's "Un nuevo poema épico neolatino sobre Hernán Cortés."

Heteronormativity   Refers to the ideology that there are only two genders and two gender roles: male and female. It refers to the ideology that seeks to *naturalize* heterosexuality as the sexual orientation and that coupling arrangements and relations exist only between people of opposite sexes. It can and does lead to heterosexism and homophobia. See Mollie V. Blackburn and Jill M. Smith's "Moving Beyond the Inclusion of LGBT-Themed Literature in English Language Arts Classrooms." See also Ernesto Martinez's *On Making Sense: Queer Race Narratives of Intelligibility*.

Homophobia   Refers to fear built on prejudices against non-heterosexual people. See Ernesto Martinez and Michael Hames-Garcia's co-edited, *Gay Latino Studies*. *See* Susana Chávez-Silverman and Librada Hernández's edited collection, *Reading and writing the ambiente*. See also Lionel Cantú's "Entre Hombres/Between Men."

Hybridity (cultural and biological)   Refers to the meeting (sometimes by force) of different cultures and people across the Américas that results in cultural and biological mixtures. See José David Saldívar's *Border Matters*. See Néstor García Canclini's *Hybrid Cultures*. See Holly Martin's *Writing Between Cultures*.

Iberian   Refers to a person or cultural product originating from Portugal and Spain. See Patricia Novillo-Corvalan's "Latin American and Iberian Perspectives on Literature and Medicine." See Frauke Gewecke's "Latino/a Literature in Western Europe." See also Suzanne Bost's and Frances Aparicio's *Routledge Companion to Latino/a Literature*.

El movimiento   The Chicano Movement of the 1960s and early 1970s where Chicano laborers, families, students, teachers, labor organizers, among others fought for equal rights to education, pay equity, and social justice across all layers of social, cultural, economic, and political life in the US.

Indigenismo   Refers to a politicized ideology that celebrates Indigenous people and culture as well as identify racial, social, historical, and political issues that have determined imbalanced relationships between the nation-state and Indigenous minorities of the Americas. See also Amaka C. Ezeife's "Code-alternation in Strengthening Indigenous Cultures and Languages."

La Malinche   Refers to the historical figure who acted as interpreter between the Nahua and the Spaniards. There is an intellectual and historical tradition in Mexico that refers to her as a *malinchista*—a traitor—because she was known as Hernán Cortés's lover. Latina scholars and creators have since reclaimed her as a smart, savvy survivor. See Ana Castillo's *Massacre of the Dreamers*. See also Martha Sánchez's *Shakin' Up Race and Gender*.

La Raza   Refers to "the race" and is used as a term of Mexican and indigenous ethnic and racial pride by Chicanos. As a celebration of non-European heritage and as a push back against celebrating the bloody conquest of Columbus, instead of celebrating Columbus Day, Chicanos will celebrate Día de la Raza. See Juan Bruce-Novoa's "The Space of Chicano Literature."

Machismo   Refers to the behavior patterns of being strong, aggressive, brave—protector of the family. It also refers to those who preserve strict gender roles in the family, often denigrating the role of women and gay or lesbian members. See Ray González's *Muy Macho: Latino Men Confront Their Manhood*.

Magical realism   Refers to a form of storytelling whereby the narrative makes no distinction nor discriminates between events that defy the laws of nature (in physics, or genetics, for instance) with those that conform to the laws of nature. See Aldama's *Postethnic Narrative Criticism*. See Aldama's "Magical Realism" in *The Routledge Companion to Latino/a Literature*.

Merengue Refers to a type of music and dance that originated in the Dominican Republic. It is popular among Latinxs in the US and all over Latin America. See Juan Flores's "From Bomba to Hip-Hop."

Mesoamerican Refers to a region and cultural area in the Americas that stretches from central California through Belize, Guatemala, El Salvador, Honduras, and Nicaragua, to northern Costa Rica. Indigenous societies flourished here before the Spanish conquest and colonization. See Arturo Arias's "EpiCentro".

Mestizaje Refers to the racial and cultural mixing of indigenous Amerindian with Europeans during the time of the conquest and colonization of the Americas. It has been claimed as a concept by Latinx scholars as a resistant decolonial worldview and political practice that seeks to remedy social, economic, and political inequality. See Juanita Heredia's *Transnational Latina Narratives in the Twenty-first Century*. See also Ilan Stavans's *The Norton Anthology of Latino Literature*.

Mestizo Refers to those born of European and Indigenous ancestry. It was used in the construction of a racial cast (casta) system in Latin America. While mestizos were becoming the dominant group during the colonial period the casta system ensured that they would have fewer rights than the European born and the white colonial-born. See Paul Allatson's *Key Terms*.

Mexican American War (1846–1848) Refers to the war between the US and Mexico that led to additional annexations by the US of northern Mexican territories, including Texas, New Mexico, and California. See Cecilia Montes-Alcalá's "Writing on the Border."

Migration Refers to the movement of people from one area to another—typically for economic reasons. See Vanessa Pérez Rosario's *Hispanic Caribbean Literature of Migration*.

NAFTA (The North American Free Trade Agreement) Refers to an agreement signed by Canada, Mexico, and the United States to create a bloc of free trade between the countries. See Ariana Vigil's "The Divine Husband and the Creation of a Transamericana Subject." See also Marta Caminero-Santangelo's "Narrating the Non-Nation."

Nahuatl Refers to a group of related languages and dialects of the Nahua people of Mexico—especially central Mexico. See Elizabeth Hill Boone's *Cycles of Time and Meaning in the Mexican Books of Fate*.

Neoliberal Refers to economic policies that favor privatization, free trade, open markets, deregulation, and reductions in government spending, favoring the role of the private sector. See Arlene Dávila's *Barrio Dreams*. See also Richard Delgado's "Locating Latinos in the Field of Civil Rights."

Pachuco and Pachuca Refers to a Mexican American (usually urban) who dresses in suits with wide-shoulders and pleated pants. These are known as zoot suits and was a style that came into fashion among Mexican Americans in the 1930s in El Paso, Texas. Pachucos used their flamboyant sartorial style to embrace and celebrate their difference from the Anglo mainstream. A pachuca is a Mexican American woman who is known for transgressing the sartorial taboos by wearing pleated pants in public. See Catherine Ramírez's *The Woman in the Zoot Suit*.

Panethnicity Refers to the clustering of various ethnicities under one umbrella group. It could be labeling all Spanish speakers as Latinx, regardless of their country of origin. Harold Augenbraum's edited, *Latinos in English*.

Pocho Is a term used (often pejoratively) by Latinxs to refer to assimilated Mexican Americans—those who had lost the culture and language of Mexico. See Marta E. Sánchez's "Pocho en español."

Pre-Columbian Refers to the huge stretch of time from the Upper Paleolithic to before the European conquest of the Americas. See Nicolás Kanelos' *Herencia*.

Pre-Columbian epistemologies Knowledge (or theories of knowledge) that grows out of non-European, indigenous concepts and formulations about matters of existence in the Americas. See Paloma Martínez-Cruz's *Women and Knowledge in Mesoamerica*.

Quetzalcoatl (the Feathered Serpent) Refers to a major Mesoamerican deity. In the Toltec culture (ninth through twelfth centuries) Quetzalcoatl was known as the god of the morning and evening star. See Karina Oliva Alvarado's "An interdisciplinary reading of Chicana/o and (US) Central American Cross-Cultural Narrations."

Rasquachismo Tomás Ybarra-Frausto's term to identify how Latinx creators are inventing anew from recycled materials to convey the worldview of the outsider. See Ilan Stavans's "*Nacho Libre*: or, The Inauthenticity of Rasquachismo."

Reggaeton Refers to a genre of music with roots in the Caribbean. See Miriam Jiménez-Román and Juan Flores's *The Afro-Latin@ Reader*.

Renaissance With civil rights gained as a result of *el movimiento*, Chicano creators, scholars, and activists began celebrating and affirming their own cultural production—a cultural production that very much had a sense of larger Third World cultural liberation movements. See Paul Allatson's *Key Terms*.

Santería Refers to a religious tradition that mixes West African (Yoruban) and Caribbean indigenous spiritual practices. See Frances R. Aparicio's and Susana Chávez-Silverman's *Tropicalizations*.

Santera In the Santería tradition, a santero or santera is an initiated priest of the orisha. See Genaro Padilla's "A Reassessment of Fray Angelico Chavez's Fiction." See also Frances R. Aparicio's and Susana Chávez-Silverman's *Tropicalizations*.

Satire Refers to a Latinx creator's use of irony and ridicule to reveal the tears in the sociopolitical fabric that makes up a given society. See Ellen Gil-Gomez's "'Facts' and the Power of the Image in *Latino USA*."

Suburbs Refers to areas in the US just outside of cities built specifically to house people—usually middle class and, because of racial segregation policies still in play till the early 1970s, largely Anglo. See Jody Agios Vallejo's *Barrios to Burbs: The Making of the Mexican American Middle Class*.

Testimonio Refers to narrative texts that grow out of the social and political upheavals that mark Latin America's history. They are based on traumatic socio-historical events. They are told from an oppressed individual perspective and speak to a communal experience as a whole. They contain devices we commonly find in literary texts such as novels and poetry. They convey a strong sense of an oral tradition. See Stephanie M. Alvarez's "Evaluating the Role of the Spanish Department in the Education of US Latin@ Students."

Translation Refers to the distillation and reconstruction in another language of Latinx literary texts. The translation process can lose nuances of language and style. In the book marketing global marketplace where English is the lingua franca, the translation process usually flows from Spanish to English. See Daniel Balderston and Marcy E. Schwartz's edited, *Voice-Overs*. See also Aldama's *The Routledge Concise History of Latino/a Literature*.

Huitzilopochtli ("Hummingbird on the Left") Refers to the pre-Columbian sun god and god of war in Aztec mythology. See Curtis Acosta's "Huitzilopochtli."

Urbanization Refers to the process whereby Latinxs are pushed to live in cities as rural, farm life becomes increasingly unsustainable. Because of redlining practices (where urban planners would red-line areas for Latinxs to live) and also familial contacts, Latinxs tended to aggregate in the same parts of US cities. See Kingsley Davis's "The Urbanization of the Human Population."

Zoot Suit Riots Refers to the summer of 1942 in Los Angeles when Pachucos (Mexican-Americans wearing zoot suits) were attacked by military and police that led to the death of one Latinx. The "riots" brought to center stage the racial tensions between Latinxs and Anglos in the US. See Catherine Ramírez's *The Woman in the Zoot Suit*.

SUGGESTED FURTHER READING

Acosta, Curtis. "Huitzilopochtli: The Will and Resiliency of Tucson Youth to Keep Mexican American Studies Alive." *Multicultural Perspectives*, vol. 16, no. 1, 2014, pp. 3–7.

Agius, Vallejo Jody. *Barrios to Burbs: The Making of the Mexican American Middle Class*. Stanford, CA: Stanford University Press, 2012.

Aldama, Arturo J., and Naomi Helena Quiñonez, eds. *Decolonial Voices: Chicana and Chicano Cultural Studies in the 21st century*. Bloomington, IN: Indiana University Press, 2002.

Aldama, Frederick Luis. *Postethnic Narrative Criticism: Magicorealism in Ana Castillo, Hanif Kureishi, Julie Dash, Oscar "Zeta" Acosta, and Salman Rushdie*. Austin, TX: University of Texas Press, 2003.

———. *A User's Guide to Postcolonial and Latino Borderland Fiction*. Austin, TX: University of Texas Press, 2009.

———. "Magical Realism." In *Routledge Companion to Latino/a Literature*, edited by Suzanne Bost and Frances R. Aparicio. New York and London: Routledge, 2012, pp. 334–341.

———. *The Routledge Concise History of Latino/a Literature*. New York and London: Routledge, 2013.

Allatson, Paul. *Key Terms in Latino/a Cultural and Literary Studies*. Oxford: Blackwell, 2007.

Alvarado, Karina Oliva. "An interdisciplinary reading of Chicana/o and (US) Central American Cross-Cultural Narrations." *Latino Studies*, vol. 11, no. 3, 2013, pp. 366–387.

Alvarez, Stephanie M. "Evaluating the Role of the Spanish Department in the Education of US Latin@ Students: Un Testimonio." *Journal of Latinos and Education*, vol. 12, no. 2, 2013, pp. 131–151.

Anaya, Rudolfo A. *Bless Me, Última*. Berkeley, CA: TQS Publications, 1972.

Aparicio, Frances R. *Listening to Salsa: Gender, Latin Popular Music, and Puerto Rican Cultures*. Middletown, CT: Wesleyan University Press, 1998.

Aparicio, Frances R., and Susana Chávez-Silverman. *Tropicalizations: Transcultural Representations of Latinidad*. Hanover, NH: University Press of New England for Dartmouth College, 1997.

SUGGESTED FURTHER READING

Arias, Arturo. "EpiCentro: The Emergence of a New Central American-American Literature." *Comparative Literature*, vol. 64, no. 3, 2012, pp. 300–315.

Augenbraum, Harold, ed. *Latinos in English: A Selected Bibliography of Latino Fiction Writers of the United States*. New York: Mercantile Library of New York, 1992.

Balderston, Daniel, and Marcy E. Schwartz, eds. *Voice-Overs: Translation and Latin American Literature*. New York: SUNY Press, 2012.

Bernal, Dolores Delgado. "Critical Race Theory, Latino Critical Theory, and Critical Raced-Gendered Epistemologies." *Qualitative Inquiry*, vol. 8, no. 1, 2002, pp. 105–126.

Blackburn, Mollie V., and Jill M. Smith. "Moving Beyond the Inclusion of LGBT-Themed Literature in English Language Arts Classrooms." *Journal of Adolescent & Adult Literacy*, vol. 53, no. 8, 2010, pp. 625–634.

Boone, Elizabeth Hill. *Cycles of Time and Meaning in the Mexican Books of Fate*. Austin, TX: University of Texas Press, 2013.

Bost, Suzanne, and Frances Aparici, eds. *Routledge Companion to Latino/a Literature*. London; New York: Routledge, 2012.

Boucher, Philip P. *Cannibal Encounters: Europeans and Island Caribs, 1492–1763*. Baltimore, MD: Johns Hopkins University Press, 2009.

Briesemeister, Dietrich. "Un nuevo poema épico neolatino sobre Hernán Cortés: la Cortesias del jesuita Pedro Paradinas." *Studia Philologica Valentina*, vol. 15, 2013, pp. 25–46.

Bruce-Novoa, Juan. "The Space of Chicano Literature." *De Colores, Journal of Emerging Raza Philosophies*, vol. 1, no. 4, 1975, pp. 22–42.

Caminero-Santangelo, Marta. "Contesting the Boundaries of 'Exile' Latino/A Literature." *World Literature Today*, 2000, pp. 507–517.

——. *On Latinidad: US Latino Literature and the Construction of Ethnicity*. Gainsville, FL: University Press of Florida, 2007.

——. "Narrating the Non-Nation: Literary Journalism and 'Illegal' Border Crossings." *Arizona Quarterly: A Journal of American Literature, Culture, and Theory*, vol. 68, no. 3, 2012, pp. 157–176.

Cantú, Lionel. "Entre Hombres/Between Men: Latino Masculinities and Homosexualities." In *Gay Latino Studies: A Critical Reader*, edited by Michael Hames-García and Javier Martínez. Durham, NC: Duke University Press, 2011, pp. 147–167.

Capetillo, Luisa. *Absolute Equality: An Early Feminist Perspective: Influencias de Las Ideas Modernas*. Houston, TX: Arte Público Press, 2009.

Castillo, Ana. *Massacre of the Dreamers: Essays on Xicanisma*. New York: Plume, 1995.

Chávez-Silverman, Susana, and Librada Hernández, eds. *Reading and Writing the Ambiente: Queer Sexualities in Latino, Latin American, and Spanish Culture*. Madison, WI: University of Wisconsin Press, 2000.

Dalleo, Raphael and Elena Machado Sáez. *The Latino/a Canon and the Emergence of Post-Sixties Literature*. New York: Palgrave, 2007.

Dávila, Arlene M. *Barrio Dreams: Puerto Ricans, Latinos, and the Neoliberal city*. Berkeley, CA: University of California Press, 2004.

Davis, Kingsley. "The Urbanization of the Human Population." *The City Reader*, edited by Richard T. LeGates and Frederic Stout. London: Routledge, 2011, pp. 2–11.

De la Campa, Román. *Latin Americanism*. Minneapolis, MN: University of Minnesota Press, 1999.

Delgado, Richard. "Locating Latinos in the Field of Civil Rights: Assessing the Neoliberal Case for Radical Exclusion." *Texax Law Review*, vol. 83, 2004, p. 489.

Elenes, C. Alejandra. "Reclaiming the Borderlands: Chicana/o Identity, Difference, and Critical Pedagogy." *Educational Theory*, vol. 47, no. 3, 1997, pp. 359–375.

Ezeife, Amaka C. "Code-alternation in Strengthening Indigenous Cultures and Languages: A Feminist Reading." *Language in India*, vol. 13, no. 5, 2013, pp. 243–257.

Flores, Juan. "From Bomba to Hip-Hop." *Puerto Rican Culture and Latino Identity*. New York: Columbia University Press, 2000.

———. "Oye Como Va! Hybridity and Identity in Latino Popular Music." *Latin American Music Review*, vol. 33, no. 2, 2012, pp. 266–268.

Flores, Juan, and George Yudice. "Living Borders/buscando América: Languages of Latino Self-formation." *Social Text*, vol. 24, 1990, pp. 57–84.

García Canclini, Néstor. *Hybrid Cultures: Strategies for Entering and Leaving Modernity*. Minneapolis, MN: University of Minnesota Press, 2005.

Gewecke, Frauke. "Latino/a Literature in Western Europe." *The Routledge Companion to Latino/a Literature*, edited by Suzanne Bost and Frances Aparicio. New York and London: Routledge, 2013, pp. 107–115.

Gies, David Thatcher. *The Theatre in Nineteenth-Century Spain*. Cambridge, UK: Cambridge University Press, 2005.

Gil-Gomez, Ellen. "'Facts' and the Power of the Image in *Latino USA*." In *Crossing Boundaries in Graphic Narrative: Essays on Forms, Series and Genres*, edited by Jake Jakaitis and James F. Wurtz. Jefferson, NC: McFarland & Company, 2012, pp. 152–173.

González, Ray. *Muy Macho: Latino Men Confront Their Manhood*. New York: Anchor Books, 1996.

Heredia, Juanita. *Transnational Latina Narratives in the Twenty-first Century*. New York: Palgrave, 2009.

Jiménez-Román, Miriam and Juan Flores. *The Afro-Latin@ Reader: History and Culture in the United States*. Durham, NC: Duke University Press, 2010.

Kanellos, Nicolás. *Herencia: The Anthology of Hispanic Literature in the United States*. Oxford: Oxford University Press, 2003.

Klahn, Norma. *Literary (Re) Mappings: Autobiographical (Dis) Placements by Chicana Writers*. Durham, NC: Duke University Press, 2003.

Lima, Lázaro. *The Latino Body: Crisis Identities in American Literary and Cultural Memory*. New York: New York University Press, 2007.

Martin, Holly E. *Writing between Cultures: A Study of Hybrid Narratives in Ethnic Literature of the United States*. Jefferson, NC: McFarland, 2011.

Martinez, Ernesto. *On Making Sense: Queer Race Narratives of Intelligibility*. Stanford, CA: Stanford University Press, 2012.

Martínez-Cruz, Paloma. *Women and Knowledge in Mesoamerica: From East L.A. to Anahuac*. Tucson, AZ: University of Arizona Press, 2011.

Martínez-San Miguel, Yolanda. "Taino Warriors?: Strategies for Recovering Indigenous Voices in Colonial and Contemporary Hispanic Caribbean Discourses." *Centro Journal*, vol. 23, no. 1, 2011, pp. 197–215.

Martin-Rodríguez, Manuel. "Aesthetic Concepts of Hispanics in the United States." In *Handbook of Hispanic Cultures in the United States: Literature and Art*, edited by Francisco Lomelí. Houston: Arte Público Press, University of Houston, 1993, pp. 109–133.

Mesa-Bains, Amalia. *Ceremony of Spirit: Nature and Memory in Contemporary Latino Art*. The Mexican Museum, 1993.

Mignolo, Walter. *Local Histories/Global Designs: Coloniality, Subaltern Knowledges, and Border Thinking*. Princeton, NJ: Princeton University Press, 2012.

——. *The Darker Side of Western Modernity: Global Futures, Decolonial Options*. Durham, NC: Duke University Press, 2011.

Montes-Alcalá, Cecilia. "Writing on the Border: English y español también." In *Landscapes of Writing in Chicano Literature*. New York: Palgrave, 2013, pp. 213–230.

Muñoz, Carlos. *Youth, Identity, Power: The Chicano Movement*. London, New York: Verso, 1989.

Muñoz, José. *Disidentification: Queers of Color and the Performance of Politics*. Minneapolis, MN: University of Minnesota Press, 1999.

Novillo-Corvalan, Patricia, eds. *Latin American and Iberian Perspectives on Literature and Medicine*. New York and London: Routledge, 2015.

Novo, Carmen Martínez. "Indigenous Appropriations and Boundary Crossings: Interdisciplinary Perspectives on Indigenous Cultures and Politics in the Andes." *Latin American Research Review*, vol. 48, no. 2, 2013, pp. 218–226.

Pabón, Melissa. "The Representation of Curanderismo in Selected Mexican American Works." *Journal of Hispanic Higher Education*, vol. 6, no. 3, 2007, pp. 227–257.

Padilla, Genaro. "A Reassessment of Fray Angelico Chavez's Fiction." *MELUS*, vol. 11, no. 4, 1984, pp. 31–45.

Pérez, Emma. *The Decolonial Imaginary: Writing Chicanas into History*. Bloomington, IN: Indiana University Press, 1999.

Perez Rosario, Vanessa. *Hispanic Caribbean Literature of Migration: Narratives of Displacement*. New York: Palgrave, 2012.

Ramírez, Catherine. *The Woman in the Zoot Suit: Gender, Nationalism, and the Cultural Politics of Memory*. Durham, NC: Duke University Press, 2009.

Rodríguez, Ana Patricia. "Refugees of the South." *American Literature*, vol. 73, no. 2, June 2001, pp. 387–412.

Rodríguez, Richard T. *Next of Kin: The Family in Chicano/a Cultural Politics*. Durham, NC: Duke University Press, 2009.

Rojas, Mary Alexandra. "An Examination of US Latino Identities as Constructed In/Through Curricular Materials." *Linguistics and Education*, vol. 24, no. 3, 2013, pp. 373–380.

Saldívar, José David. *Border Matters: Remapping American Cultural Studies*. Berkeley, CA: University of California Press, 1997.

Sánchez, Marta E. "Pocho en español: The anti-pocho pocho." *Translation Studies*, vol. 4, no. 3, 2011, pp. 310–324.

Sánchez, Martha. *Shakin' Up Race and Gender: Intercultural Connections in Puerto Rican, African American, and Chicano Narratives and Culture (1965–1995)*. Austin, TX: University of Texas Press, 2005.

Sánchez-González, Lisa. *Boricua Literature: A Literary History of the Puerto Rican Diaspora*. New York: New York University Press, 2001.

Shorris, Earl. *Latinos: A Biography of the People*. New York: W.W. Norton, 1992.

Stavans, Ilan. *The Norton Anthology of Latino Literature*. New York: W.W. Norton, 2011.

——. "*Nacho Libre*: or, The Inauthenticity of Rasquachismo." In *Latinos in Narrative Media: Participation and Portrayal*. New York: Palgrave, 2013, pp. 111–116.

Torres, Lourdes. "In the Contact Zone: Code-switching Strategies by Latino/a writers." *MELUS*, vol. 32, no. 1, 2007, pp. 75–96.

Torres-Padilla, José L. *Writing Off the Hyphen: New Critical Perspectives on the Literature of the Puerto Rican Diaspora*. Seattle, WA: University of Washington Press, 2011.

Valdez, Luis. *Early Works: Actos, Bernabe, Pensamiento Serpentino*. Houston, TX: Arte Publico Press, 1990.

Vigil, Ariana. "The Divine Husband and the Creation of a Transamericana Subject." *Latino Studies*, vol. 11 no. 2, 2013, pp. 190–207.

Villa, Raúl. *Barrio-Logos: Space and Place in Urban Chicano Literature and Culture*. Austin, TX: University of Texas Press, 2000.

Villenas, S., et al. "Chicanas/Latinas Building Bridges." *Chicana/Latina Education in Everyday Life. Feminista Perspectives on Pedagogy and Epistemology*, edited by Dolores Delgado Bernal et al. New York: SUNY Press, 2006, pp. 1–9.

INDEX

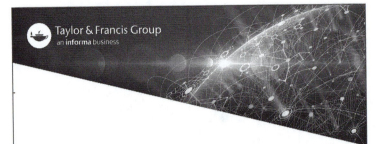

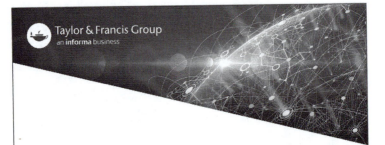